Twayne's United States Authors Series

EDITOR OF THIS VOLUME

Warren French
Indiana University

Robert Lowell

Second Edition

TUSAS 176

Robert Lowell

ROBERT LOWELL

SECOND EDITION

By RICHARD J. FEIN

State University of New York
College at New Paltz

TWAYNE PUBLISHERS

A DIVISION OF G. K. HALL & CO., BOSTON

First edition copyright © 1970 by Twayne Publishers, Inc.
Revised edition copyright © 1979 by G. K. Hall & Co.

Published in 1979 by Twayne Publishers,
A Division of G. K. Hall & Co.
All Rights Reserved

Printed on permanent/durable acid-free paper and bound
in the United States of America

First Printing

Library of Congress Cataloging in Publication Data

Fein, Richard J., 1929 -
Robert Lowell.

(Twayne's United States authors series ; TUSAS 176)
Bibliography: p. 206 - 18
Includes index.
1.   Lowell, Robert, 1917 - 1977—Criticism and
interpretation.
PS3523.089Z66   1979   811'.5'2   79-1126
ISBN 0-8057-7279-0

For my mother,
and in memory of my father.

Contents

About the Author

Born in Brooklyn, New York, in 1929, Richard J. Fein attended Brooklyn College, where he received his B.A. and M.A. degrees, and New York University, where he received a Ph.D. Dr. Fein is currently Professor of English and Coordinator of the Jewish Studies Program at the State University College, New Paltz, New York.

He has taught at Hunter College and the University of Puerto Rico. During 1971 - 72, Professor Fein was appointed Fulbright lecturer in American literature at the University of Madras.

Professor Fein has written articles on modern war poetry, on nineteenth-century American literature, on Jewish-American literature, and on Yiddish literature. His articles have appeared in such journals as *Southern Review, Sewanee Review, PMLA, The New England Quarterly, The Centennial Review, Judaism,* and *Midstream.* His own poetry has appeared in *The Nation, Quartet, University of Kansas City Review,* and *Response.* His translations of Yiddish poetry have appeared in *Present Tense.*

A fellow at the Max Weinreich Center for Advanced Jewish Studies from 1975 to 1978 and a recipient of a grant from The National Foundation for Jewish Culture, Richard J. Fein is currently co-editing an anthology, *The Yiddish Poem Itself.*

Preface to the Second Edition

This second edition is revised and expanded: one chapter has been entirely replaced; another has been removed; one has had material added; one has been substantially revised, and new chapters have been added. At the least, all chapters have undergone some stylistic changes. I have also added two personal essays as a prologue and an epilogue. My hope is that they extend the range of the book. In addition, the annotated bibliography has been brought up to date.

Prompted by the recent and sudden death of Robert Lowell, this edition, unlike the first one, presents evaluations and conclusions under the sad recognition that the poet's work is no longer in process. My preferences will be clear to any reader.

I appreciate having received a grant from the State University of New York, which enabled me to devote one summer toward the writing of this second edition.

RICHARD J. FEIN

Preface to the First Edition

This study, which traces the development of Robert Lowell's poetry from the early work to the present, discusses the works as they have appeared. The book strives for some overall view of Lowell's work and for a sense of his position in American literature and in modern poetry. However, I stress those works that in my view are central to Lowell's meaning and to his development and that particularly bring forth a sympathetic response from me. The poetry that is only briefly mentioned sheds light on the poems and the play discussed at length. For example, I do not devote a separate chapter to Lowell's first book, *Land of Unlikeness,* as the best work was rewritten and reintroduced in Lowell's second book, *Lord Weary's Castle.* To this second book I devote a long chapter, and whatever is important about *Land of Unlikeness* is referred to in this chapter. The same method is used for some other works by Lowell: his translation of Racine's *Phaedra* and his reinterpretation of Aeschylus's *Prometheus Bound* are handled in terms of his other works, especially the dramatic trilogy, *The Old Glory.*

Although I do not intend to make claims for Lowell's work beyond the level of its artistic accomplishment, I enthusiastically discuss a poem or an entire book when the poem or book demands nothing less. Other poems or works by Lowell engender critical reservations. Essentially, however, I confirm the feeling that Lowell's voice is a major one in American poetry of this century.

The study is conceived in a centrifugal pattern, moving from the particular volumes and their key poems to important issues of concern to Lowell's poetry in general and to the culture at large. Yet those cultural concerns are not divorced from the way the poetry itself forces us to reflect upon them. The poems are not regarded or used as merely stepping stones to other matters. The larger and extra-poetic issues are but another way of seeing what the poems themselves are about.

Biographical material, which is kept to a minimum, is principally introduced in relation to the poetry itself. Some information about Lowell's life and career is presented in the opening chapter, since it bears upon his development as a poet and as the kind of man the poetry itself talks about and dramatizes. Essentially, this book is a study of Lowell's poetry and what that poetry means.

I must confess a debt to many critics whom I have read over many years. They are too numerous to mention, and it would seem gratuitous for me merely to list names. I must, however, single out M. L. Rosenthal, who was one of my very few teachers who ever taught me how to read a poem. I am of course also indebted to the many scholars and critics who have written about Lowell's work, and I have indicated that indebtedness in the course of the study. I also suspect that they have led me toward insights that stemmed from their writings.

Colleagues and students have also assisted me by going through the manuscript or challenging my ideas. Mrs. Vincenza Pentick was a great help, and I owe much to Mr. Herbert Ruhm, whose criticisms were candid and whose suggestions were generous. Without his encouragement, I am not sure I would have been able to give final shape to the book. I wish to thank my wife for her understanding and assistance. I also want to express appreciation for the grant from the State University of New York, which enabled me to work on the book one summer. In addition, my students in the course, "Studies in Contemporary Poetry," increased my understanding of Lowell's work. I am keenly aware that I have taken and built upon some of the ideas they shared with me when we read Lowell in that spring of 1968 which was overwhelmed by "chance assassinations."

Finally, I must warn the reader that he will find two critical approaches in this book. One derives from the poem-oriented New Criticism which deeply influenced me when I was in graduate school. The other approach stems from those socially concerned critics, like George Steiner, Irving Howe, and Alfred Kazin, who have had a great impact on me since graduate school. Also, I must admit, that different books by Lowell bring forth different kinds of responses. It is said that after a time biographers begin to resemble their subjects. My own stylistic development and problems, I sometimes think, resemble on a lower level Lowell's development from *Land of Unlikeness* to *Life Studies*.

RICHARD J. FEIN

State University College
New Paltz, New York

Acknowledgments

Portions of the book have appeared previously, sometimes in altered forms, in the *Ball State University Forum, The Literary Review, The New England Quarterly, PMLA, Sewanee Review* and the *Southern Review*. I am grateful to their editors for allowing me to use this material.

Acknowledgment is also due to:
Farrar, Straus & Giroux for permission to quote: Selections from *77 Dream Songs* by John Berryman. Copyright © 1959, 1962, 1963, 1964 by John Berryman. From *Day by Day* by Robert Lowell. Copyright © 1975, 1976, 1977 by Robert Lowell. From *The Dolphin* by Robert Lowell. Copyright © 1973 by Robert Lowell. From *For The Union Dead* by Robert Lowell. Copyright © 1956, 1960, 1961, 1962, 1963, 1964 by Robert Lowell. From *History* by Robert Lowell. Copyright © 1967, 1968, 1969, 1970, 1973 by Robert Lowell. From *Imitations* by Robert Lowell. Copyright © 1958, 1959, 1960, 1961 by Robert Lowell. From *The Old Glory* by Robert Lowell. Copyright © 1964, 1965, 1968 by Robert Lowell. From *Life Studies* by Robert Lowell. Copyright © 1956, 1959 by Robert Lowell. From *Prometheus Bound* by Robert Lowell. Copyright © 1967, 1969 by Robert Lowell. Reprinted with the permission of Farrar, Straus & Giroux, Inc.
Harcourt Brace Jovanovich, Inc. for permission to quote excerpts from *Lord Weary's Castle* and *The Mills of the Kavanaughs* by Robert Lowell; copyright © 1946, 1948, 1951, 1974, 1976 by Robert Lowell.
New Directions Publishing Corporation for permission to quote an excerpt from *The Cantos,* copyright © 1948 by Ezra Pound. Viking Penguin Inc. for permission to quote from *Herzog,* copyright © 1961, 1963, 1964 by Saul Bellow.

Chronology

1917   Robert Traill Spence Lowell, Jr., the only child of Com-
        mander R. T. S. Lowell, USN, and Charlotte Winslow,
        born in Boston, March 1.
1935 - Attends Harvard.
1937
1937 - Transfers to and graduates from Kenyon College, where he
1940   majors in Classics and is a student of John Crowe Ransom.
1940   Converts to Catholicism; marries the novelist Jean Stafford.
1941 - Editorial assistant for Sheed & Ward, publishers.
1942
1943   Indicted for violation of the Selective Service Act. Sentenc-
        ed to a year and a day; serves five months.
1944   *Land of Unlikeness.*
1946   *Lord Weary's Castle*, awarded Pultizer Prize for Poetry.
1947   Consultant in Poetry at the Library of Congress.
1947 - Awarded Guggenheim Fellowship.
1948
1948   Divorces Jean Stafford.
1949   Marries the critic Elizabeth Hardwick.
1950 - Trip to Europe.
1953
1950   *Poems: 1938 - 1949.* Father dies.
1951   *The Mills of the Kavanaughs.*
1954   Mother dies.
1957   Daughter, Harriet Winslow Lowell, born.
1959   *Life Studies,* awarded the National Book Award.
1961   *Imitations,* awarded the Bollingen Prize; *Phaedra.*
1964   *For the Union Dead*
1965   *The Old Glory; Selected Poems.* Rejects an invitation to a
        White House Arts Festival in protest of American's foreign
        policy.
1967   *Near the Ocean.*
1969   *Prometheus Bound; Notebook 1967 - 68; The Voyage.*
1970   Revised and expanded edition of *Notebook.*

1972   Divorces Elizabeth Hardwick, marries novelist Caroline
        Blackwood and moves to England.
1973   *History; For Lizzie and Harriet; The Dolphin.*
1976   *Selected Poems.*
1977   *Day by Day.* Dies in New York, September 12.

CHAPTER 1

Prologue: Memories of Brooklyn and Robert Lowell

In discussing any writer, or in coming to terms with him, we must avoid the trap of mere abstract evaluation, and try to reproduce the actual conditions of our relation to him.

—Allen Tate, "Our Cousin, Mr. Poe"

THE library was a place by itself within the sandstone, white brick, academic-looking, and obscurely named Samuel J. Tilden High School. All that I knew about Tilden was that he was robbed of the presidential office he should have had and that we shared the same middle initial. But if there was always something puzzling for me about the school's name, the library was freedom. It wasn't crowded and it didn't smell like the cafeteria. Its tables were of shellacked wood, not like the ones in the cafeteria, whose dark green surfaces resembled calcified ink blotters, or some frozen thick bile, and were impervious to anything spilled on them. The more daring students would chip away at the stuff with penknives, and every piece wedged out was some kind of victory against this tough substance the school asked us to eat on.

The library was different—clean, quiet, and usually not crowded. Huge windows gave light to the large room, and there was plenty of space between the tables and the wooden shelves.

Before you were allowed to enter the library you had to deposit your books with a student clerk behind a cage in an alcove on whose shelved walls were square, numbered metal tags placed every foot or so. The clerks would store your books behind the cage on a shelf, in return for which you received a tag which allowed you to enter the library. Even then I thought that I was turning over my books to some miniature concentration camp but that my body was allowed to escape into the freedom of the library. Unintentionally, the

17

whole process became a symbol to a teen-ager's mind—leave your
school texts behind the cage while you enter the room where you
can read what your heart picks. The library was a place of freedom
for me; my school self was on a shelf behind a cage, and the institu-
tion wanted it that way. It was one of the few occasions in my
school career when the authorities and I seemed to be in some
secret agreement whereby I could imprison the institutional me and
escape into my real self. I could never hear the word *library* without
thinking of being liberated. It was a beautiful and inviting word to
me, like something growing on a tree. Sometimes it means that to
me now. Occasionally it meant that when I was a graduate student.

There were three of us who would meet in the back of the huge
room, near the magazine rack and in front of the librarian's office,
as if we wanted to invade the office and get still further back. We
always talked politics. With *Vital Speeches*, the *Congressional
Quarterly*, and the *New York Times* around us, we endlessly dis-
sected the follies of America. America was only a body to be
lacerated by our sharp, unrelenting minds which were filled with a
bitter idealism.

A senior in Tilden High School, moping into my future in 1947 -
48, I picked from the school library one day a new book of poems
entitled *Lord Weary's Castle*, by Robert Lowell. A thin black book,
except for the dull gold imprint of the title, author, and publisher
on its spine, its color, size, and title were different from most books
I read, despite the fact that I was used to reading poetry. It was
different from the big anthology of poems collected by John Kieran
that I borrowed from the neighborhood public library, with
Kieran's sparse, handsome, striking Aryan face on the front cover.

I think I picked up this book of poems, *Lord Weary's Castle*,
because I had never heard of a title like that before. Certainly both
its title and very smooth, dark cover were different from a collection
of Carl Sandburg's poems I had bought somewhere for a dollar,
with a picture of wheat on the front of the dust jacket. This book
was also unlike my paperback anthology of American poetry with its
shiny red and blue cover, a book I carried into the army and
pocketed and thumbed for years until one day it must have crumpled into oblivion. Only a James Russell Lowell, not a Robert
Lowell, was in that collection that went all the way back to Anne
Bradstreet.

Lord Weary's Castle was different from any other book I knew. It
did not look at all like some of the thick biographies and

autobiographies I read. Not at all like Jack Dempsey's *Round by Round* or Konrad Heiden's *Der Führer* or Teddy Roosevelt's account of his hunting trips in Africa or those many exposés of native fascist movements I found as exciting as novels. This little book of poems was also unlike the Modern Library Giant edition of John Dos Passos' *U.S.A.* There was a title I could sink my teeth into; there was an author whose name always meant to me pathways into America. How could the elusive, vaguely self-negating title of *Lord Weary's Castle* stand alongside that three-lettered epic? How could the slender book of poems (a phrase I learned from the *New York Times* Sunday book reviews) stand up against *U.S.A.*, which literally could hide the poetry between its pages? After all, could Lowell's *Lord Weary's Castle* have an impact on me comparable to Dos Passos' trilogy, which for a week after I read it convinced me I was a Communist? What possible conversions could lie in that book of difficult poems?

Certainly it was also different from my Modern Library edition of Whitman's *Leaves of Grass* with its forest green, soft cardboard cover (here was a book I knew by the color of its cover), or different from the Modern Library Giant edition which I later took out of the library and which had even more of Whitman's poems and some woodcut illustrations.

At any rate I was to find no fellow traveller on a Brooklyn trolley car who was reading *Lord Weary's Castle* as I had found a slightly older girl next to me one day reading *Leaves of Grass*. I was so anxious to talk to her about "Song of Myself" that even though I knew it could be taken for a mere pass, I excitedly asked what she thought of Whitman's poem. Her un-Whitmanesque and cold response set me completely aback. I crouched back into myself—all I had wanted to do was to talk to her about the poetry. I mourned inwardly. Weren't all readers of Whitman's poetry soul-mates of some sort? "And who but I should be the poet of comrades?" "Camerado, this is no book,/Who touches this touches a man." No, poetry never turned out to be exactly the same thing as life. The thought of how poetry could lead into its equivalent in life always tormented me.

Why *did* I take *Lord Weary's Castle* from the shelf? I can't think of anyone more ill prepared than I was for understanding the book. Even my love of poetry did not train me for this kind of work; maybe some obscure Poe poems would have been more to my bent. I was contrary to *Lord Weary's Castle*. Generally speaking, poetry

was for me either the Whitman longings of "Crossing Brooklyn
Ferry," or the hope and optimism of Sandburg's *The People, Yes,* or
Oscar Wilde's "The Ballad of Reading Gaol," whose last word in
the title and whose line "And all men kill the thing they love" in-
toxicated me. I used to recite passages from Whitman, Wilde, Sandburg, and others near a window at home from which I could see the
poles of trolley cars emit blue sparks on making initial contact with
the overhanging electric wires. What could I be doing with such an
intellectual and baroque book as *Lord Weary's Castle* except that its
very title seemed a distant cousin of Wilde's title? I was riper for a
book like Henry Roth's *Call It Sleep.*

My political interests could not have instructed me to pick up
that book of poems. How could I have known that the author of
Lord Weary's Castle had been sent to jail during World War II as a
conscientious objector? I didn't know he had done time for a
political cause even after I had read his book. Did I know from his
poems that he was mocking a false New England tradition while
ironically upholding its true revolution? Did I know that in his
poems the poet was showing us his religious rebellion and his conflict with his father and his family? Did I know that the book was
born of some postwar refugee spirit? How could I have known these
things at the time? I hardly understood the poems. Then what attracted me to the book, made me take it home? There was a gap
between my everyday interests, even my ordinary literary interests,
and this particular book of poems, a gap that more than a decade
later I could only begin to bridge, a gap that some part of me must
have earnestly wanted or felt it couldn't escape. It was a gap that
separated my everyday self from my imagination which was
hungering for something else. It was a gap I secretly and puzzlingly
wanted between my mind and the world's reality I thought I was
committed to. I think reading *Lord Weary's Castle* was my first intellectual taste of alienation.

I must have also chosen the book because, snide-minded as I was,
no one else in the entire school, I thought, would ever read it. Or it
was a book only the unhappy few would read. Years later when
someone might take the book out he would know that once there
was a student who had tackled this difficult book. That I understood
little of the book hardly mattered. I had my name down as its
borrower—though I couldn't escape the feeling that somehow it
had borrowed me. It was a mixture of puzzling, shameful, confused,

and precious motivations that led me to take the book off the shelf, to scan it, and then check it out. I carried the book home like some special dark shield against the world. I entered *Lord Weary's Castle* (the title still fascinates me so much that I can't refrain from repeating it) as my retreat and my fortress.

How to describe my reactions to that book? The book was a swirl, and I can still feel it! Without my understanding it, the poetry shook me up, spun something inside of me. I think it was the first time I ever read anything that I didn't understand but that moved me, that touched me though it wasn't clear to me. To this day I cannot pick up my own copy (purchased long since at a Fourth Avenue bookstore in New York) without feeling that swirl or turmoil, as if the poems leave their book and storm around my head. In all, I think the poems came at me in a way I could only come close to explaining by quoting a passage from Lowell's imitation of Eugenio Montale's poem "Dora Markus":

> Your restlessness makes me think
> of migratory birds diving at a lighthouse
> on an ugly night—
> even your ennui is a whirlwind,
> circling invisibly—
> the let-ups non-existent.

The poems were the birds, and my mind was the entire scene of the birds storming around the lighthouse.

Though the title *Lord Weary's Castle* always intrigued me—what a mysterious title of grandeur and tiredness—I never understood it. The fact that the poet explained the title in an introductory note didn't seem to help me. No formal explanation would have made me completely understand the strange way the title possessed me. I can understand that title better now as over the years worn edges and seams of white have broken through the dark cover of my own copy. But, then and now, the title meant more than the note explaining it as part of an old ballad about a mason who built Lord Weary's castle but received no payment for his labors. I did not intellectually, or artistically, understand the title, but it appealed to me deeply, to some noble but frustrating sense of my adolescent self. I was seventeen years old, torn between imitating Oscar Wilde writing "The Ballad of Reading Gaol" and making speeches as a United States senator fighting for democracy overseas and at home.

Lord Weary's Castle's Latin epigraph was as alien to me as anything could be; I knew that there was something deep within this book that I could never share. I did feel some intense, despairing, and apocalyptic religious sensibility in the book, for which at the time I had little sympathy. But I did find some poems about war that moved me. True, many details and references escaped me, and I was often lost in the woods of the poems. But even though I couldn't name the trees, I did feel the forest I was in. It was not simply a forest of my ignorance, but a darkness of experience the poems were pulling me into. I could feel something terrible about war in this poetry, and I could feel something in the poems that spoke with the authority of history, of some permanent experience.

Nobody in the book quite suffered as I thought I suffered, and nobody in the book seemed to come from my kind of family. But somewhere in my imagination I must have been enthralled by a rhetoric about death that confused me and yet that finally revealed a conclusion I felt I understood.

France

(From the Gibbet)

My human brothers who live after me,
See how I hang. My bones eat through the
    skin
And flesh they carried here upon the chin
And lipping clutch of their cupidity;
Now here, now there, the starling and the
    sea
Gull splinter the groined eyeballs of my sin,
Brothers, more beaks of birds than needles
    in
The fathoms of the Bayeux Tapestry:
"God wills it, wills it, wills it: it is blood."
My brothers, if I call you brothers, see:
The blood of Abel crying from the dead
Sticks to my blackened skull and eyes.
    What good
Are *lebensraum* and bread to Abel dead
And rotten on the cross-beams of the tree?

I had no idea that the poem was based on a passage by Villon; had no one to instruct me that it was an Italian sonnet (whose sestet, I later dutifully learned and still later dutifully taught, was supposed to resolve the problem expressed in its octet); I probably even missed the Christian image at the end and must have had to look at the word *gibbet*. But I could see and hear the victim, knew that his situation and sorrow were as old as the Old Testament, and understood without instruction the connection of the poem and its German word to recent military and political ventures. But something else was there in the poem, another element that throughout the book had a hidden appeal to me: "the starling and the sea / Gull splinter the groined eyeballs of my sin. . . ." I don't think I have ever understood that passage and still hope that no student of mine ever calls upon me to explicate it for him. But I am sure that when I was seventeen and a half and was reading *Lord Weary's Castle* I was excited over lines like that, and the book seemed to have them on every page. Whatever they meant, and it didn't really matter what they meant, there was something about the corkscrew imagery that got to me, that went into me in ways Oscar Wilde's refrains and Whitman's *saluts au monde* could not.

Much older and wiser by degrees, I think I now understand some of those poems in *Lord Weary's Castle*, but I critically distrust such poetic rhetoric: so much manner but what meaning? Yet I can still recall the secret, almost sexual thrill of reading such poetry. The poetry was invading me against my will, unlike the other poetry I was reading which I could swim in. It was the first time in my life that I went out of my way to read and reread something I didn't understand. I couldn't defend this work to anyone, hardly explain it to myself, but I was secretly drawn to it. Now I think of Emerson's words near the end of "The Poet": "An imaginative book renders us much more service at first, by stimulating us through its tropes, than afterward when we arrive at the precise sense of the author." How could my harried guidance counselor have ever known I was on my long way to graduate school as an English major?

The two poems from *Lord Weary's Castle* that impressed me most of all were the two major elegies, "In Memory of Arthur Winslow" and "The Quaker Graveyard in Nantucket," one about the death of the poet's grandfather, the other about the death of the poet's cousin in the navy during the war.

Again, I felt uncomfortable with some of the Christian concerns in the poems. (The work of T. S. Eliot, years later, first encouraged me to feel I could come to terms with and freely respond to a Christian poem or a poem indebted to Christian experience and knowledge.) But something else in Lowell's poems did appeal to my

imagination and enabled me to put aside any uncomfortable un-
religious feelings I may have had. To this day the ending of the second stanza from "In Memory of Arthur Winslow" is thrilling for me
to read. Here is the entire stanza:

> Grandfather Winslow, look, the swanboats
>   coast
> That island in the Public Gardens, where
> The bread-stuffed ducks are brooding, where
>   with tub
> And strainer the mid-Sunday Irish scare
> The sun-struck shallows for the dusky chub
> This Easter, and the ghost
> Of risen Jesus walks the waves to run
> Arthur upon a trumpeting black swan
> Beyond Charles River to the Acheron
> Where the wide waters and their voyager
>   are one.

The mid-Sunday or any-other-day Irish didn't interest me, nor their
weekend play in some garden or other, and I must have had to look
up the name *Acheron*, but there was and still is something
marvellous about the merging of the Christian and the pagan experience in the poem; it was the mixture that I found exciting and
different. I was thrilled that the poem "took place" in Boston, not
simply the real Boston of which I knew nothing but a Boston that
was both a real *and* a mythical place. Stranger though I was to the
city, the poet was not, and he made certain that my imagination
knew this Boston where his grandfather died. My imagination knew
it knew. Since I have gone to college, Boston has conjured up for
me a place called the Common where Emerson once strolled with
Whitman, but it is also a place where swanboats I never saw (what
my imagination did with that!) floated on a river where Grandfather
Winslow, King Arthur, and I voyaged, the three of us making one
myth.

   The poem that impressed me even more, that took me up and
swirled me about at the same time it was knotted and gnarled with
sounds and rhythms that threatened to overwhelm me, was "The
Quaker Graveyard in Nantucket." Its conclusion stirred me up. The
poem contains all the life and violent contradictions of Genesis.
Something of its affirmation of life coming up out of a sense of
divine destruction and turmoil appealed to me at the time.

> The empty winds are creaking and the oak
> Splatters and splatters on the cenotaph,
> The boughs are trembling and a gaff
> Bobs on the untimely stroke
> Of the greased wash exploding on a shoal-
>　　bell
> In the old mouth of the Atlantic. It's well;
> Atlantic, you are fouled with the blue
>　　sailors,
> Sea-monsters, upward angel, downward fish:
> Unmarried and corroding, spare of flesh
> Mart once of supercilious, wing'd clippers,
> Atlantic, where your bell-trap guts its spoil
> You could cut the brackish winds with a
>　　knife
> Here in Nantucket, and cast up the time
> When the Lord God formed man from the
>　　sea's slime
> And breathed into his face the breath of life,
> And blue-lung'd combers lumbered to the
>　　kill.
> The Lord survives the rainbow of His will.

Years later, during our honeymoon on Martha's Vineyard, my wife and I took an excursion to Nantucket to see that graveyard (and the island Melville's Ishmael shipped out from). The field of weeds with stones slanted into the earth was a large lot which happened to be a cemetery. It wasn't the crowded and elegant city of tombs and plots I was used to seeing in New Jersey and Long Island. It was the first graveyard I had ever seen that was open to ocean and air. It looked as if it were falling apart and in a few years would be unrecognizable. I don't know what I expected, maybe God himself blowing through the field and around the stones. He was blowing through those whipped-up lines in the poem, wasn't He? Whenever I wonder about what attracted me to *Lord Weary's Castle* I think of this force blowing through "The Quaker Graveyard in Nantucket."

I suppose it was in the cards for me to write a part of my Ph.D. dissertation on Robert Lowell and still later on to write a book about him. And as his books appeared I was more interested in the later work than in the poetry of *Lord Weary's Castle*. Although I am open to the argument that *Lord Weary's Castle* is the best book he produced, I still would surrender it for *Life Studies* if I had to choose between the two and if only one book of Lowell's poetry could remain with me. The sensibility in *Life Studies* is more gracious and vibrant than the one housed (or locked) in *Lord Weary's Castle*. Such poems from *Life Studies* as "A Mad Negro Soldier Confined at Munich," "To Delmore Schwartz," "Words for Hart Crane," "Memories of West Street and Lepke," "Skunk Hour," speak more immediately to me than anything in *Lord Weary's Castle*. These are the poems, *Life Studies* is the book, I wish I could have written. They are the kinds of struggles of awareness I wish I could put into poetry. The poems to the Negro soldier, to Schwartz, and to Crane honor other men in a way that honors the poet who can write such poems, and they are the kind of honorings to which a reader must respond.

Obviously, *Life Studies* is the book I am in love with. It is second only to *Leaves of Grass* in American poetry. In addition, only *Walden* and *Moby Dick* make me feel such a passion that I wonder if I don't physically change as I think of these books. In particular, *Life Studies* is for me a great work because it is the first book that brings to American poetry the Russian spirit of poetry. *Life Studies* is a book in which the political and private consciousness of the poet urges the reader to remain human by being loyal to his freedom and to his turmoil. That striking atmosphere of Russian literature that encourages a character to fathom his depths and to surface with a rich and contradictory sense of his feelings—an embarrassing self-betrayal that turns out to be a touching self-discovery—is also evident in *Life Studies*. In his own fashion, Lowell responds to the question raised prophetically by Dostoevski in *Notes from the Underground:* "Can a man who attempts to find enjoyment in the very feeling of his own degradation possibly have a spark of respect for himself?" Lowell pursues this question in *Life Studies*, particularly in the final and culminating poem, "Skunk Hour." In *Life Studies* the poet's art defends our human confusions against the forces of restriction and betrayal. Partly born of the Joe McCarthy era, *Life Studies* expresses the deepest and most moving kind of confessions about one's past. And in *Life Studies*, as Alfred Kazin has put it, "twentieth-century poetry comes back to its great tradition as plain speech; comes back, in Pasternak's phrase, 'to its sister, life.' "

Life Studies (and Lowell's play *Benito Cereno*) appeal to our sense of our situation, with its poems about an incarcerated Negro, the disturbed, poor, and drunken poets, the poet jailed as a conscientious objector, the poet breathing his freedom above the garbage pail; and with the play's confrontation between the American and the Negro, each playing a role for the other.

However, even after having acknowledged the attraction of *Life Studies*, and of some of Lowell's other works, I must confess that *Lord Weary's Castle*, nonetheless, appeals to two other (and related) parts of me: the graduate school self, the explicator of difficult lines; and the late teen-ager, high-school self who, from whatever motivation, took down the book and was swirled around by a poetry he never really understood but that moved his imagination. What is still so compelling about that book's compulsive rhetoric? Does the way it insists on the excess of its language reflect my own inclinations for language alone to create the world I inhabit? Does the book's rhetorical insistence parallel my own emphatic yet inverted desires to find in words the basis of my action in the world? I stand by *Lord Weary's Castle* ready to criticize its overcharged language, its rhetorical and overdone religious pleas, at the same time that I am prepared to read it as I did for the first time, captivated by its language jumping out of itself.

CHAPTER 2

Lowell's Career

The two first American Hathornes [sic] had been people of importance and responsibility; but with the third generation the family lapsed into an obscurity from which it emerged in the very person of the writer, who begs so gracefully for a turn in its affairs.

—Henry James, *Hawthorne*

THOUGH born into a famous Boston family, Robert Lowell had always been more interested in relatively unknown or unsung members of his family than in his literary or culturally prominent forebears. Not James Russell Lowell or Amy Lowell, the poets of the family, but his civic and military ancestors interested him.

A member of his mother's family, Edward Winslow, arrived on the *Mayflower;* the first of the Lowells did not get to these shores until 1639. The Winslows (and the Starks, other maternal relatives) occupied a prominent place in the history of the colonies and at the time of the Revolution. The Lowells, of course, were influential in the development of New England. These ancestors afforded a rich and contradictory tradition for Robert Lowell. That significant role of the family in the past caused him, as one of its descendants, to question and distrust the official culture. Josiah Winslow, commander-in-chief of the colonial forces in the brutal Indian battles known as King Philip's War, was an ancestor of Robert Lowell, who was very conscious of the military aggressions of his country. Yet as his poetry also attests, Lowell could indicate admiration for members of the family who were officers in the Revolution and in the Civil War, and he mourns and mocks the impotent naval career of his own father. He also respects some of the civic achievements of his ancestors. Lowell's increasing sense of himself as a poet committed to some public role may have been related to his profound and critical understanding of the roles his ancestors once played in the history of the country, especially in the history of

28

New England. Lowell's sense of his family is important, therefore, to his poetry and to his views of himself and of his country.

By the middle of the twentieth century both branches of the family no longer possessed the cultural influence they once had. If the prose and poetry of *Life Studies* are any indication, Robert Lowell was born into a family whose earlier postures and ambitions diminished to those frustrations and anxieties that might overshadow any middle-class domicile in which the father is a failure and the mother nags him and their son with her ambitions. As a result, *Lord Weary's Castle* and *Life Studies* show Lowell as striving for some redeemable sense of the family's once-important civic and military roles. The overall impression, however, is that the family's position has declined.

From his sense of some family failure, one related to the history of the country, Lowell emerges. In "In Memory of Arthur Winslow," Lowell's grandfather is almost a commercial parody of the energy of his Revolutionary ancestors; and the failures of the poet's father are relentlessly displayed in *Life Studies*. In both the prose and in the poetry of *Life Studies*, Lowell exposes the burdens of identity he felt in his family and tells us about his search for himself through and beyond his family name. Much of Lowell's career can be viewed, therefore, as his special search for his *true* ancestors and relatives. Moreover, his own rebellions are sometimes related to his ability to rediscover the family's past, and they are sometimes part of his struggle to go beyond the certified but damaged inheritance. The origins of Lowell's commitment to and rebellion from tradition lie in his sense of his family.

Even his formal education represents some of his uneasy relationships to family expectations. After attending schools selected by his mother, Lowell eventually transferred from Harvard University (only recently presided over by a relative, Lawrence Lowell) to Kenyon College—a switch that was one of his many family "betrayals," but some were tolerated more than others. By changing colleges, Lowell indicated his desire to receive a vigorous education in a school where poetry was being written as well as taught. At Kenyon poetry was at one and the same time part of the tradition and part of one's own efforts. At Kenyon Lowell studied under John Crowe Ransom, roomed with Peter Taylor, and met Randall Jarrell. Like Ezra Pound and T. S. Eliot, who also found fellow writers at the University of Pennsylvania and at Harvard, and whose academic majors were Romance languages and philosophy, respectively, Lowell did not choose English as a major but the Classics. Influenced by the half-ironic advice of Ford Madox Ford, Lowell found that reading Classical literature was a way of keeping in touch with humanity. Like Pound and Eliot, Lowell came to the study and writing of poetry in English through an ambitious academic training. Before going to college, Lowell, as a student at St. Mark's School (one of whose headmasters during the nineteenth century was an occasional poet named Robert Traill Spence Lowell) received encouragement in his poetic endeavors from one of the teachers there, the poet Richard Eberhart. Lowell's young earnestness with Allen Tate and Ford Madox Ford also speaks for his poetic seriousness. As a young man, he had planned to do an anthology with Tate; and even when he was an undergraduate, he had assisted Ford Madox Ford in putting together his book, *The March of Literature*.[1] There is something Miltonic about Lowell's preparations to be a poet, though we must exclude the broad-minded sympathy that Milton's father showed for his son's ambitions.

Lowell's early poetry, intellectually and rhetorically intense, displayed the textual concerns of the New Critics, whose influence through Ransom and Tate he personally felt. His early work also showed the influence of John Donne, Gerard Manley Hopkins, Dylan Thomas, and Jonathan Edwards. Like so much of modern poetry (and of modern art in general), Lowell's poetry was going to go to extremes in the technical and intellectually idiosyncratic demands it would make upon itself. Indeed, John Crowe Ransom found Lowell's work so overloaded that he was disinclined to include it in the *Kenyon Review*, of which he was editor.[2]

Lowell's first book, *Land of Unlikeness* (1944), displays the clotted style and the gnarled intellectuality of his early poetry. His second book, *Lord Weary's Castle* (1946), shows a maturer resolution of these matters. And by the time of *Life Studies* (1959), Lowell could look back and almost find himself a stranger to his earlier work. His entire career reveals a plunging into one kind of style, eventually to be replaced by another, just as he has left one kind of home for another. Yet there is also a looking back and a returning to old ·materials—a desire to tighten or loosen previous concerns and styles in the poetry. The initial poem of *Lord Weary's Castle*, "The Exile's Return," captures the rhythms of return and estrangement at an early point in Lowell's career.

Curiously, during college, Lowell was fascinated by the poetry of

William Carlos Williams, unfashionable though such an interest
was in his circles. He even tried, he said, to write in the Williams
manner,[3] although we do not see the Williams influence surfacing
until *Life Studies*. Hart Crane may be regarded as the intermediary
talent, in Lowell's development, between the verbal pyrotechnics of
the poets who influenced his first two volumes and the
"democratic" gestures of Williams, whom Lowell in later years increasingly acknowledged as an important poet. Possibly Lowell had
to go through the rhetorical phase of his first volumes in order to
return to an even earlier view he had had of his poetry, a view
which he could not accept until he felt he had tried the interesting
tones and experiments of "modern poetry."

From his development it appears that Lowell had put aside one
part of himself in order to learn from the textual skills of the New
Critics, his *personal* teachers, as a student will do when he comes
under some brilliant masters; then he rediscovered that part of
himself temporarily put aside, a passionate rediscovery precisely
because it marked a self-acceptance and a self-identification.
Lowell's poetry combines both his urge to exploit the modern inheritance, exemplified in the work of Eliot and Pound, and his
desire to free himself from it. In general, Lowell's development
shows itself to be something like Yeats's, as he moved from some
modish, though not for him artificial, style, to the personal constructions of his later work.

Similarly, Lowell's conversion to Catholicism in 1940 and his subsequent deconversion sometime later in that decade convey the
rhythm of commitment followed by a restlessness. (It was also during the 1940s that he married and then later divorced novelist Jean
Stafford.) The conversion to Catholicism seems to have been a step
Lowell took partly out of a need to "structure" his despair through
appropriate figures or values found within the Church. Lowell may
have also taken the step of conversion as another means of testing
himself against the family patterns he was supposed to inherit (just
as his refusal to serve in World War II represents another version of
that testing). Robert Frost's observation that a man like Franklin
Delano Roosevelt could amount to something despite the
guarantees of his family position applies to Lowell's career, for
Lowell has seemingly always felt a need to exploit and yet to surmount the questionable inheritance. Lowell's religious conversion
and political conscience, however, should not be relegated to merely an esthetic or a family strategy. Finally, as with T. S. Eliot,

Lowell's moral conversions, political and religious, have a value independent of his personality or of his poetry; but keenly felt through the poetry is the man who is searching for and even discovering his passions.

In the 1940s and during World War II Lowell, after trying to enlist in the navy, finally decided to become a conscientious objector and to oppose what he considered America's increasingly brutal waging of the war. Sentenced to a year and a day, but serving only five months, Lowell merged his religious and social rebellion during his wartime protest. Such a merger, though on a somewhat altered level, was to reoccur during the 1960s when Lowell objected to American intervention and fighting in Vietnam. As an act of protest against the war, he publicly rejected President Lyndon Johnson's invitation to a White House Festival of the Arts.

In the early 1950s Lowell spent several years in Europe, eventually returning to Boston, where he also did some teaching. In the early 1960s, with his second wife, the critic Elizabeth Hardwick, and their daughter, Harriet Winslow Lowell, he moved from Boston to New York. Perhaps this important move from New England can be considered as another kind of conversion on his part, another attempt by him to go beyond "the Boston heritage," as well as a reflection of the current attraction of the New York literary scene. In 1972, Lowell divorced Elizabeth Hardwick and married the novelist Caroline Blackwood, settling in England with stints of teaching at Harvard. At the time of his sudden death in September of 1977, it appears that Lowell was planning to spend more time in the United States while his family remained in England.

In summary of some important factors of Lowell's career: while he moved from Boston to New York to England, New England remained a permanent part of his imagination; he converted to and then was converted from Catholicism; he objected to America's brutality and refused to serve in World War II, yet in his poetry he is fascinated by the military hero; his highly conscious sense of literary tradition was fused with his desire to "make it new"; he was critically attached to his New England ancestors and to what they had made of themselves. In all of these ways, Lowell has made us feel that in reading his work we are in contact with those experiences of examination, choice and re-discovery that make up a man's identity and self-knowledge.

CHAPTER 3

Visiting Lord Weary's Castle

When a reality of human existence has completed its historic course, has been shipwrecked and lies dead, the waves throw it up on the shores of rhetoric, where the corpse remains for a long time. Rhetoric is the cemetery of human realities, or at any rate a Home for the Aged. The reality itself is survived by its name, which though only a word, is after all at least a word and preserves something of its magic power.

—Jose Ortega y Gasset, *The Revolt of the Masses*

A S the visitor to the Metropolitan Museum of Art enters the fifth room of the European Paintings Collection, a room "longitudinal as Versailles," he notices alongside the near right wall two glass cases set at eye level, each above a wooden base. Inside the rectangular glass enclosures are two pieces of military equipment, probably created only for display purposes.

In the glass case on the right, about fifteen feet diagonally from the entrance, there is raised on a metal shaft a parade helmet from the time of Louis XIV (ca. 1700). Made of silver, with mountings in bronze, chiseled and gilded, this heavy helmet of thirteen pounds and six ounces most likely served for state occasions rather than for actual military use. On the top of the helmet lurks a fabulous monster with the tail of a snake sliding down the back of the helmet and tapering to the head of an arrow near the base. The body of this lizard-like lion, with its feet clutching a bronze strip raised at the top of the helmet and also tapered toward the back, sprouts the wings of a pterodactyl. A pointed tongue sticks out from its wolfish face. Projecting a little over the front edge of the helmet is the face of a bear. Above this face, three bronze folds curl upward. All embellishments are in bronze and look like gold.

About fifteen feet to the left, the visitor finds the second glass case. Here again is displayed a military piece from the time of Louis XIV, this one a parade shield, also made of silver with mountings in bronze, chiseled and gilded. (Both objects, except for the bronze decorations, look as though they were made of black marble, with perhaps a hint of purple.) Again that heavy weight (thirteen pounds, eleven ounces) suggests that this piece also served for state occasions rather than for real defense in a war. In the middle of this oval shield is the head of a bronze Gorgon: creased forehead; thick eyebrows arching downward, like lumps dripping from the wrinkled forehead, into the bridge between the fiery eyes; both eyeballs converging diagonally downward in the direction of the snorting nose; nostrils reared back. The mouth is wide open, a peculiar circle, a few upper teeth showing, the tongue striking out over a thick lower lip. Arcs of anger or of age are etched under the eyes and around the sides of the mouth. Around the entire face is a braided pattern of entwined golden snakes that threaten to envelop the face and crawl all over the shield.

Between these two cases that hold the helmet and the shield is a large canvas of Nicolas Poussin's "The Rape of the Sabine Women." Above this canvas is an even larger picture entitled "The Building of Carthage." A red carpet begins between the two cases and runs down the middle of the long floor.

Both of these military artifacts, shaped presumably for state occasions, reside behind glass in frozen splendor. They are showpieces, and turning from them while standing on the red rug, one looks down the room and sees the long walls tiered with canvases. The helmet and shield from the age of the Sun King serve as unintended introductory guardians to this long room crowded with European art. In their cultivated hardness, in their sophisticated glory reduced to show and inspection, these two objects might serve as emblems, as metaphors we can appropriate for consideration of Robert Lowell's first significant book of poems, *Lord Weary's Castle*, published in 1946.

I   *Title and Tone*

In *Lord Weary's Castle* Lowell shows himself in touch with English poetic traditions and with the myths, value systems, and dimensions of history that make up American and European heritages. Lowell sets up the poems in the book as studied works that express a fascination for and discontent with the Western culture in which they are so grandly, unhappily, and intelligently immersed.

The book's title comes from an Irish ballad about a nobleman who refused to pay his debts after having had his fine castle built. Lord Weary's refusal to meet his obligations to the mason who built his home for him results in the destruction of his family by the angry and unpaid builder. Lord Weary's is a depleted nobility. On one level, the title may refer to the culture or a system of belief the owner has no right to claim as his own because he has not honored the terms and obligations of its creation. One poem in the book, "The Death of the Sheriff," refers to Priam's father, Laomedon, who hired Poseidon to build the walls of Troy but who refused to pay when the work was completed. For this default, Laomedon's daughter is abducted and his sons killed, except for his son Priam, who remains alive long enough to see the doomed city and *his* many sons destroyed by the Greeks, aided by Poseidon. That castle of the title may also refer to the world created by God but turned into all sorts of commercial, military, religious, or familial establishments which are constructed at the expense of the owners' debt to God and to other men. That mason may also be seen as representing the exploited lower class, the true creators of value, who will take their ultimate revenge on selfish owners.

Lord Weary's Castle is Lowell's effort to house his sensibility in an older world of Catholic belief, of classical themes, of American experience, of European history, of inherited poetic forms he fiercely energizes. It is the strenuous book of a poet all wound up and ready to spring from his almost unbearable present into the past. One inviting aspect of the past is that it always seems more structured than our present. Even their "chaos" looks more orderly to our eyes than our historical moments. And of course the past can be meaningfully appropriated for our own turmoil.

Still and all, has there ever existed a reader not puzzled or disturbed by *Lord Weary's Castle?* The reader weathers not only all that knowledge rammed into the poems, all those allusions, all that heavy historicity, and a prosody of wrenched anger, but also an insistence on attitudes that almost seem dictatorial on the part of the poet—dictatorial to history, to God, to the poet himself, and to his rhythms: "The fathoms of the Bayeux Tapestry: / God wills it, wills it, wills it: it is blood.'" One wants to squirm out of lines like that. Despite the fact that a great deal of history is on the poet's side, the charge against God seems less pressing than the poet's own obsession.

Some thirty years after its publication, *Lord Weary's Castle* is

puzzling and impressive in its insistence on God's forceful will in
the domain of history; in its dedication to the idea of some furious
religious commitment; and in the hidden self of the poet (whose
presence in the book can now be seen more clearly than originally).
The poems have a frozen grandeur, almost defying anyone to crack
through them. They are polished showpieces on display in the
museum of Lowell's troubled mind. Some of the poems sound like
glorious, manic thrusts at history's turmoil:

> The eagles gather as the West invades
> The Holy Land of Russia. Lord and glory
> Of dragonish, unfathomed waters, rise!

Not many poets during the forties could simultaneously damn
Napoleon and Hitler in lines like that. But might not Lowell have
overdone things a bit by demanding that God's anathemas and the
ruin of nations converge?

Two points may be made here: one is the obsession with war that
dominates Lowell's book; the second is the histrionic quality of the
war in some of the poems. Lowell opens the poem "War":

> Where basilisk and mortar lob their lead
> Whistling against the cloud sheep overhead,
> Scarlet or green, before their black-tongued Sire,
> The massed battalions flounder into fire
> Until the furnace of affliction turns
> A hundred thousand men to stone and burns
> The poor dead in the summer grass.

Sometimes the war seems like some gigantic scene out of a pageant
of Revelations. (One of the strains of *Lord Weary's Castle* is due to
the difficulty of coupling pity to such a clenched, apocalyptic
language.) It is as if Lowell stages history, especially war, in the
poems.

But we can also look at the opening part of the justly praised
"The Quaker Graveyard in Nantucket" (dedicated to a cousin killed
at sea). There we find descriptions of war that have a strenuous immediacy about them, in the sense that a forceful wave pounds on
the shore this moment but at the same time has carried that energy
from afar:

> A brackish reach of shoal off Madaket,—
> The sea was still breaking violently and night

Had steamed into our North Atlantic Fleet,
When the drowned sailor clutched the drag-net. . . .

. . . .

Sailors, who pitch this portent at the sea
Where dreadnoughts shall confess
Its hell-bent deity,
When you are powerless
To sand-bag this Atlantic bulwark, faced
By the earth-shaker, green, unwearied, chaste
In his steel scales: ask for no Orphean lute
To pluck life back. The guns of the steeled fleet
Recoil and then repeat
The hoarse salute.

Here is a muscular immediacy that any reader must respect and might admire and a warning that a reader is compelled to contemplate as Lowell in much of *Lord Weary's Castle* grapples with the awful results of military ventures.

II *Religious Poetry*

Although *Lord Weary's Castle* is by a Catholic convert, religious belief is a dour thing in the book. Lowell addresses the Virgin Mary from afar and can only convert her into a strange, small statue at an English shrine where "once the penitents took off their shoes." Presumably not many people come there anymore. And should the world again retreat to Walsingham, it will discover that Mary herself is now divorced from "Calvary's cross . . .[and] crib at Bethlehem."

Any one of the women in the book, like Katherine of "Between the Porch and the Altar," or the dying Mary Winslow, is felt more immediately than the Virgin Mary and the salutations to her. It would seem that Lowell was trying to invoke a figure of compassion that he himself did not believe in. Furthermore, he tries to petition this virginal figure in a century when only a few artists or writers could approach her with any assurance. Maybe a Rouault could invoke her. At one and the same time Lowell would have been on more interesting and also traditional ground if, during World War II, he had tried to describe in his poetry someone on the order of Catholic pacifist Dorothy Day.

In *Can These Bones Live?* a book of essays about American literature, Edward Dahlberg makes a comment pertinent to these considerations of Lowell's work. Dahlberg felt compelled to complain that "there is no Magdalene, not even a Mary or a Martha, in the Puritan Testament; woman does not exist in these literary masterpieces, in *Moby-Dick*, or in *Walden*. There has never been a *Mater Dolorosa* in America, Our Lady of Succor."[1] *Lord Weary's Castle* (no haven), Lowell's addition to the Puritan Testament of American literature, also exemplifies Dahlberg's mournful observation. Lowell was striving for a Virgin Mary who, however, was unavailable to him on a number of levels. No wonder Lowell could look back to this book years later, years during which his mother, his wife, and his daughter came to occupy bold places in his poetry, and wonder how he ever wrote it.

Despite his efforts to invoke Mary, to refer to God's justice, to steep the book in an apocalyptic religious imagery, this is the poetry of a man who does not believe in a loving God, in the mercy of the Virgin Mary, or in the offerings of priestly grace as much as he believes that man invokes his doom during World War II. Referring to the military acts of the 1940s as well as to their gross recrudescence two decades later, Lowell observed about himself in September, 1967: "I have never gotten over the horrors of American bombing."[2] Surely here we find the real beliefs, the real source of the imagery, that haunted *Lord Weary's Castle*—that title image of a nation-state built and owned by a callous man whose sons will pay for his sins. (As the Latin epigraph to the book indicates, Lowell conceived of his poems as payment to God for freedom from sin. Lowell, unlike the lord of the title, and unlike the family oriented to a military and public career, of which he was an unlikely scion, offered up his poetry as a commemoration to the martyrdom of saints and as a counterclaim to the aggressive lives of men.)

One of the tensions of *Lord Weary's Castle* results from Lowell's reaching for a Christian redemptive meaning for the experience he sees about him, a meaning in which he believes only partly. The pictures on the title pages of *Land of Unlikeness* and *Lord Weary's Castle* are shapes of violence augmented but not redeemed by religious awareness. On the title page of the first book a fiendish gargoyle is wrapped around a cross, snorting and grimacing into the distance, beyond the page, seemingly beyond the reader and any human appeal. On the second book's title page, a naked Cain takes a demonic glance backward at his fallen brother and skulks away from the contorted, stricken body. These pictures dramatize the

concerns of the poetry. It is a poetry rarely touched by the
Catholicism of an Erasmus, who looked upon human experience
and tolerantly observed: "A thing is not godless simply because it is
imperfect."[3]

Perhaps the only way Lowell felt he could "do" *Lord Weary's
Castle* and prevent that dour faith from collapsing in on itself was to
shore it up with monumental slabs of history, fierce props main-
taining and pressuring contemporary scenes of destruction. Or he
could try to bolster the figures of Mary and God through an
overcharged language that would insure their firm presence. The
very stylistic virtuosity of the book may, at first glance, conceal the
gap between the supposed Catholic commitment and the book's
true despair (a despair, ironically, met and possibly transcended in
its opening secular poem, "The Exile's Return"). Writing all of
those poems so formally propped up, chiseled, and gilded,
sometimes entwined in rhyme, and containing all that heavy, mold-
ed history, Lowell might have hoped that doom would be both
comprehended and propitiated by such technique. God's insatiable
demand for blood might be expressed and withstood by the poet's
own forced-march repetitions and militancy of sound. The stunning
style of *Lord Weary's Castle* may be partially explained by Lowell's
need to hold together with great will and expertise what he fears
will burst all mental sets. Indeed, if poetic technique and religious
imagery had not been on Lowell's side when the war and history
rose against his mind, he, like those Quaker sailors he describes,
might have been "swallowed up quick." Style and references combine to make the book a monument to the urge to incorporate the
difficult present into a culturally strategic past that tends to make
the contemporary turmoil a showpiece of permanent history. Much
of the book is calculated as a means of withstanding present despair,
but it never really reaches this achievement. Not artistic technique
hammered into the poems—the poet wills it, wills it, wills it: it is
form—nor religious faith so testily striven for, nor a knowledgeable
invocation of the past will finally save the mind of the poet from
simply having to face the turmoils of history or of his own life
without built-in religious or historical explanations.

Sometimes it is a mental strain to read *Lord Weary's Castle* as its
tempestuous descriptions, invocations, allusions, nervous caesuras,
and sinuous alliterations take over a passage. Reading the book then
becomes an effort to ride out the accumulation as Lowell works up a
scene:

When the whale's viscera go and the roll
Of its corruption overruns this world
Beyond tree-swept Nantucket and Wood's Hole
And Martha's Vineyard, Sailor, will your sword
Whistle and fall and sink into the fat?
In the great ash-pit of Jehoshaphat
The bones cry for the blood of the white whale,
The fat flukes arch and whack about its ears,
The death-lance churns into the sanctuary, tears
The gun-blue swingle, heaving like a flail,
And hacks the coiling life out: it works and drags
And rips the sperm-whale's midriff into rags,
Gobbets of blubber spill to wind and weather,
Sailor, and gulls go round the stoven timbers
Where the morning stars sing out together
And thunder shakes the white surf and dismembers
The red flag hammered in the mast-head. Hide,
Our steel, Jonas Messias, in Thy side.

Despite the appeal at the end of such a passage (magnificent after its fashion), there was really no way for Lowell to help his unbelief, particularly as the imagery was speaking for what Lowell really believed. The art of the book, its true psychic energy, is dedicated to the churning world, to violent history, rather than to appeals to Jesus Christ to save mankind from itself, to blunt man's weaponry. In Lowell's view, the sanctuary, or Christ's body (despite a final nervous appeal), is a terrain at the mercy of weapons. Lowell no more expects that salvation, it would seem, than he expects to temper the wrenching imagery that dominates the book. Even that appeal to Christ depends upon violence done to Him. As for Mary, she is "too small for her canopy". She oddly sits waiting for an unwilling world to come to her Walsingham shrine, a shrine that in any case would now strike the visitor as being devoid of religious transcendence. What really exists for the imagination that created *Lord Weary's Castle* is the movement of the ocean, the motions of war, and that terrific energy that can be knotted in a man's mind. That mind often, for Lowell, is identified with the ocean, which is where "The Quaker Graveyard in Nantucket" ends. Its wind-moiling graveyard affected by strenuous ocean tides is God's "proving ground." If God is anywhere in *Lord Weary's Castle*, He is in that graveyard-womb of the ocean. It is an ocean whose depths and fierceness are more inspiring than the gurgle of "Shiloah's whirlpools." It is in these depths of the ocean that Lowell seeks his God.

III   *War Poetry*

In a speech delivered on the eve of World War II and later revised for a book called *Man's Quest for God*, the noted Jewish
religious philosopher Abraham Joshua Heschel spoke in terms that
coincidentally describe the strife and imagery of Lowell's first two
volumes. Said Heschel, in Europe, in 1938: "Emblazoned over the
gates of the world in which we live is the escutcheon of the demons.
The mark of Cain in the face of man has come to overshadow the
likeness of God."[4] Man's land of unlikeness was the region of the
coming war, a war that overshadowed Lowell's mind as he wrote
the poems for *Land of Unlikeness* and *Lord Weary's Castle*.

A deep impression of the second and better book is Lowell's
dread of war, particularly of saturation bombing, which is one
reason he became a conscientious objector. An offshoot of this dread
is his sense, as early as World War II, of the new American imperium. In the opening poem of *Lord Weary's Castle*, "The Exile's
Return," Lowell describes the victorious Americans as "unseasoned
liberators." Theirs is a parody of ancient European conquests, as
"torn-up tilestones crown the victor." During the war Lowell indicted America's violations, violations that most minds registered
and still register as having been militarily desirable. Lowell's opening poem makes one wonder, harking back to the book's haunting
title of futility, if "the Yankee commandant" who took over the ancient home and city of the exile did so only to inherit the very kind
of military and cultural aggressions that made Germany itself invite
catastrophe. Similarly, Laomedon's Troy, built on deception and
irresponsibility, fell to Greece, a victory that in turn cost Agamem-
non his family and his own life. *Lord Weary's Castle* raises the kinds
of thoughts that bewilder Prometheus as he is chained to his rock in
Lowell's imitation of Aeschylus's drama.

What Lowell detected in the mid-forties during the war, his
poetry bore witness to in the 1960s and 1970s. Despite, indeed
because of, his refusal to serve in that earlier war, he "saw" the
possibility of a Vietnam in the very victory during World War II.
The sons of those "unseasoned liberators" come by the end of the
1960s to "fall in small war on the heels of small / war." This poet is
our historian.

On an even larger scale, as Lowell's *Lord Weary's Castle* shows
us, American aggressions go all the way back to the wars against the
Indians, in particular to King Philip's War, when the Governor of
Plymouth was Lowell's ancestor Josiah Winslow. (Robert Lowell

has really projected himself into that ballad about the children who pay for the sins of Lord Weary. The aggressions of the Lowells are sometimes found in the book, indicating some of the author's inheritance, his rich, troubled sense of America. Through a loyalty to the truth of family history Lowell's contemplative, withdrawn spirit found itself driven to issues of historical importance.)

This pattern of aggression eventually haunts the nation that undertakes it, just as the figures of Cain and Abel trouble *Lord Weary's Castle*. They are the primeval aggressor and victim who bother Lowell's imagination. Actually, Cain appears under different names—Napoleon, Charles V, Blucher, Louis XVI. Lowell is haunted by the Cain-general, who murders for national aggrandizement and for glory, and by the Abel-victim—Indians, cousin Warren Winslow, a German "blue-lipped priest" killed by Allied phosphorous bombs, and the many unnamed victims of "jellied fire." Sometimes the Cain-Abel figures merge in the persons who end up as victims of their own aggression: Quaker sailors on the Pequod crusade, the victim of the gallows in "France" who sought *lebensraum*, and, to circle around again, Louis XVI.

Some of the poems of *Lord Weary's Castle* can be appreciated as Lowell's attempt to bestow a voice upon the victims of military conquests. And the poem about Dante meeting the bloodied Ghibelline soldier in Purgatory ("In time of war you could not save your skin") expropriates an older literary-historical scene in order to express a contemporary concern about victims, about an enemy, in war. The same can be said about Lowell's concern for the wars with the American Indians (see "At the Indian Killer's Grave," "Children of Light," "Concord") or for Mennonites, Doukabors, and Israelites, persecuted sects opposed to military service (see "At a Bible House," "In the Cage"). This book of 1946 portrays Lowell's identification with the victims of war, including, and perhaps especially, the victims of American aggression.

Many of these victims are condensed into the spaniel described in "1790." "Mucked with tar," the poor dog is the image of the ordinary man who serves his society on call, who returns "on the double-quick" to its mistress only to have its back gratuitously broken by Louis XVI, three years before he himself was guillotined.

The poetry of *Lord Weary's Castle* is testimonial to the ways in which World War II hardened America's moral sense during military conquest. Now, years later, after having seen some of the bitter fruits of that hardness in Vietnam, his readers can further appreciate the consciousness that Lowell was keeping alive in the poetry of *Lord Weary's Castle*. Not even the just purposes of World War II (to which a severe Lowell gives no deference) prevented him from seeing what was actually happening to our sensibility. Akin to the lonely integrity of Jonathan Edwards, the courage of his alienated convictions enabled Lowell to witness the truth of that increasing and unthinking military brutality.

It is as if this postwar book is telling us that, whatever else, Lowell will never shake off that consciousness that so dominated his mind as a young man: "I have never gotten over the horrors of American bombing." We have come to share Lowell's obsession. If Lowell as a poet speaks for us it is not because he was free to choose this theme that has always been near the heart of his poetry.

There is one poem in *Lord Weary's Castle* that, by using the military theme, strives for an openness to God's redemptive spirit that is rare in the book.

Taking place in a part of Bridgeport, Connecticut, where there was a defense plant during World War II and where Lowell spent some time after being released from federal prison in the spring of 1944 for violation of the Selective Service Act, "Colloquy in Black Rock" is one of the most interesting and difficult religious expressions in the book. In this poem, written in celebration of the Feast of Corpus Christi, the religious and physical turmoil of the narrator is related to Hungarian workmen who donate their blood to soldiers. Prototype of those soldiers, and for whom the Hungarian church is named, the body of "Stephen the martyre was broken down to blood: / Our ransom is the rubble of his death." The war's destructive process is converted into a paradoxical confirmation of the process through which Christianity and God's presence are felt. The poem uses the war to assert that once the world is "broken up," the spirit of God is able to enter men. This idea is expressed in conclusion of the poem through an overpowerful image, probably derived from Gerard Manley Hopkins:

> Christ walks on the black water. In Black Mud
> Darts the kingfisher. On Corpus Christi, heart,
> Over the drum-beat of St. Stephen's choir
> I hear him, *Stupor Mundi*, and the mud
> Flies from his hunching wings and beak—my heart,
> The blue kingfisher dives on you in fire.

In this strange and forceful poem Lowell converts images of dive-bombing and wartime murder into the "destructions" that make men accessible to Christ's influence, just as Christ himself is ab-

sorbed by men only after his body is "broken down to blood."
(Unhappily, Lowell's closing image reminds me of his description of
one of the victims of Allied bombings: "one more blue-lipped
priest, the phosphorous / Melted the hammer of his heart to fire."
The kingfisher is still the dive-bomber.)

In "Colloquy in Black Rock" Lowell willfully manipulates the
war's violence in order to register the idea that only out of some up-
heaval of the spirit will God touch men. Not until they have fiercely
crumbled the false "set," the false consciousness, will men find
themselves worthy and receptive to the darting kingfisher. A comparable idea resides at the end of "Christmas Eve under Hooker's
Statue," where we are told we will not escape our wars "Till Christ
again turn wanderer and child," an almost impossible task since the
Christ child is usually dead in the poetry of *Lord Weary's Castle*.

This Christ-child-as-death is related to the fear of war that
dominates the book. Repeated imagery, as usual, is telling: "Jesus,
in the harness," is curiously like Charles V, "clamped in his black
and burly harness," and reflects Lowell's complaint to the Crucifix:
"How can your whited spindling arms transfix / Mammon's un-
bridled industry, the lurch / For forms to harness Heraclitus'
stream!" Christ, whether as a child or as the crucified adult, is
another way of registering that sense of war, of men's destruction of
other men, of commercial or state aggression, that is felt throughout
the book. Christ could no more "turn wanderer and child" in
Lowell's poetry at the time than Jesus could throw off the harness.
Furthermore, the distraught descriptions of the Christ child are
related to the glimpses we get of some sour New England
childhood. It is as if, in Lowell's state of conversion, Christ cannot
be a source of innocence and joyful inspiration; nor can He even
grow up to the crucifixion and then resurrection but is doomed to
die as a child—an abortive hope.

At the time of *Lord Weary's Castle* the significant tradition for
Lowell has really hardened or become knotted up within itself; he
wishes for a new force to enter his life but can only make rhetorical
gestures toward it. What he really believes in most deeply is the
surging ocean at the end of "The Quaker Graveyard in Nantucket."

As previously mentioned, even in the sixth section of "The
Quaker Graveyard. . . ," "Our Lady of Walsingham," which
offers an expression of Christian tenderness rarely felt in Lowell's
poetry, the figure of Mary is strangely inaccessible. She is "too
small for her canopy" and "There's no comeliness / At all or charm

in that expressionless / Face with its heavy eyelids." She is impassive, restrained, unlike the Revelatory-like guns, the turmoil of ocean and its monsters that possess the rest of the poem. The reader begins to feel that all of Lowell's descriptions of Mary are his moving yet failed quests for a redemptive figure.

It is the stormy and majestic welter of man's experience that the poem has all along conveyed and that it registers in the conclusion; already cited in the "Prologue" to this book, beginning "Atlantic, you are fouled with blue sailors. . . ." (See p. 25) The poem exploits the contradiction between its dedication—"For Warren Winslow, Dead at Sea"—and its epigraph: "Let man have dominion over the fishes of the sea and the fowls of the air and the beasts and the whole earth, and every creeping creature that moveth upon the earth."

The effort of the poem is to move between the fact of man's violent death at sea and God's promise of dominion to man. It is man's fate to ride the waves between the drowning and the promise, and the conclusion celebrates this condition. The final line—"The Lord survives the rainbow of His will"—confirms the idea that despite the cousin's fate mentioned in the dedication and despite the unrealizable promise of the epigraph, there is a realm of continuous struggle which is celebrated in the last stanza. The poem's final line is the poet's re-dedication to the never-ending turmoil of human experience. The poetry of *Lord Weary's Castle* finally emphasizes not redemption but reimmersion in our contradictions, even a fascinated dedication to our turmoil, inherent in God's creation. The ocean at the end of "The Quaker Graveyard in Nantucket" is Lowell's recognition that the contradictions and energies of life itself finally fascinate him beyond Christian images of redemption.

An obvious difference between *Lord Weary's Castle* and *Life Studies* is that in the later book Lowell opens himself up to that "blue kingfisher" in ways he could not do at the time of the earlier book. *Life Studies* reveals a grace and an availability to a spirit of redemption that Lowell could never manage to find or exhibit in *Lord Weary's Castle*. Lowell once wondered, comparing these two books, ". . . whether my poems are religious or whether they just use religious imagery. I haven't really any idea. My last poems don't use religious imagery, they don't use symbolism. In many ways they seem to me to be more religious than the early ones."[5]

Like the shield and helmet in that glass case in the museum, the

images of Christ and Mary in *Lord Weary's Castle* are housed for
show. They are addressed, approached, rhetorically. They are
religious figures, religious images, for the poet's imagination and
skill, not simply the son and mother of God to whom he appeals,
just as those military pieces are for display rather than for use, esthetic hailings to some glory.

In Lowell's development such images would be replaced along
with that almost willed poetry through which they are expressed.
They were to be forsaken for women like Katherine of "Between
the Porch and the Altar," or Anne Kavanaugh, or the poet's wife,
mother, daughter. Christ and Mary were to be abandoned. They
never really worked for Lowell, at least as far as a reader of his
poetry can tell. They were figures from the museum of belief. (A
similar pattern can be worked out in Lowell's search in his poetry
for a statue that is alive, not a museum piece or simply a monument
to the past. The stern pose of the Union general in "Christmas Eve
under Hooker's Statue" contrasts with the vibrations of St.
Gaudens' Civil War relief of Colonel Robert Gould Shaw—looking
at that frieze, "William James could almost hear the bronze
Negroes breathe." The statue of Persephone in "The Mills of the
Kavanaughs" might be considered some midway point between the
Hooker statue and the figure of Shaw celebrated by Lowell in "For
the Union Dead.")

As the later titles, *Life Studies* and *Notebook*, suggest, the
museum pieces give way to direct impressions, seemingly careless,
unfinished, unstructured, yet vibrant, touching, and formed out of
almost casual and curious poetic and psychological subtleties. (How
different the invocation of history or of scenes from past literary
works in *Lord Weary's Castle* is from *Life Studies*, in which Lowell
seems to stumble upon his own contemporaneity, with the past slip-
ping in casually and strangely and with a kind of profoundly absent-
minded relevance.) The at best half-dead Christ child of *Lord
Weary's Castle* and the narrator's equivalent in that volume—the
stern, angry child—are altered to the poet-child of *Life Studies* who
misses his grandfather, mockingly mourns the failures of his father,
and finds childhood a great source of pity and keen observation.
Lowell's remark about the *Life Studies* poems that "In many ways
they seem to me to be more religious than the early ones," is astute
self-criticism.

If reading *Lord Weary's Castle* is somewhat like seeing those
Louis XIV pieces of artifical military splendor at the Metropolitan

Museum of Art, then reading *Life Studies* is like moving from those glass cases to a Rembrandt face or a Van Gogh chair. At such a moment we feel we are less viewing objects in a museum than observing a person or a piece of furniture that tells us we are both livers and observers and that what we observe observes us back. This is something of what we mean when we say that a work of art is like life. In such a case the work of art is greater than the museum that holds it, and it seems destined for more than a wall or a glass case in a museum. Something along these lines is the difference between *Lord Weary's Castle* and *Life Studies*. *The Mills of the Kavanaughs* is the bridge between these two landmarks in Lowell's career.

CHAPTER 4

Transition: The Mills of the Kavanaughs

> . . . a character which succeeds in interesting its author may elicit from the author latent potentialities of his own being. I believe that the author imparts something of himself to his characters, but I also believe that he is influenced by the characters he creates.
>
> —T. S. Eliot, "The Three Voices of Poetry"

IT is useful to look at *The Mills of the Kavanaughs* (1951) as a bridge between *Lord Weary's Castle* and *Life Studies,* as a step toward the confessional poetry and the descriptions of other people that comprise Lowell's next and crucial collection of poems. *The Mills of the Kavanaughs* is also a book in which Lowell makes his first moves from religious faith to doubt. This third book also happens to contain two long poems, "Falling Asleep over the Aeneid" and "Mother Marie Therese," that are among Lowell's finest whether or not they relate thematically to the rest of his work. *The Mills of the Kavanaughs* is a book that can be easily underrated or pigeonholed; a consideration of its relationship to Lowell's work as a whole should not ignore some of the individual achievements included in the book.

Lowell's third book displays a concern for private lives. It is almost a Victorian book, about people who can confess and explore a loss in their lives at their leisure or in terms of some permanent setting to their lives. The poems are principally monologues on the dead, or on a life of stagnation; and Lowell himself is burying his Christian consolation in these poems. This "set" background of meditation occurs most significantly in "The Mills of the Kavanaughs," "Falling Asleep over the Aeneid," and "Mother Marie Therese." By the end of the book a more frenetic confessional tone appears. In its focusing on a special pathos of private lives, *The Mills of the Kavanaughs* is the closest Robert Lowell has ever come to Randall Jarrell's kind of poetry.

Dramatic monologues, these poems are in the "second voice" (to use T. S. Eliot's term), the voice of the poet talking to other people. Yet, these monologues, it is important to note, are essentially spoken by people to themselves or to imaginary listeners. The person speaking is an isolated figure. However, to the extent that Lowell can create characters who are not just extensions of his own voice and thoughts, to the extent that the poems present other people thinking, and not just the poet making sure that his thoughts are in the poem, Lowell has attracted readers who may feel that they have had enough of *his* apocalyptic Catholicism or tortuous turmoil. A common complaint, voiced by Randall Jarrell among others, is that people in Robert Lowell's poetry tend to sound like Robert Lowell.

In these poems the self-inspection is done by the characters themselves, though sometimes, as in the case of "Her Dead Brother" and "Thanksgiving's Over," the situation is cryptic and is finally clear, we suspect, only to the poet. Both of these poems are like overcharged fragments of an Ingmar Bergman movie: they are forced, even sensational poems. Yet we can see in "Thanksgiving's Over," and in some other poems in the book, that Lowell is trying to cope with the subject of mental breakdown or personality disorder—an important subject more satisfactorily handled in his next book, *Life Studies*.

The way in which the themes of incest and adultery, real or imagined, appear in *The Mills of the Kavanaughs* is strange: more often than not, these themes of illicit love turn out to be melodramatic—less a situation of real guilt, a convincing experience, or a genuine, tragic theme than an excuse for the author to fish in tempting waters. The themes of incest and adultery are only believable and poetically achieved at last when Lowell translates Racine's *Phaedra* (1961).

Almost all of the poems in the book are a mixture of dreams, memories, even hallucinations. The power of recalled experience, or of dreamed experience, is evident here. *The Mills of the Kavanaughs* shares with *Life Studies* an intensity of memory. These people remember well—too well. Occasionally relief, occasionally a recovery of some old glory, memory is persistent; and its details are usually a burden. However, as speakers move from religious belief to unbelief, their particular memories of past belief are sometimes reenergized for the mind's new secular drama.

In this third book of Lowell's a secular consciousness replaces the Christian one insisted upon in his earlier work. *The Mills of the Kavanaughs* is the point at which the epigraphs to Lowell's books change from Latin to English (and finally to none at all). Considering the rhetorical excess of the Christian consciousness in *Lord Weary's Castle*, a shrewd reader of that second book might have predicted its demise in the work to follow. When Randall Jarrell, in reviewing *Lord Weary's Castle*, expressed the idea that a movement from constriction to liberation was the principle of Lowell's development, he was indeed such a reader.[1] Instead of classical myths working with the Christian consciousness, as occurs in "The Quaker Graveyard in Nantucket" and "In Memory of Arthur Winslow," those myths now house a secular sensibility that longs for, but has relinquished, a religious dimension to its consolations. In these secular monologues over the dead, mental breakdown is a major concern. Lowell is moving from the religious bone and gristle of *Land of Unlikeness* to the painful flesh of *Life Studies*. This demise of Christian explanation and Christian motifs in *The Mills of the Kavanaughs* makes way for the opening poem in *Life Studies*, "Beyond the Alps," his farewell to Rome.

In "Beyond the Alps" Paris comes to replace Rome, just as Anne Kavanaugh finds that the best function of the Douay Bible is that of a silent opponent in solitaire. She herself is her only opponent, her only salvation. Or to register this religious shift in different terms, in the title poem, "The Mills of the Kavanaughs," Persephone replaces Mary as the significant female figure, but first and foremost the reader feels the presence of Anne Kavanaugh in the poem, the human woman herself. After *Lord Weary's Castle*, the women in Lowell's poetry become wives in difficult relationships with their husbands, not just rhetorical Mary figures. Lowell might have borrowed Anne Kavanaugh from Wallace Steven's "Sunday Morning" or from any one of a number of poems by Jarrell.

I   *"The Mills of the Kavanaughs"*

"The Mills of the Kavanaughs" is a poem we read because it is by an author who interests us. Even if the poem, despite its length and portrayal of character, does not fully let us know why Anne Kavanaugh and her husband have their differences, or why Harry

Kavanaugh must leave the navy, or why on returning home he wastes away, this poem with its sad marriage, failed naval career, and demise of an old American family comes to interest us because Lowell finally absorbs these themes into *Life Studies*. The family in Lowell's poetry is a structure within which a victim-member continues his efforts at survival. Sometimes the family means an inherited house the inheritor cannot quite live up to or cannot live in without feeling uncomfortable. The Kavanaugh motto—"Cut down we flourish"—*is* the motto of the Winslows, Lowell's mother's family. It is through confessions, through a cutting back to the roots, that Lowell tries to flourish, as we come to see in *Life Studies*.

Yet "The Mills of the Kavanaughs" does retain our interest apart from the fact that the poem is by Lowell or is related to his other work. Anne Kavanaugh is one of the most interesting persons we ever know in Lowell's poetry. She engages us because of her full being, because of her efforts to understand herself and her situation. The poem appeals also because of the way in which the myth of Persephone merges with the life and thoughts of this Maine widow. The action of the poem occurs on September 22, the date of Persephone's death. From its beginning we see a statue of the goddess on the grounds of the Kavanaugh estate, a statue which haunts the imagination of Anne and which is also linked to her courtship and her life with her now-dead husband. The Persephone myth is not just a spool around which to wind the thoughts of the woman or the facts of her life; the myth is something Anne herself takes into her consciousness, sadly and readily uses to think about herself. Like Persephone's life in Hades, Anne's with Harry Kavanaugh is a marriage into death from which the woman can only partly escape; therefore, the myth influences the way Anne sees and thinks about herself. Toward the end of the poem, she thinks of ancient Roman gods rising from the pool on marble knees:

> "They watch like water-polo players—their eyes,
> Stars of a recognition, no disguise
> Or veil will hinder, now that they have found
> Me then Persephone, gone underground
> Into myself to supplicate the throne
> And horn of Hades to restore that stone,
> Imperial garland, once the living flower,
> Now stone—Harvest, my mother's, only dower
> To the dark monarch, and the futile dead
> In Hades, where I lost my maidenhead."

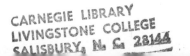

This knotty passage indicates Lowell's search in his poetry for a statue whose public figure and classical pose are metamorphosed into something vital. Lowell's interest in Ovid (a poet whose influence is felt in "The Mills of the Kavanaughs") is related to his desire to convert public statues and the frozen postures of heroes and gods into new and lively forms for our understanding.

At the end of the poem Anne again thinks of herself and of Persephone:

> "Although God's brother, and himself a god,
> Death whipped his horses through the startled sod;
> For neither conscience nor omniscience warned
> Him from his folly, when the virgin scorned
> His courtship, and the quaking earth revealed
> Death's desperation to the Thracian field.
> And yet we think the virgin took no harm:
> She gave herself because her blood was warm—
> And for no other reason, Love, I gave
> Whatever brought me gladness to the grave."

The Persephone myth intensifies the situation of Anne Kavanaugh because she thinks about the myth in terms of her own life. To the extent that Lowell succeeds not only in bringing the myth to bear upon contemporary experience but also in allowing us to see how the woman is compelled to think about the goddess, the myth is not superimposed upon the poem; the myth is a necessary aspect of the speaker's consciousness. Anne Kavanaugh, who ponders Persephone just as she considers her own dreams, cannot avoid thinking of the goddess married to death. The consciousness of Anne Kavanaugh marks a certain growth in Lowell's poetry and indicates one way in which he could come to appeal to those readers who are overwhelmed and put off by the religious turmoil of *Lord Weary's Castle*.

"The Mills of the Kavanaughs," however, is still not strong enough to overcome its closet-drama qualities, its tendency to stage a setting, and the poet's urge at times to tell us what Anne is doing or thinking: too often we are told, "she thinks" or "she dreams and thinks." In the plays, or in such later poems as "A Mad Negro Soldier Confined at Munich" and " 'To Speak of Woe That Is in Marriage,' " Lowell's people are more convincing, more immediate—they find their own language. Meanwhile, the monologue in "The Mills of the Kavanaughs" is dramatic enough to make us feel interested in this woman who wonders about herself in terms of the story of a mythical woman who gave up part of her life to death and had no choice; for Anne Kavanaugh's marriage into an old American family is a marriage into a family that has nowhere to go except into debt, disgrace, and extinction. Although she was poor, her marriage is finally less a step up the social ladder than a marriage into death and self-analysis. At this point arises the question that always haunts the readers of Lowell's poetry: Can Lowell ever avoid being a moving poet about some final American defeat? Is it finally true that, through depicting such characters as Anne Kavanaugh and the old man who falls asleep over the *Aeneid*, Lowell (like Edwin Arlington Robinson) sees the humanity of his characters *only* in their defeat?

Whatever the limitations of "The Mills of the Kavanaughs," it is a poem that a reader with a fondness for Lowell's poetry will find always drawing him back. Lowell's poetry would be that much weaker and more austere without the consciousness and the personality of an Anne Kavanaugh somewhere in it. As with the women of Randall Jarrell's poetry, Anne evokes the pity of desire and loss.

Just as Anne Kavanaugh must solve her confusions without religious aid, so Lowell's poetry in this book moves from the consolation of religious belief (such as it was) to the individual's struggle with no such consolations available. In this respect, "The Mills of the Kavanaughs" is indeed Lowell's version of Wallace Stevens's "Sunday Morning." Jerome Mazzaro indicates what is at stake in this change in Lowell when he notes that "The Mills of the Kavanaughs" abandons contemplation of religious truth for the continuation of other modes of belief and behavior. This development not only indicates that some of the earlier poetic wrenchings and rhetorical contemplation will be tempered, but that Lowell may now be on his way toward writing plays or writing poetry about other people, dramatizing *their* situation. In *Life Studies*, we see that Lowell's ability to create other lives in his poetry is related to his ability to create interesting versions of himself as well. Also, as Mazzaro observes, Lowell's poetry will make itself more available to readers who sense their own lives in terms of ordinary history and events rather than in apocalyptic quests for absolutes.[2]

In the best sense of that much abused term, *The Mills of the Kavanaughs* is a transitional volume; it shows us the poet's development.

II   *"Falling Asleep Over the Aeneid"*

"In Dreams Begin Responsibilities" Delmore Schwartz titled his most famous short story, taking the phrase from one of Yeats's books, and reflecting the Freudian idea that in their dreams men are artists compelled to imagine their condition.

Just as Schwartz's story is about a man who imagines the ineluctable family influences on his life, so Robert Lowell's "Falling Asleep Over the Aeneid" is about an old man dreaming of early influences in his life. The old man in Lowell's poem has his dream because some unfulfilled responsibility to the past has bothered him since childhood.

While reading the *Aeneid* one Sunday morning in Concord, an old man dozes off and misses a church service. He falls asleep and dreams about the passage he has just been reading. That is the scene (Book XI, lines 30 - 100) in which Aeneas attends the funeral service for his friend Pallas, killed by the enemy Turnus. The old man dreams that he is Aeneas, though he is also Pallas in part of the dream.

After he awakes, the old man remembers a scene eighty years earlier when he was also reading Vergil. On the heels of this memory, he recalls another scene at the time of the funeral of his Uncle Charles, an officer in the Civil War. Since the poem suggests that both these scenes occurred around the time the boy was eight, the old man is some eighty-eight years old at the time of his dream. Since the military funeral scene of his Uncle Charles occurs either late in the Civil War, or shortly thereafter,[3] the old man is dreaming in Concord either during or just after World War II, eighty years later. Images in the poem reflect that latest war.

"Falling Asleep Over the Aeneid" thus embraces four wars: the struggle for the founding of Rome (with references to the Second Punic War); the American Revolutionary War (one of its early battles was in Concord); the Civil War; and World War II. The old man, ironically from Concord, can no more escape history and his sense of war then he can escape his dreams. However, he is finally unsure about his relationship to the military tradition built into the epic he is rereading and part of the family-national responsibilities he is expected to uphold.[4]

"Falling Asleep Over the Aeneid" is about a civil war within the old man, a conflict that has been within him all his life. Fascinated by the military pose, the old man dreams he is Aeneas the empire-founding hero, but he dreams he is also Pallas—the dead Pallas who can't help asking, "Who am I, and why?" Pallas also merges with the dead hero, Uncle Charles, whom the boy-old man admires but could never emulate. The dreamer is a man who has been puzzled all his life by his relationship to a family, a history, and a literature that honors war. What should be his responsibilities as a result of his profound connection to these values? Without that puzzlement there would have been no dream. The distance is not very great between this dreaming, reminiscing old man and the moody, remembering narrator of "My Last Afternoon with Uncle Devereux Winslow," in *Life Studies*. Both are poems, to quote a remark Lowell once made about "For the Union Dead," "about a child maturing into courage and terror."[5] An older man remembering scenes from his boyhood and puzzling over his loyalty to those early scenes has been one source of Lowell's poetry. One of the themes finely realized in Lowell's poetry is this memory of childhood: not the recollection and description of a child's early days as they were actually felt and lived in the past, but that time and those emotions as they are remembered and reflected upon by an older man who ponders the relationship between childhood and adulthood. Lowell is a poet of childhood seen from the retrospect of the brooding adult. If, as it has been suggested, one of the great themes in Lowell's work is the experience of aging, then that theme was anticipated through his portrayals of an adult's recurrent brooding over childhood, trying to connect past and present. (The recurring visit to graveyards in Lowell's poetry, especially family graveyards, also reflects the hold of the past on the poet's life.)

The old man's sense of war is related to family history. It is a family history in which shame is mixed with pride, confusion with honor, lineage with betrayal (the *Lord Weary's Castle* syndrome), and heroism with uncertainty, as the old man at the end only uses the dead uncle's sword as a kind of cane to lean on. In this declining, limited way the octogenarian associates himself with the weapon and the heroism of the uncle. Now this might be a plausible resolution of the dreamer's problem, but the old man isn't really satisfied. For, like Lowell, he is both fascinated and appalled by the potentialities in that sword. He can neither wield nor deny the sword. (How urgently, yet almost vindictively, Lowell himself tried to convert the sword into a cross in *Lord Weary's Castle!* Was becoming a militant Catholic pacifist a kind of inverse reflection of that family-military, religious, national heritage he half-admired,

half-rejected, and could never really cope with?) The old man who
has fallen asleep over the *Aeneid* and who has dreamed his lifelong
puzzlement in connecting heroism to war undergoes the same conflict vital to much of Lowell's poetry, where an attraction to certain
heroes of war shimmers alongside the desire to replace that image of
the military hero, or at least to reshape that image.

As a child Lowell "played Napoleon in my attic cell" and
remembered "two hundred French generals by name / from A to
V"; but as a young man he put aside childhood things and became
"a fire-breathing Catholic C.O. . . . telling off the state and president, and then/sat waiting sentence in the bull pen. . . ." (See
"Memories of West Street and Lepke.") Lowell's conflict is conveyed by those very initials at the end of that pacifist-dragonish
phrase, as the abbreviation for "commanding officer" is replaced by
the same abbreviation for "conscientious objector."

Other moments in Lowell's poetry bear upon the inheritance and
conflict of the old man in the poem. Lowell writes that as a child he
was brought to tears by an old print of a French soldier dropping his
"sabered eagle" and about to be killed by an English soldier. (See
"Buttercups"; he also refers to the same scene in "Waterloo" in
History.) And in "91 Revere Street" he admits, "I enjoyed being
allowed to draw Father's blunt dress sword," a pleasure repeated in
the poem "Commander Lowell." At the end of Lowell's play *My
Kinsman, Major Molineux* (but not in the Hawthorne story which is
the basis of the play), the young Robin is given the sword of his
deposed relative to keep as a souvenir. He is holding it when he
observes,

> Look, the lights are going out,
> The red sun's moving on the river.
> Where will it take us to? . . . It's strange
> To be here on our own—and free.

Confusion and shame mix with honor and heroism in Lowell's sense
of the military exploits of his ancestors who played significant roles
in the founding of the country. Lowell also wrote a poem critical of
some of those ancestors, entitled "At the Indian Killer's Grave" and
containing an epigraph by Hawthorne about *his* fierce ancestors.

Lowell's attitude toward his ancestors is as poignant and double-
edged as Hawthorne's were toward his forebearers. Lowell discovered that despite, or rather because of, his name he had to labor

for his tradition. This is a responsibility especially encumbent upon a man when it appears that all he has to do is inherit a tradition and fit into it.

If one function of the dream in "Falling Asleep Over the Aeneid" is to dramatize the conflict the old man feels, we can also say that another function of the poem is to dramatize the same conflict felt by Lowell. It is a conflict between the appeal of the military hero and an obsession with military acts of destruction. The old man is fascinated by, rather than admiring of, Aeneas. He cannot separate his sense of Aeneas's military exploits from his respect for the military exploits in the family tradition, exemplified by his Uncle Charles. Yet his uncle is not unrelated to descendants of Aeneas who have climbed "The knees of Father Time, his beard of scalps, / his scythe, the arc of steel that crowns the Alps." The problem of the old man would disappear if he could either deny and denigrate the appeal of the military hero or celebrate the hero's presence and reenact this military heroism. This conflict is at the heart of Lowell's poetry and reflects that moment in American culture when military heroism is still honored though the military impact has been increasingly destructive.

There lingers, however, the one positive sign of the military hero in Lowell's poem. That is the dead image of Uncle Charles who, in the line of Robert Gould Shaw, once paraded with "his colored volunteers." (See "For the Union Dead.") The Uncle Charles of the poem seems to be a fusion of Shaw, Charles Russell Lowell (a cousin of Lowell's who fought in the Civil War and whom he admires; see the poem about him in *History*), and Major Mordecai Myers, an officer in the War of 1812, and an ancestor whom Lowell fondly celebrates and "creates" in "91 Revere Street."

Lowell's attraction to Major Myers can be compared to Herman Melville's interest in his grandfather, General Peter Gansevoort, a hero in New York State during the Revolutionary War. After the business failure of his father, Melville fell back upon the image of his military grandfather, just as Lowell opens up his prose memoir, which largely deals with the failures of his father, by thinking of Major Mordecai, the substitute military-hero father. In addition, the old man of "Falling Asleep Over the Aeneid" is like Melville's character Pierre in that he, too, recalls a war hero in the family. Both Melville and Lowell had fathers who were failures, fathers whose sons then went into the family past for images of military heroism to reply upon, that heroism not disconnected from civic virtue. Lowell is an important figure for our sense of an American literary and cultural tradition that is real, not an academic creation. Lowell conveys in contemporary terms some of the dilemmas Hawthorne and Melville felt.

The conversion of military death and deed into significant social acts that sustain the ideals of the society is celebrated in the figures of Shaw, Charles Russell Lowell, and Major Mordecai Myers. In this way Lowell is able occasionally to transcend his dread of and fascination for the military hero, a dread and fascination that occupy a great deal of his work. In this form of transcendence the military-civic hero, like Shaw, replaces the Caesar-Napoleon military adventurer and carries forward the military exploit as civic vision. The old man can only partly envision that metamorphosis in "Falling Asleep Over the Aeneid," but in "For the Union Dead" Lowell is able to turn the trick. And perhaps this accounts for Robert Penn Warren's comment to Lowell about "For the Union Dead": "That's one of your best, I expect. One of your very best." [6]

Lowell himself is of interest because his poetry is based in part on his family which has its "roots in the national past," which has "a public name"—all those "advantages" most Americans never possessed but which they were supposed to look upon admiringly. Children were encouraged to feel by the culture and by early schooling that such advantages only became problems if they didn't possess them. With those advantages, a person was really at home in this country. Later it turned out, however, that to struggle for one's heritage, even to be its adversary in certain ways, was to have the advantageous and exhilarating position. It is by taking a questioning attitude toward his inheritance, by being puzzled, even embarrassed by it, that Lowell has cut a significant figure. Somewhat like Edith Wharton, who also had to challenge family and class prestige in order to touch the values of conscience and sensibility, Robert Lowell had to move against his family situation. Like Edith Wharton, he had to "expose."

Since in a democratic culture all (or most) members are unsure as to what a viable family-cultural inheritance means, the career and poetry of Robert Lowell have been particularly illuminating. He has especially conveyed the problem of "family background"; it is the scenery of a great deal of his poetry. If Lowell had trouble in relating to the national past, then many of his readers may discover in him the high drama of what they feel in themselves, people who have never been connected to the American past through family. If those with immigrant backgrounds have trouble in relating to the national past, how curious a reflection of that dilemma is Robert Lowell, who has made that past viable and alive by questioning it, by having conflicts over it, by rejecting parts of it. In this way his poetry has found a role through and beyond its family origins. Lowell had been at once shrewd and fortunate enough to reconnect himself to his family in this questioning way. However, if Lowell found much in his family background both restrictive and questionable, there was also much that he found and half-created into figures who were attractive and even inspiring. And by working out his relationship to his relatives through the poetry he found a liberation of sorts. Three of those ancestors to whom Lowell was attracted—General John Stark, Major Mordecai Myers and Colonel Charles Russell Lowell—were men with military roles in the Revolution, the War of 1812, and the Civil War, respectively. They are figures of achievement and admiration to Lowell. Just as the old man dreaming in Concord recalls his Uncle Charles, Lowell recalls in "91 Revere Street": "I was proud of our Major Mordecai. I used to stand dangerously out in the middle of Revere Street in order to see through our windows and gloat on this portrait's scarlet waistcoat blazing in the bare, Spartan whiteness of our den-parlor."

In his admiration of officers like Shaw, Charles Russell Lowell, Stark, and Myers; in his ambiguous fascination for Che Guevara; in his fear of Caesar, Hannibal, and Napoleon; in his description of peace-marchers who "step off like green Union Army recruits/for the first Bull Run"; in his shame but attachment to colonial ancestors who fought in wars against the Indians; in the mock condemnation of his father's impotent naval career; in his own conscientious objection during World War II—in all of these associations we find ample evidence of Lowell's critical attachment to the military figure. He is carrying forward his attraction for the man of military action along with his fear of such a figure. A statement attributed to the late Japanese novelist Yukio Mishima I am forced to think would have haunted Lowell if he had known it: "I have long since thought I wanted to die not as a literary but as a military man."[7] That sentiment would have been appreciated by the Robert Lowell who confessed once that the relative "I'd most like to have known myself" was not one of those poets and public officials in the family past, but "my military cousin Charles Russell Lowell,"[8] the student turned cavalry officer.

Beyond that military admiration, however, Lowell also leads us to

the response of William James to the monument honoring Robert
Gould Shaw and his black volunteers. At the time he made the
dedication speech for St. Gaudens' frieze, James called for poets to
celebrate not only Shaw's military courage but also that lonely civic
courage which in time of peace enables a man "to risk his worldly
fortunes all alone in resisting an enthroned abuse."[9] Imagining a
heroism equivalent to an act of military courage and pondering the
troops on the far side of Shaw and his horse, "William James could
almost hear the bronze Negroes breathe." In his poem about Shaw,
in *For The Union Dead,* Lowell was able to draw upon the kind of
dedication and spirit unavailable to the old man in Concord who
cannot move beyond the unresolved conflicts of his family-military
dream. Like Anne Kavanaugh with her Persephone, the old man
with his Vergil and family memories tries to resign himself to his
puzzling life.

III   *"Mother Marie Therese"*

The Canadian nun who thinks about "Mother Marie Therese"
begins by remembering the secular appeal of the dead sister:

> Old sisters at our Maris Stella House
> Remember how the Mother's strangled grouse
> And snow-shoe rabbits matched the royal glint
> Of Pio Nono's vestments in the print
> That used to face us, while our aching ring
> Of stationary rockers saw her bring
> Our cake.

Mother Marie Therese partly surrendered her worldly inclinations
for the Church:

> Was it not fated that the sweat of Christ
> Would wash the worldly serpent? Christ enticed
> Her heart that fluttered, while she whipped her hounds
> Into the quicksands of her manor grounds
> A lordly child, her habit fleur-de-lys'd
> There she dismounted, sick; with little heed,
> Surrendered. Like Proserpina, who fell
> Six months a year from earth to flower in hell;
> She half-renounced by Candle, Book and Bell
> Her flowers and fowling pieces for the Church.

Certain of her own language and remembrances, the speaker celebrates this idiosyncratic nun whose interests and life-style vie with the colors, forms, and expectations of the Church. The old nun remembers Marie Therese (the name of a Bourbon queen, mother of Marie Antoinette) as a force that has permanently left her life. The speaker, who by now has ordered her own life, recalls Mother Therese as once representing for her a fling at life. Like the old man in "Falling Asleep Over the Aeneid," this remembering nun indulges in reveries in order, in her fashion, to remain faithful to a once-noble and striking figure who left her years ago by drowning. The nun keeps the memory of Mother Therese by recalling her in opposition to the demands of the Church. The usual restricted passion of nuns' lives is found wanting when put beside the fire and indulgence of Sister Marie Therese, whose secular interests continued to conflict with, or lie uneasily alongside, her religious obligations. Those secular interests make her come alive for the reminiscing nun.

Mother Marie Therese kept up with Bourbon politics, read Rabelais, and enjoyed riding and hunting. Described in terms contrary to the "stern virginity" of the lives of nuns, she is the very opposite of Chaucer's dainty, over-sophisticated prioress. She is drowned off Saint Denis' Head (the name of the French patron saint derives from the Greek god Dionysus); and, to further the interesting posture of Mother Marie Therese, the nun thinks of her as "she welters on her back. / The bell-buoy, whom she called the Cardinal, / Dances upon her." The nun who speaks the poem remembers in her own terms, and the poem succeeds in the way the voice in the poem is genuinely that of the nun who remembers and describes the other woman who once entered her life. The passages at the beginning of this discussion, and the lines just quoted, display the tones of the reminiscing nun as her speech is influenced but not overwhelmed by the conduct or the language of Mother Marie Therese, who is genuinely felt through the thoughts of the nun. The nun's memory appropriates the poem and is engaging as she incorporates as best she can the idiosyncratic passion of the life she honors.

Like Anne Kavanaugh and the old man who dreams, the reminiscing sister alone appreciates the significance of the person who came into her life. When people mourn the dead in *The Mills of the Kavanaughs* they honor, as best they can, something mysteriously vibrant in their lives. Their remembrances are both a

statement of some confusion and a tribute to some partly felt nobility. Their remembrances, different as they are in particulars, reflect
one of the epigraphs to the title poem, a passage from William
Carlos Williams's *In the American Grain:* "Morals are the memory
of success that no longer succeeds."

The speaker of "Mother Marie Therese," like Anne Kavanaugh,
like the old man with the *Aeneid,* like the woman of "Her Dead
Brother," and like Michael in "Thanksgiving's Over," must locate
and live with her turmoils and regrets but without too much
assistance, if any at all, from religious views. *The Mills of the
Kavanaughs* dramatizes secular sensibilities who can refer to Christian motifs (and, of course, to classical ones), but who are finally lost
in their world with no sure footing except that of their ability to
reminisce painfully and dramatically. Their honest confessions or
remembrances are all they have. The poems of *The Mills of the
Kavanaughs* point the way past the energized religious "consolations" of *Lord Weary's Castle* and toward the furies of *Life
Studies* that resist being appeased through the old forms of ordering
and making sense of experience.

CHAPTER 5

Life Studies: *An Overall View*

It is a violence from within that protects us from a violence without. It is the imagination pressing back against the pressure of reality. It seems, in the last analysis, to have something to do with our self-preservation; and that, no doubt, is why the expression of it, the sound of its words, helps us to live our lives.

—Wallace Stevens, *The Necessary Angel*

"the experience of each new age requires a new confession. . . ."

—Emerson, "The Poet"

I   *Part One*

WHAT excited the reviewers about *Life Studies* still attracts the reader: the exploration of the self and the stance of that self in the world. The informal yet structured poetry and the informal yet analytical self that emerge in *Life Studies* have not failed to be of interest, and the range of personalities in the book remains engrossing. Despite its seeming anarchy and disjointedness, its sense of Lowell trying himself on for size and sorting out his experience and knowledge, *Life Studies* is the most structured book Lowell wrote. The organization of the book as a whole is the tightest and clearest he ever made—not to mention, for the moment, the hidden tautness of some of its poems. The shape of *Life Studies* (and, in a lesser way, the arrangement of some of the other books) brings to mind Yeats's strategies in putting together his poems in a volume. In particular, *Responsibilities, The Wild Swans at Coole,* and *Michael Robartes and the Dancer* are books whose very structures reflect the poet's reaction to historical and personal issues, to political and poetic concerns, and his feel for the interplay of all these matters. Indeed, to think of Lowell trying to strip himself of his previous style, his earlier debts, and his outworn com-

63

mitments, and of his seeking a wider sphere for his art inevitably recalls Yeats and his development.

At the time the material of *Life Studies* (1959) was going through his mind, Lowell said that he was traveling on the West Coast, reading his poetry three or four times a day and wondering how he was going to record the new ideas he had—the accomplishments of *Lord Weary's Castle* (1946) didn't seem to fit the thing he wanted to do. Yet the new book, like "the ductile anchor" of Whitman's spider, was launched out of what preceded. *Life Studies* was first written in the "closed style" of the earlier volume and then recast into the new, "looser" patterns.

The organization and content, as well as the art, of *Life Studies* signify talent moving on from previous achievements. Part One, including "Beyond the Alps," "The Banker's Daughter," and "Inauguration Day: January 1953," is a bridge from previous books. The first poem is a religious work that spins off from *Lord Weary's Castle;* the second, a refugee from the lives and reminiscences of *The Mills of the Kavanaughs;* the third, an expression of political fear, a secularizing of an earlier poem like "Christmas Eve Under Hooker's Statue."

Some of the passages in the opening poems of *Life Studies* are reminiscent of the style of *Lord Weary's Castle*, such as the jamming of alliteration and rhyme in lines like "the costumed Switzers sloped their pikes to push,/ O Pius, through the monstrous human crush . . ." in the opening poem of the book, which is Lowell's farewell to Rome and his own previous styles.

By beginning with "Beyond the Alps," this book of premeditated radical departures begins with a poem constructed out of a sonnet sequence and the ten-syllable line, again a hint of the skillful use of traditional form in *Lord Weary's Castle*. (Note also the way that Lowell shapes "Inauguration Day: January 1953" into a distortion of the Italian sonnet, dividing the stanzas into nine and five lines, the rhyme scheme itself abrasively affected.) Such formal (dis)-connections to the past serve to warn the reader that in this new collection the classic poses are "breaking up." The couplet from the final sonnet of "Beyond The Alps" is broken off from its preceding twelve lines, and the poem itself is about the poet's restlessness in leaving Rome for Paris, religion for modernism.

The last poem from Part One, "A Mad Negro Soldier Confined at Munich," indicates Lowell's growing ability to bring other persons into his poetry. It also displays a new kind of imagery that Lowell would use increasingly. Under control, after his escapades, the soldier concludes by describing the routine hospital world that keeps him and others in check:

> . . . . "We file before the clock,
>
> and fancy minnows, slaves of habit, shoot
> like starlight through their air-conditioned bowl.
> It's time for feeding. Each subnormal boot-
> black heart is pulsing to its ant-egg dole."

This imagery of a policed life pervades Lowell's work from here on, as if the tumultuous "mind" of *Lord Weary's Castle* is partially tamed. This poem about rebellion, disturbance, and a forced return to normality and control points toward the problems of the fourth part of the book, which includes Lowell's own working out of what in the beginning is the task of the confined soldier: the task of keeping his identity alive despite the pressures on him.

The neo-Pavlovian atmosphere, the prepared, lobotomized creature wired for controlled behavior (like those hyphenated words), in line as he should be, along with the others—these elements are present and foreshadow not only Lowell's experience taken up later in the book but also that policed atmosphere felt in so much of his poetry written during the 1960s: "The Mouth of the Hudson," "The Public Garden" (a revision of "David and Bathsheba in the Public Garden"), "The Drinker," "The Opposite House," "Central Park." Imagery of a man's puzzling aloneness, heightened through some restrictive communal setting, remains at the heart of Lowell's poetry.

"A Mad Negro Soldier Confined at Munich" also establishes the tone of personal anguish felt throughout the book. The poem does not explicitly relate the poet to "A Mad Negro Soldier," yet (keeping in mind all of *Life Studies*), the reader feels silent and deep relationships between the author of *Life Studies* and that soldier, just as within the poem the soldier's condition and problems are connected to "We" and all the other "fancy minnows, slaves of habit."

It is pertinent to recall that the city where the soldier is confined was the scene of a rebellion—the failed 1923 *putsch* that signalled Hitler's political career—as well as, in 1938, of a notorious political betrayal (Neville Chamberlain's sellout to Hitler to win "peace in our time"). The place name of the title becomes a metaphor for the dilemma of the deranged Negro soldier as he wavers between an uncontrollable self-expression and an institutionalized docility in a city noted for its irrational subversions and diplomatic betrayals. Yet within that Negro soldier's rebellion against pacification lies an urge for life not to be denied or imprisoned. Part One, especially in its opening and closing poems, foreshadows the directions and difficulties of the rest of *Life Studies*.

II *Part Two*

An autobiographical fragment, "91 Revere Street" fits well into the scheme and concerns of the volume. The autobiographical section is written in prose and automatically relates to the prosiness of the poetry Lowell is creating in the book.

The fragment opens with Lowell's romantic indulgence of his distant relative Major Mordecai Myers, a military and civic figure, possibly Jewish, whose forthright and respectable stature during the early years of the country contrasts sharply with the poet's washed-out, ex-naval-officer father. (The Jewish consciousness is so pervasive in American literature following World War II that here we even find a Lowell opting for something of that identity.) Family furnishings, like those in some of the poems later on in the book, are keenly remembered and are invoked as psychological relics of the family's past that haunt Lowell's mind. The descriptions of absurd family situations and friends also adumbrate the situations described in the last part of the book. Lowell's remembrances of his childhood set the scene for and help to clarify his problems that occupy some of the later poems. The droning, half-lazy prose style fits the sense of doldrums that Lowell evokes in his memoir, despite occasional outbursts of character (another tie to the condition of that mad Negro soldier). That style helps create a boring world that Lowell as child and poet seeks to escape. A Portrait of the Poet as a Child, "91 Revere Street" conveys the same grimy-morose-inspired childhood that Lowell conveys in his imitation of Rimbaud's "The Poet at Seven."

In one particularly good passage from "91 Revere Street," Lowell remembers a Christmas Eve when his father (who is thinking of leaving the navy for a business career) in the middle of dinner is peremptorily ordered by his superior officer to return immediately to the Boston Navy Yard. In bed that evening, Lowell, the boy, thinks of his saddened Christmas Eve; he has a deflating vision of his father and his father's pirate-sailors storming an altar which turns out to be a cash register. The holiday sounds of the Salvation Army Band mingle with the noises and songs of drunken sailors and with the shrill telephone voice of the boy's mother bawling out her husband's superior officer. After complaining to the admiral of the Navy Yard that he has left her defenseless this Christmas Eve, the mother goes into her son's bedroom, telling him how comforted she is to have a man in the house. The child can only reply, "I am not a man . . . I am a boy."

The prose piece foreshadows the difficulties of the poems to come and seeks to establish that prose context for the poetic studies in life to follow: the failure of the father; the insistent influence of the mother; the loneliness of the boy as he is dwarfed by adults, is aggressive toward friends, and spends some years at what is principally a girls' school. Lowell remembers an embarrassing moment in that school, when a little girl left on the floor a golden puddle that spread toward Lowell's chair; later on, the principal of the school came in to instruct the children that there is "nothing laughable about a malaise." The autobiographical fragment emphasizes the drudgery Lowell felt as he was reared in his family. Some of the anecdotes and incidents, however, like some of the people introduced, are drawn out and boring. The descriptions of the Annapolis classmate and lifelong friend of Lowell's father are particularly overdrawn, even though it is clear that Lowell is ludicrously trying to find some heir to the military pose once held by Major Myers, something worth being nourished by.

"91 Revere Street" is a fitting prose accompaniment to the poetry of *Life Studies*. In its context, the memoir suggests that prose is not altogether different from poetry (a connection that fascinated Lowell after the writing of *Life Studies*) and asks the reader to make connections between the prose portrait of the life of the young Robert Lowell and the moments in his life to appear in Part Four of the book.

III   *Part Three*

Part Three, the central section, is dedicated to writers and establishes the literary and intellectual context of the disruptions, breakdowns, and fitful recovery of powers that dominate the book. By forceful indirection, the four writers, whose names make up the titles of the poems—"Ford Madox Ford," "For George Santayana,"

"To Delmore Schwartz," "Words for Hart Crane"—prepare us for the estrangement, illness, and idiosyncratic achievement celebrated in the last part of the book. Their plight, intelligence, honesty, and absurdities are shared or nurtured by the author of this book. These writers become to Lowell the "American" equivalents of the numerous Russian writers who were purged, exiled, or hounded to death; they honor and deepen *Life Studies* with their presence. In a sense they are to Lowell's imagination and intellectual dedication what John Synge and other friends and writers were to Yeats in his sad celebration "In Memory of Robert Gregory." Lowell, like Yeats, wishes to honor these men, "With some appropriate commentary on each."

Three of the four poems were written to dead writers, and the one to Schwartz was probably written after his and Lowell's breakdowns. Of the four writers, one died in want; one, in exile, dramatized the ironies of fame and faith; one was driving himself to death; and one had already killed himself. Lowell's replacements for the Lionel Johnson and Ernest Dowson whom Yeats appreciated and whom Ezra Pound honors and mourns in "Hugh Selwyn Mauberley," these writers are part of any modern poet's unavoidable heritage. The very names of these writers are for Lowell names of poems, and each poem is a statement of love. The estrangement and defeat of these men are part of their accomplishment and significant being. These writers, like the mad Negro soldier in Munich, not only deepen Lowell's plight as he seems to share their fate but are also a sustaining force. Without their presence in one form or another, *Life Studies* could not have been written. Ezra Pound linked Ford's poetry to the prose tradition of English poetry,[1] and Santayana considered himself both a Catholic and an atheist. Both of these men reflect Lowell's own development from *Lord Weary's Castle* to *Life Studies*, from "Colloquy in Black Rock" to "Beyond the Alps."

In a remark quoted by an interviewer in 1953, we get a sense of how at least one of these writers, even in his act of self-destruction, served as a lifeline for Lowell as he thought about or interpreted the writer's actions. Lowell remarked on Hart Crane's death "that when Crane leapt off the fantail of the ship into the Mexican Gulf he did not wish to commit suicide, but rather . . . had only an intense desire to cool and wet his exhausted body."[2] For such a reason, Lowell immersed himself in the lives and experiences of *Life Studies*.

The best of the poems in Part Three is the last, "Words for Hart Crane," a sonnet whose unorderly rhyme and prosody at first conspire to rob the poet of his traditional and stately accented ravings—but not quite. The poem shrewdly expresses the poet's difficulties, especially if the anarchy of accents in the second line quoted below is compared with the traditionally iambic pentameter of the first line. Like "A Mad Negro Soldier Confined at Munich," Crane honorably, intensively, and individually speaks his anguish. After referring to the corruption of literary prizes in his time and acknowledging that few considered why he spent time "stalking sailors," Crane asserts:

> "Because I knew my Whitman like a book,
> stranger in America, tell my country: I
> *Catullus redivivus*, once the rage of the
> Village and Paris, used to play my role
> of homosexual, wolfing the stray lambs
> who hungered by the Place de la Concorde.
> My profit was a pocket with a hole.
> Who asks for me, the Shelley of my age,
> must lay his heart out for my bed and board."

The poem has the effect of Crane's acting out the words handed to him by Lowell, or the words are really Crane's with Lowell acting as the recorder of them. The last two lines of Crane's confession state the task for reader and poet as they meet in this book, for Lowell himself does "lay his heart out." Laying out the heart forms the fraternity of the four writers, each of whom bares himself in the poem dedicated to him. Lowell might say, in the words of Edward Dahlberg about some American expatriates in Europe, including Crane, "I salute these men; for though now dead they cure my own life; only the deceased can save us."[3]

IV   *Part Four, Section One*

Part Four of the book, itself subtitled "Life Studies," takes the most risks: though prepared for previously, it is the rawest part of the book. In it, the family moments are wryly recalled, and the poems are the most personal. This material is what the earlier parts of the book encourage Lowell to deal with: the difficulties of his relatives and his family, as well as his own difficulties, that Lowell wants his poetry and himself to face and still survive. Divided into

two sections, the first section of Part Four begins with the poet's
memories of grandparents and relatives during the 1920s. While
such poems as "My Last Afternoon with Uncle Devereux Winslow"
and "Grandparents" are serious and sad portraits of relatives
engulfed by time as the poet-child looks on and remembers, they
are also filled with precious, absurd details that both defy and
heighten the seriousness. Sometimes Lowell presents the family and
its troubles only to deflate the people and to make of family difficulties not a burden of duty and tradition, but a pathos and an absurdity that allows the poet a freer sense of himself.

As early as "In Memory of Arthur Winslow," Lowell describes his
relations as impoverished inheritors of a one-time Pilgrim and
Revolutionary New England. Lowell, an interesting representative
of the American aristocracy of family, has done for himself what in
larger terms has been described, in the words of Philip Rieff, as "a
revolution of the rich by which they have lowered the pressure of
inherited communal purpose upon themselves."[4] Having done so,
Lowell finds himself more willing and able to bring into the poet's
circle the fates of "A Mad Negro Soldier Confined at Munich" and
of Hart Crane. Lowell is also preparing to describe himself in a
poem like "Skunk Hour" at the end of the book. By the time he
gets to "Memories of West Street and Lepke," he has turned over
some of the older, orderly, and recognizable communal-family purposes to the man scavenging trash cans who "has two children, a
beach wagon, a helpmate, / and is a 'young Republican.' "

Part Four builds toward the poet's adult life by either working
away from the past or back to it. The chronology of the poems is
moving, although the sequence belongs to every man. The son
becomes a husband and a father in his turn. The generations go
forward, but consciousness can suddenly shift back. When an illness
of his daughter reminds Lowell of his own childhood, he compares
himself to her. The child-observer in the section's opening poem
about the death of his uncle, "My Last Afternoon with Uncle
Devereux Winslow," becomes a few poems later, in "During
Fever," the adult-observer watching the illness of his own child.
Some deep inability to escape the past lies in these poems.

The cast of *Life Studies* is rich, perhaps too rich. The members of
the family include the grandfather, whom the grandson calls "my
Father," and the aunt who practiced on a dummy piano and who
once did not appear for her own recital. Family rumor has it that
she jilted an Astor. An uncle is dying at twenty-nine, and the poet's

father goes downhill all the way while the mother reads the psychiatrist Menninger at night and discusses her husband's character with her son. Odd details, relationships askew, pervade this family portrayal and personal history. After the grandfather's death, the poet inherits the family farm with its stained billiards-table cloth on which "I doodle handlebar / mustaches on the last Russian Czar." The seemingly careless off-rhymes in such a poem as "Grandparents" advance the informal affection that the child Lowell felt for his grandfather. The poem's rhyme "structure" suggests a disorganized overthrow of order. The rhymes are so casual, seemingly so accidental, as to be a rhyming equivalent of doodling. Yet the slapdash reference to the Czar also turns into a comic-serious foreshadowing of the frightening descriptions of the gangster Lepke in a later poem in which Lowell treats his rebellion during World War II, a rebellion with the deepest personal and social implications. *Life Studies* has a marvelous way of mixing the serious and the comic—they become part of one experience.

When the poet is in a mental hospital, the family nurse (a witch of sorts) ties "gobbets of porkrind in bowknots of gauze" on trees to help feed the winter birds; the tub in the hospital is "vaguely urinous from the Victorian plumbing"; and, because of his political conscience, the poet ends up in jail with the leader of Murder, Inc. As a wry, Chekhovian note of the entire family absurdity, "Lowell" is misspelled "Lovel" on the coffin carrying the poet's mother home from Italy. The inherited family tradition is indeed deflated, the very name lowered to some absurd comic level, a mismanagement of family name and love.

Lowell may be accused of stretching his material and his intent. The portrayal of his down-and-out father in poem after poem leads to the doubts raised by M. L. Rosenthal when he wondered just how much a man can demean and try his father in public without suffering himself.[5] There isn't anything Lowell's father can do right, from cutting meat to making money, from saving money to playing golf, from handling his wife to ordering his naval and commercial careers. Each morning toward the time of his death he is "inattentive and beaming." We have too much of Lowell's father in this book.

The love Lowell feels for the isolated and idiosyncratic Ford Madox Ford or for the dying George Santayana is never felt for the father. Lowell probably meant to both exorcise the father and indicate his ties to him, but what most impresses us is the relentless

exposure of his father's weaknesses. The son has obviously
destroyed the father (Lowell is a remorseless Stephen Dedalus), but
the destruction does not result in the son's emotional or intellectual
independence from parental authority. At times the son's is a cheap
victory. Lowell once wisely observed: "The worst grievance is the
limitation inherent in any poet's character. . . . That central
limitation is far more serious than a few bad lines."[6]

Yet, after all is said and done, part of Lowell's intent is not
to usurp the father or to express the kind of conflict recorded years
earlier in "Rebellion." In the father's absolute failure, Lowell is
posing the situation of a son growing into his own maturity without
the father as any kind of guide. Childhood and the child's manhood
are difficult burdens in Lowell's poetry. The poems about the
father, overdone as they are, are nevertheless the logical portraits of
the orphan spirit, the myopia of being, that haunt the poet. These
poems constitute, in effect, Lowell's "Letter to His Father." Finally, these poems are Lowell's sad, disappointed notations on the
failed ideal of a proper and exhilarating military energy. If the
poems of the second section of Part Four are better than those in
the first section, we cannot be sure that those earlier poems do not
help account for the impact of the final poems in that second section.

All of Part Four, "Life Studies," the section that takes the most
risks, must have had a special meaning for Lowell. In the recording
he made for the Yale Poetry Series, he first reads "The Quaker
Graveyard in Nantucket" (dedicated to a cousin), then "Beyond the
Alps," and then all of the poems from this last part (the family circle) of *Life Studies*. By the end of the first section of Part Four, the
relatives, who have taken over from the literary figures, are dead in
their turn—the poet is alone with his family, with himself. As family
heir in *Life Studies*, Lowell feels, in the words of T. S. Eliot, "Not
fare well,/But fare forward, voyagers."

V *Part Four, Section Two*

Of the four poems concluding the book and making up the second section of Part Four, two deal with marriage, one with Lowell's
opposition to American policy during World War II, and the final
one with the poet-protagonist's mental plight. This part is the
maturest one of the book; and, if there are victories and defeats of
character in *Life Studies*, they stand out in these final poems. These

last poems compose a related but separate section because their concerns are what Lowell has been raising all along, but the poet finally moves out, artistically and personally, on his own.

" 'To Speak of Woe That Is in Marriage' " started out as a translation of Catullus and, alongside "Man and Wife," presents a devastating portrait of a marriage. These marriage poems are in the two principal voices Lowell has worked out for himself in the book. " 'To Speak of Woe . . .' " is uttered by an objectively created character, like the mad Negro soldier and Hart Crane; "Man and Wife" is in the voice of the poet-protagonist. The woman who speaks of woe (her title words are the Wife of Bath's), no less than the poet who created her, has to scheme her way to survival. In this poem and in "Man and Wife," Lowell continues the tradition of George Meredith and Thomas Hardy in the poetry of "modern love," to explore the way men and women make victims and captives of each other. Lowell does not write love poetry as much as he writes poems about marriage.

The other two poems which open and close this last grouping in *Life Studies*, "Memories of West Street and Lepke" and "Skunk Hour" confirm and vivify the book's title. They are both about the poet's struggle for survival and the terms of surviving. In "Memories of West Street and Lepke," Lowell, the son of a naval officer and the descendant of an old American family noted for its dedication to public and military service, examines his experience as a conscientious objector during World War II. He recollects that emotional event from the strangely tranquil vantage point of the following decade.

Twice Lowell had volunteered for service but twice was rejected for nearsightedness. By the time he was finally called up, America was halfway through the war; and Lowell found himself opposed both to saturation bombing, which especially meant the killing of civilians, and to the demand for unconditional surrender. He refused to appear for induction in September, 1943; and he even failed to appear for arraignment. Finally, in October, the *New York Times*, in an article headed "A 'Boston Lowell' is a Draft Dodger," reported that Lowell had pleaded guilty of violating the Selective Service Act.

A month before, in a letter to President Roosevelt, Lowell announced his intention to refuse military service, contending, according to the *Times* report, "that the Allies were fighting as ruthlessly as their opponents." Denied the status of a conscientious objector,

Lowell, as already noted, received a year and a day for refusing to be inducted, though the usual sentence was three years; and he served five months in the penitentiary in Danbury, Connecticut. In fixing the sentence, the judge told Lowell, "You are one of a distinguished family, and this will mar your family traditions."[7] By 1943, Lowell had become, therefore, doubly a renegade to his family; a convert to Catholicism (in 1940) and a conscientious objector—and both themes lie behind the poem "Rebellion."

In "Memories of West Street and Lepke," Lowell, the rebellious young man, has survived to "The tranquillized *Fifties*" and to his own age of forty; to a safe, academic life of sorts; and to the decade when, under the influence of Senator Joseph McCarthy, many men were forced to betray former political passions, to undergo some "agonizing reappraisal," and to confess their past. At the same time, some terrible complacency had settled over American life. What is the confession of the poet in these circumstances?

In the opening stanza of the poem only the description of the poet's daughter, nine months old, suggests a revitalized life, new possibilities—"Like the sun she rises in her flame-flamingo infants' wear." Like W. D. Snodgrass in "Heart's Needle," Lowell sensitively brings together a troubled world, a self in turmoil, and the "saving" image of the growing daughter. After all that dredging up of family matters in the preceding poems of *Life Studies*, the image of the young daughter comes as an unexpected delight; for the poet, perhaps, as much as for the reader. Yet the sad note is never lost as we are told that the child is young enough to be the poet's granddaughter; some sense of lost years filters into the poem. At the same time, the poet wonders if he should regret his past rebellion; and he half-mockingly compares his present affluence and soul-searching with the image of a good citizen who makes a living by scavenging trash cans.

Lowell humorously and self-deprecatingly talks about his present self and his formerly rebellious self. Should he reject his "seedtime" when he was "a fire-breathing Catholic C.O." and told off the authorities? Maybe he has rejected that fierceness with his present life: teaching once a week, book-worming in pajamas, and living on Henry James's "hardly passionate Marlborough Street." He is ill at ease whether in the swim of protest or while living some semipatrician, orderly, Bostonian life.

Like T. S. Eliot, Lowell suffers sometimes from a self-deprecating assessment that belies the vitality the poem is about or that must have motivated it in the first place. Just as Eliot, as critics have pointed out, may tiresomely refer to himself as the aged eagle, Lowell never tires of being the prisoner of himself, or of wrapping himself up in his turmoil. The danger lies in the uncritical self-posturing and in the poet's potential disloyalty to a vibrancy the poem deals with elsewhere. Also, the question (with a touch of awkward diction), "Ought I to regret my seedtime?" is partly a rhetorical self-indulgence; for the poem, with its oddly comfortable Boston setting, only halfheartedly considers such a regret a possibility. In the 1960s the poet was to win fame among those generally unaware of poets by criticizing President Johnson about the barbarities of the Vietnam war. (Stephen Spender once remarked in a lecture that when the Bostonian Robert Lowell had criticized the President from Texas he was above all being a Lowell.) Furthermore, in cold war symposia of the 1960s, Lowell continuously chose positions similar to those of his "seedtime." Lowell's response to Cassius Clay's unwillingness to serve during the Vietnam war reminds us of the poet's own problem and its resolution in the 1940s: "Refusal to report to the army is certainly the most effective way a young man can protest an unjust war."[8] His stature in the 1960s is partially explained by the fact that he, too, had once been jailed for protesting a war. (These "radical" inclinations of the sixties, incidentally, may have also been acts of contrition for the severe anti-communism Lowell felt during the forties.)

Yet "Memories of West Street and Lepke" should be appreciated as an effort by Lowell to reassess his previous position as conscientious objector and to question his current, oddly respectable status; indeed, the poem is the poet's honest urge to question what his prose statements and his life affirm. The political act, the ideological commitment made in prose, when turned into poetry is not simply repeated in a heightened language but is exposed to psychological and social complexities which the act and statement cannot fully deal with or admit to. The relationship between Lowell's act of being a conscientious objector, his extra-poetic statements on war, and "Memories of West Street and Lepke" points up the difference between the man in the world and the man in his art: the art acknowledges and exploits complexities that a man mutes or deflects in order to act. As Lowell once observed, paraphrasing T. S. Eliot, in prose a man writes what he wants to believe; in poetry, what he must.

A close look at "Memories of West Street and Lepke" enables us to see how the poem conveys the poet's searching and wondering in a weird, maladjusted, dry-rotting world that his "seedtime," his irony, and his conscience cannot entirely avoid. The first three stanzas register the poet's situations:

> Only teaching on Tuesdays, book-worming
> in pajamas fresh from the washer each morning,
> I hog a whole house on Boston's
> "hardly passionate Marlborough Street,"
> where even the man
> scavenging filth in the back alley trash cans,
> has two children, a beach wagon, a helpmate,
> and is a "young Republican."
> I have a nine months' daughter,
> young enough to be my granddaughter.
> Like the sun she rises in her flame-flamingo infants' wear.
>
> These are the tranquillized *Fifties*,
> and I am forty. Ought I to regret my seedtime?
> I was a fire-breathing Catholic C.O.,
> and made my manic statement,
> telling off the state and president, and then
> sat waiting sentence in the bull pen
> beside a Negro boy with curlicues
> of marijuana in his hair.
>
> Given a year,
> I walked on the roof of the West Street Jail, a short
> enclosure like my school soccer court,
> and saw the Hudson River once a day
> through sooty clothesline entanglements
> and bleaching khaki tenements.
> Strolling, I yammered metaphysics with Abramowitz,
> a jaundice-yellow ("it's really tan")
> and fly-weight pacifist,
> so vegetarian,
> he wore rope shoes and preferred fallen fruit.
> He tried to convert Bioff and Brown,
> the Hollywood pimps, to his diet.
> Hairy, muscular, suburban,
> wearing chocolate double-breasted suits,
> they blew their tops and beat him black and blue.

At first the poet seems to be merely biding time, to be wandering amid his present thoughts and his recall. The first impression the reader gets is that of a weak, lolling, lackadaisical mind. The poet is "only teaching." The language seems slack, participial phrases stretching out matters. The poet's indulgent use of clichés, as if he were taking the path of least resistance in reminiscing about the past and assessing the present, adds to the reader's sense of the speaker's soft, decaying consciousness. Stock phrases—"bookworming," "hog a whole house," "so out of things" (from the last part of the poem)—and some overall tired animality contribute to this impression. (Lowell even invents a packaged phrase—"the tranquillized *Fifties.*") Yet underneath this slack surface another impression is conveyed, one of violence and hardness. Clichés of violence can also be found in the poem: "fire-breathing," "blew their tops," "beat him black and blue." Deep within the poem's apparent softness lies something tough and frightening, a mechanical, unthinking brutality. The poet fears not only the flabbiness but also the violence overtaking him and his world, just as in the first stanza his self-mocking position is partially eclipsed and usurped by the man "scavenging filth in the back alley trash cans." Also, it seems as if Lowell again connects himself to the tendencies of his father (whose conversation, according to the prose memoir, was often sprinkled with clichés), yet he finally surmounts the connection through his own shrewd indulgence of the phrases.

At the end of the poem we come across the mentally tough slogan "agonizing reappraisal," a phrase that during the tenure of Secretary of State John Foster Dulles in the Eisenhower years was used to describe a supposedly painful rethinking of American foreign policy. In employing the phrase himself, Lowell not only indicates how *Life Studies* grew out of the atmosphere of the 1950s, but uses his own plight to rescue the phrase from its fate as a political cliché. At the same time, he ambiguously connects himself to the deceptive language of the time.

The final, and fourth, stanza continues to show some of the poet's self-deprecation, his fallen view of himself—he was "so out of things" in prison. But the poem also leads to a world of submerged violence, for the fellow prisoner who taught Lowell how to make his bed

> . . . pointed out the T shirted back
> of *Murder Incorporated's* Czar Lepke,
> there piling towels on a rack,
> or dawdling off to his little segregated cell full
> of things forbidden the common man:
> a portable radio, a dresser, two toy American
> flags tied together with a ribbon of Easter palm.

Flabby, bald, lobotomized,
he drifted in a sheepish calm,
where no agonizing reappraisal
jarred his concentration on the electric chair—
hanging like an oasis in his air
of lost connections. . . .

Lepke, the patriotic murderer, represents in his dumb way the state
of national life; his is an executive position in an efficient corporation whose task is to destroy human beings. This gunman Prufrock,
"Flabby, bald, lobotomized," is symbolic of his time, related as he
is to the "hairy, muscular, suburban" pimps who are, in turn, dis-
quietingly a variation of that scavenger of filth with his "two
children, a beach wagon, a helpmate." These descriptive phrases
are not interchangeable, but they do suggest relationships, a
frightening, hidden common cause of destruction. They are all
patriots, destroyers.

But where is the poet in all of this? In certain ways he is related to
Lepke, whose "sheepish calm" is like the state of "I" at the beginning of the poem and at the conclusion of the two poems immediately prior to this one, "Waking in the Blue" and "Home After
Three Months Away." In these last two poems Lowell thinks about
having been in the mental hospital: "We are all old-timers, / each
of us holds a locked razor"; and "I keep no rank nor
station. / Cured, I am frizzled, stale and small." As Jerome Mazzaro
has pointed out, "This 'sheepish figure' of Lepke turns on the
earlier figures of Lowell and Lowell's father, recalling Lowell's own
sense of being lobotomized and tranquillized and the Commander's
loss of hope."[9] Lepke, like Lovel, is another version of Lowell.

The poet's fate is tied to that of gangsters and other outcasts. Yet,
if the poet and the gangster, as literature often affirms, share a
secret life (they are not only outcasts, but their health and security
are dependent upon their ability to live off their antisocial behavior
or ideas), the figure of the gangster Czar, as well as that of the two
Hollywood toughs, also strikes a position different from that of the
poet. The poet feels himself a part of the time's dry rot, but "no
agonizing reappraisal" dominates the murderer's mind as it does
the poet's. For Lowell, survival and continuation always mean self-
analysis; and his ability to investigate himself is his own heroic act
even in a time of doubt, deprecation, and destruction of personality.
The poet is a Prometheus chained to himself. If in this situation the

poet is a criminal (and shares his situation with criminals), his is also another role, one related to a man's ability to make and investigate his own courageous decisions.

VI "*Skunk Hour*"

"Skunk Hour," the last poem of *Life Studies*,[10] is, as Lowell has said, "not entirely independent, but the anchor poem in its sequence." A fit conclusion to the book, it is the culmination of the book's trouble and turmoil; it is also the key poem of survival within the swirl of existence. "Skunk Hour," the final itemizing of the confessional accounts, is also about a man's honest survival amid the disappointments, the rebellions, the losses, and confusions strewn all about his life.

Within the poem, and within the book it concludes, there is a loyalty to the truth and a commitment to the vibrant voices of self-knowledge. Like Elizabeth Bishop's "The Armadillo," a poem dedicated to Lowell and one which he said on "rereading suggested a way of breaking through the shell of my old manner," "Skunk Hour" (which in turn is dedicated to Miss Bishop) offers the mind illumination through its ability to imagine destruction. The poet survives the labyrinth of disorder by depending upon the devious pattern. The poet, like the skunks at the end, searches "in the moonlight" (a traditional light for the mad) for something to eat and grow on and, finding it in the garbage pail, "will not scare." This final poem of the book can be viewed in one of two ways: as a final succumbing to the "ant-egg dole" and "back alley trash cans," or as a paradoxical victory for the poet while "free-lancing out along the razor's edge" and while undergoing the "agonizing reappraisal." The poem is not a victory exactly, or entirely; but it speaks for a person's hard-edged ability to live within the truth of his frightening yet life-giving reality. The poem can be likened to Dante's situation in *Inferno*, where he is described as one "going this pilgrimmage through the sick night" (Canto V, 1.89).

"Skunk Hour" was begun, Lowell has said, after he returned from numerous readings on the West Coast, when he questioned his old style, which seemed to hide his real concerns and which "many times offered a stiff, humorless and even impenetrable surface," and when he was finding it difficult to complete poems he had started. The poem's origin in frustration supports its position as

anchor poem of *Life Studies*. During this San Francisco experience
and his readings, Lowell found himself writing prose. This fact
alone explains why he attached the prose autobiographical fragment
to *Life Studies*—to show us what kind of writing he had been doing
and trying out while he was working on the poems for the book. It
was at this time, Lowell said, that he began to feel "that the best
style for poetry was none of the many poetic styles in English, but
something like the prose of Chekhov or Flaubert."[11]

A takeoff on Pound's remark that poetry should be at least as well
written as prose, this statement conveys Lowell's effort to throw off
the earlier influences of Hopkins, Dylan Thomas, Allen Tate, and
Donne; it also indicates the achievements and risks of the book.
Unlike the earlier poetry, the surface of *Life Studies* is immediately
visible; the rhetoric does not "stand in the way." As with the prose
of Chekhov or Flaubert, what is seemingly direct and apparent on
the surface turns out to have resonances deep, mysterious, and
puzzling in a new way. The reader immediately feels this
strangeness in the poem, and the puzzled feeling increases as he
goes through the first half of "Skunk Hour":

>Nautilus Island's hermit
>heiress still lives through winter in her Spartan cottage;
>her sheep still graze above the sea.
>Her son's a bishop. Her farmer
>is first selectman in our village;
>she's in her dotage.
>
>Thirsting for
>the hierarchic privacy
>of Queen Victoria's century,
>she buys up all
>the eyesores facing her shore,
>and lets them fall.
>
>The season's ill—
>we've lost our summer millionaire,
>who seemed to leap from an L. L. Bean
>catalogue. His nine-knot yawl
>was auctioned off to lobstermen.
>A red fox stain covers Blue Hill.
>
>And now our fairy
>decorator brightens his shop for fall;

> his fishnet's filled with orange cork,
> orange, his cobbler's bench and awl;
> there is no money in his work,
> he d rather marry.

As John Berryman and John Frederick Nims have shown in their illuminating discussions of the poem, "Skunk Hour" is either deceptively simple or deceptively anarchic—its particulars are striking and distinct but also curiously isolated and disconnected, like the remarks of a Chekhov character. (No discussions of the poem can avoid honoring the critiques and explanations offered by Berryman and Nims. Their studies are brilliant homages to the poem, and all subsequent readers are indebted to them.)[12]

Strange qualities attach themselves to the identities of these islanders. The heiress is called "hermit" and, despite her money, lives in a spartan cottage. She seems more masculine than feminine (contrasting with the decorator), and her idiosyncratic effort to regain privacy is only her perverse way of opposing her time. We are abruptly told "she's in her dotage," the summarizing line of the opening stanza; and the feminine yet harsh, abrupt rhyme with "cottage" and "village" rings up her character.

Other confusing roles are suggested in the opening stanzas: "Her son's a bishop," which parallels the last phrase summing up the heiress. Yet, despite the hint of parallel idiosyncrasies, the stanza suggests that the mother and son are far apart and do not speak to each other, or even see each other—so close yet so far apart, like other family relationships in *Life Studies*. (The stanza brought to Berryman's mind a similar situation of a mother and a son in Chekhov's story "The Bishop.") The fact that a farmer is a selectman is not in and of itself strange, but the social fact that the rich woman's hired hand is a village official does suggest topsy-turvy identities and relationships. The old woman wants to emulate a Queen Victoria presence, but she is in the wrong century and has no court to speak of (her farmer has more political power than she does), except perhaps for her sheep—the hermit heiress metamorphoses into a weird shepherdess.

Everybody has roles in the first half of the poem, but they are askew, or these people have no working relationships that insure tradition, order, stability; like other characters in *Life Studies*, the people in "Skunk Hour" are isolated in their roles. The strangely contradictory and "ill" roles continue in the next stanzas. The millionaire, who is in financial trouble, is just a "summer millionaire"; he must sell his pleasure craft to the lobstermen. An ironic reversal of the fairy decorator who converts practical objects into decor, the rich man must turn over his pleasure ship to the practical pursuit of catching lobsters. The term "lobstermen" suggests a strange animal takeover, in keeping with the conclusion of the poem and with much of the imagery of *Life Studies*. The relationship of these fishermen to the millionaire (they are social inferiors who turn out to be superior and who usurp the other's role) parallels that of the heiress and her farmer in the first stanza.

Moreover, as with the heiress, there is something ludicrous about this millionaire, who seems more like a fugitive from a manufacturer's showroom or from some child's storybook than a dignified rich man. His "nine-knot yawl," like other phrases difficult to pronounce ("Nautilus Island's hermit / heiress"; "Thirsting for/the hierarchic privacy"), indicates Lowell's perverse insistence on not mellifluously describing matters as they are at this hour. Even the language works against notions of stability and security, against the forming of harmonious relationships. Poetry at this hour is in the condition of the people of the poem; therefore, art and life connect through the appropriate style. Hugh Staples has pointed out that the rhyme scheme of each stanza varies from, yet reflects, the rhyme in the opening stanza.[13] Even the rhyme schemingly advances the spirit of the poem, a pattern of disorder. The form is there to be upset.

Finally, in this first half of the poem the fairy decorator confuses matters, as shown both in his person and in the way he transforms trade equipment into so much bric-a-brac. (The poem is one weird metamorphosis.) The fourth stanza also suggests a parody of traditional poetic diction, a snickering at the way a mediocre poet might have described one season's change into another—"And now our fairy / decorator brightens his shop for fall." The language of a false, sentimental artist is evoked in the fourth stanza, the language of a hackneyed romantic, like the decorator. Lowell's phrases also weirdly echo each other—"there is no money . . . , / he'd rather marry"—and suggest strange matings between people and their activities. The many incidental details about the characters in the poem seem irrelevant or foreign to one another, or oblique to the persons themselves. Although the details seem to be carelessly thrown into the poem, their prosaic motley creates a disturbing pattern, a pattern the reader feels as he moves through the rest of the poem.

Halfway through the poem now, and having set the scene and having described other persons living through this animal hour, the narrator is ready to speak about himself. He recalls that "One dark night" in "my Tudor Ford" he spied on lovers in cars. He acknowledges, "My mind's not right" and then returns to the present moment:

> A car radio bleats,
> "Love, O careless Love. . . ." I hear
> my ill-spirit sob in each blood cell,
> as if my mind were at its throat. . . .
> I myself am hell;
> nobody's here—
>
> only skunks, that search
> in the moonlight for a bite to eat.
> They march on their soles up Main Street:
> white stripes, moonstruck eyes' red fire
> under the chalk-dry and spar spire
> of the Trinitarian Church.
>
> I stand on top
> of our back steps and breathe the rich air—
> a mother skunk with her column of kittens swills the
>   garbage pail.
> She jabs her wedge-head in a cup
> of sour cream, drops her ostrich tail,
> and will not scare.

His illness in its way seems no worse than the general "life" that he peers at and that has been present in the poem and in the book all along. Like Hamlet's "sick intelligence," his illness measures that larger life. The poet sees the mechanics of love as a kind of death; his illness bequeathes to him the power and burden of observing human behavior. His self-descriptive phrase, "My mind's not right," echoes the description of the heiress, "she's in her dotage." His Tudor Ford seems as absurdly noble and commercial as many of the other facts registered in the first half of the poem. (Perhaps it is some odd echo of the writer described earlier in the book.)

Also, like the heiress and her sheep, the millionaire selling his boat to lobstermen, and the decorator's use of fishing equipment, the poet has his own animal through which we can come to understand him. Although a strange animalism comes to dominate *Life*

Studies, it is an animalism that may metamorphose into a cunning survival. The poet's daughter "rises in her flame-flamingo infants' wear," and the skunk-mother has an ostrich tail, with perhaps some pun lurking in the bird's name.

Life Studies may be Lowell's totemic book of poems. Like those skunks, the poet will not scare; he insists on being true to himself, true to where he must search for survival. As John Frederick Nims points out, in the pun on "soles" the poet shares his fate with these insistent animals, that mother skunk and "her column of kittens." Just as she leads her charges to eat wherever and whatever the food is, this poet has been raiding the food locker of his life. There is something disturbing but also brave about the poet's stance—a reclamation in "the rich air" of the self. The imagery of the final stanza suggests the ego's self-persistence despite the confines of illness, personal and public.

VII   Life Studies *in Context*

Life Studies is not only an important collection of poems in the development of Robert Lowell; it is also a seminal book in the history of American poetry. It not only takes its place along the route of American poetry; it helps establish the terrain. It can be said of *Life Studies*, as of Walt Whitman's *Song of Myself* and of T. S. Eliot's *The Waste Land*, that American poetry could not be the same after Lowell's book was published.

At the conclusion of his summary view of modern poetry, "From Poe to Valéry," T. S. Eliot claims that the *art poétique* which he traces from the American to the French writer has gone as far as it can go. Although a lapse into barbarousness after all that sophisticated consciousness is undesirable, Eliot says, we now probably require an esthetic that both utilizes and moves beyond the kind of poetic achievement established from Poe to Valéry. In this essay, written in 1948, Eliot modestly points toward an esthetic beyond the one that he himself was so prominent and successful in establishing. Eliot's final words in that essay about the burdens of consciousness and organization and the urge to be free of such burdens point toward the kinds of concerns and efforts displayed in *Life Studies*.

Indeed, Lowell's poetry from *Lord Weary's Castle* to *Life Studies* is a case history of what Eliot is talking about. Like Yeats, whose career reflects the history of English poetry from the hothouse mood of the 1890s to the difficult temper of "modern" poetry, Lowell's career measures the development of modern poetry from the hard surface, the intellectually brilliant writing (replete with self-conscious literary references), to a poetry that does not exactly deny this tendency but that is low-keyed, approaching the informalities and laxities of prose. Lowell has epitomized an important phase of our literature and culture. From a religiously charged and traditionally formed poetry to an unrelenting secular search for the self in a language that works like a safety razor that adjusts and readjusts the edges of its blade, Lowell has given shape to our rueful yet inspiring ties with the past and our contemporary puzzlement.

Life Studies is important in terms of the history of American poetry. In his valuable study, *The Continuity of American Poetry*, Roy Harvey Pearce speaks of the dialectic in American poetry between what he calls the Adamic poem (Whitman's *Song of Myself*, the poetry of Emily Dickinson, or that of Wallace Stevens), a poem that "makes us aware of the operation of the creative imagination as an act of self definition," and the mythic poem (Eliot's *The Waste Land*, Pound's *The Cantos*, Crane's *The Bridge*) in which the poet looks outward from beyond the assumed persona, not to an inexhaustible communal self (à la Whitman) but to a form of order beyond the self, one "established" by the culture. Pearce sees both types as overdetermined efforts, and to him Stevens and Eliot represent the finest expressions of the two modes. But if there is a poetry that conveys both modes at the highest level, it is Lowell's. In *Life Studies* and in *Lord Weary's Castle* he had already done so. Lowell learned from both William Carlos Williams and T. S. Eliot.

In talking about the nature of the American epic and the role of poetry in a democracy and basing his discussions on de Tocqueville's observations in *Democracy in America*, Pearce, without referring to Lowell, makes us think of him:

It may well be that for us a definition of the person is *per se* a definition of the hero . . . the author of the American epic must be his own hero, as his epic is the record of his struggle to make something of himself and of his world which constitutes his central subject. Thus in some way or another he must tell all; he wills himself to be incapable of dissembling or repression, lest something of the creative self be left out. These are the ungainlinesses of his compulsions, which neither he nor we can escape. [14]

What could be more descriptive of *Life Studies?*

Who would have thought that it would be a Lowell and a poet owing so much to the Poe-Valéry *art poétique* who would take his place alongside Whitman at the heart of American poetry? The roots of Lowell turn out to be deep indeed, and he came closer to absorbing chaotic America, her predicaments and her possibilities, than he or his readers or his family might have foreseen.

Life Studies was also the first major statement in the mode that, fortunately or unfortunately, has come to be called "confessional poetry," a term no one would think of applying to Eliot, Pound, or Auden—no matter how openly or secretly confessional their poetry at times might appear to be. Of the writers of the generation before Lowell's, only Williams at times might be considered a confessional poet. Yet this kind of poetry has become familiar in the works of W. D. Snodgrass, Anne Sexton, Sylvia Plath, and in Allen Ginsberg's "Kaddish" and in the quieter poetry of Philip Larkin. Certainly there is inherently no more magic or power in confessional poetry than in the poetry of Richard Wilbur or of Theodore Roethke.

Yet, in the way Lowell has done it, he has given us not only a striking *art poétique* but at some deep level has allowed the age itself to come through. Alfred Kazin has aptly referred to the literature of the 1960s as one of self-pity. Perhaps that literature reflects the feeling that a man's last stronghold against a usurping culture, his true source of life in the "air-conditioned bowl," is his inner self. Certainly *Life Studies* and the confessional poem fit this view and this situation in which a man finds himself. In this case, the artist's investigations into, and advertisements of, himself, if well done, become his way of making a human connection with himself and with other persons.

As confessional poetry, *Life Studies* can be considered in the light of observations made by Philip Rieff, who in his study of a shifting mode of being in America, *The Triumph of the Therapeutic*, sighs: "We are, I fear, getting to know one another. Reticence, secrecy, concealment of self have all been transformed into social problems; once they were aspects of civility." Yet, as Rieff then speculates, "Self knowledge again made social is the principle of control upon which the emergent culture may yet be able to make itself stable." *Life Studies* is the *art poétique* rising out of the kind of world Rieff is describing, including the further idea that "Modern man has himself disenchanted the world; only his inner life harbors residues of enchantment."[15] This inner life harbors a painful kind of enchantment, to be sure; and, for some of Lowell's readers, this enchantment is too self-pitying and too self-important. For more sympathetic readers, it is possible to discover in the literary, per sonal, and familial disturbances of Lowell's poetry a convincing parallel to social disorder, to our need to trace and transcend our sense of chaos. This role can be coaxed from *Life Studies* and from its anchor poem, "Skunk Hour." Lowell's work comes to play the kind of cultural role inevitably undertaken by significant poetry. As the title suggests, *Life Studies* gives us our life—as it is; as we might enlarge it.

VIII   *Coda: Family and History in* Life Studies

Robert Lowell's *Life Studies* was published in 1959, the year that also saw the appearance of Norman Mailer's *Advertisements for Myself,* Norman O. Brown's *Life Against Death,* and Saul Bellow's *Henderson the Rain King.* Along with these, *Life Studies* anticipated some of the indulgent and dramatic expressions of self that were to become literary signatures, public displays, and even political phenomena, before the end of the next decade. The publication of these books in the same year supports the notion that by the 1960s the new and last frontier for some Americans was to be their own selves. We are now witnessing the cultural career of the ego—this last realm that might define itself in terms of freedom, mystery, unexpected possibilities. Appearing when it did, Lowell's *Life Studies,* like Brown's and Mailer's and Bellow's books, profoundly registered and propelled an obsession with the self—personality as antidote to the restrictions of politics and culture—which was to mark the shift from the 1950s to the 1960s.

Possessed by a sense of history, yet simultaneously immersed in several recent decades, *Life Studies* conveys some of the deepest concerns of its age.

The poem, "A Mad Negro Soldier Confined at Munich," implicitly capitalizes on the politically volatile role of that city in twentieth-century struggles for power. Munich is an appropriate place for the confinement of that soldier who becomes representative of some malaise in which individuals drift between a manic assertion of self and an institutionalized docility. Associated with social subversion and with false agreements which supposedly insure peace but really point toward war, Munich has become a psychological metaphor. It stands for the treacherous terms of political experience, the predicaments of survival. It symbolizes fear of self-

betrayal, betrayal by others, the restrictions of history. Munich
leads to West Street.

One of the effective connections between decades occurs in
"Memories of West Street and Lepke." This poem begins in the fifties, moves back to the forties, and prefigures some of the difficulties of the sixties and beyond. Lepke in jail, clearly, is an extension of that mad Negro soldier. Lepke also represents the exaggerated fears Lowell has about himself in the beginning of the
poem, and, as mentioned previously, is reminiscent of Lowell's
father, who earlier in *Life Studies* is described as a warning and a
fear to his son: "And to judge from my father, men between the
ages of six and sixty did nothing but meet new challenges, take on
heavier responsibilities, and lose all freedom to explode." Lepke's
fate and docility and the subduing of that mad Negro soldier
overshadow Lowell's descriptions of himself. The fear of not being
able to feel and to act on the basis of those feelings appears in a
number of Lowell's poems. The phrase describing Lepke, "no
agonizing reappraisal," affirms the presence of the 1950s in the
book and connects Lowell's personal fears to the troubles of the age.
"Memories of West Street and Lepke" is a good example of how
Lowell's concern for the drama of his own experience leads to the
stage of history.

Lowell's remembrances and personal situations have the ability
to loom beyond themselves. In "To Delmore Schwartz," Lowell
pictures himself and Schwartz as Harvard outcasts from society. He
quotes Schwartz's parody of Wordsworth in a run-down Cambridge
house in 1946, "*We poets in our youth begin in sadness; / thereof
in the end come despondency and madness.*" This traditionally
romantic role of the poet takes on a particular historical and familial
poignancy because from 1784 to 1943 (except for one decade), a
member of the Lowell family served Harvard University in some official capacity, once even as President during the youth and young
manhood of Robert Lowell. Ferris Greenslet in *The Lowells and
Their Seven Worlds* also points out that "The nineteenth century
opened with the three branches of the Lowells well entrenched, or
starting under the most favorable auspices, in the professions and
pursuits of the three ruling classes of New England, the law, commerce and the Congregational ministry."[16] And in the first third of
the twentieth century, three Lowells made names for themselves as
astronomer, educator, and poet. None of this distinction, however,
is acknowledged in Lowell's memoir, "91 Revere Street." Nor does

his closer maternal side, the Starks and the Winslows, show any like capacities, at least none that Lowell would honor while growing up. (One wonders if the family demise was as evident as Lowell makes us feel.) At any rate, the member of a once-distinguished family has certainly registered the diminishing prestigious role of that family and appears on the scene to haunt, criticize, and also pay unexpected homage to that family. Paradoxically, by taking this submerged path back to the family, Robert Lowell comes to redeem or salvage something of a social role for them.

Lowell's belittling portrait of his father in *Life Studies*, his unrelenting disappointment in his father's way of life, can now be seen as something more than his private problem. Lowell's difficulties with his father, and the way his father's abortive naval career moved against Lowell's boyhood and poetic fascination for the Napoleonic military adventurer, relate to larger and more interesting matters.

Either as naval officer or later as a salesman-executive type, the father was unequal to the son's imaginative demands of him. The elder Lowell's shift from a naval to a business career only increased the disrespect or the sense of failure that the son felt for the father. (Even though Lowell loved his idiosyncratic grandfather Winslow, who is sometimes referred to as "father," he cast doubt on Arthur Winslow's capitalistic ventures and contrasted the grandfather's misplaced business energies with the military, civic, and artisan skills of colonial ancestors, the old family heroes.) The Lowell father-and-son antagonism not only expressed a personal disappointment but dramatized a disapproval felt by many sons who still long for their father to take on some historic role. What is at stake in Lowell's rejection of his father is the child's longing for the parent who displays a bravery and a glamour beyond the calculating bourgeois role. Lowell suffered from the parent who could not inspire the son's imagination. It is a family drama that reveals the problem of a meaningful inheritance from one's parents. In Lowell's case, the drama is played out against the background of a family engaged in the history of America and the very existence of the problem evinces a decline in the historical role of that family.[17]

Lowell seeks that longed-for heroism in an ancestor from the first half of the nineteenth century, Major Mordecai Meyers, a distant relative of whom his imagination can make something. Lowell seeks some lost family historical role in this figure from the past, a patriarch, possibly Jewish, who lived almost one hundred years.

Lowell is not only attracted to family military officers but particularly to those who fight for just social causes. Major Myers, Lowell tells us in "91 Revere Street," "sponsored an enlightened law exempting Quakers from military service in New York State. . . ." (The Robert Lowell who has his "Memories of West Street and Lepke" would appreciate his ancestor's efforts on behalf of conscientious objectors.) And Lowell in "For the Union Dead" honors the military image of Robert Gould Shaw, a Civil War soldier and family acquaintance whose leadership of a black regiment had an idealistic impulse that is still admired a century later.

To some extent, Major Myers is a substitute for the failed father in *Life Studies*. Yet, finally, what could Lowell's father have given the son equal to the image of the heroic he was seeking? Nothing less than his father sailing home from Pearl Harbor, like Odysseus returning to Ithaca, could have satisfied this Revere Street Telemachus. Lowell mentions more than once how as a boy he loved to hold his father's dress sword (with gold braid), loved to play with toy soldiers, and memorized the names of French generals. Considering this fascination with the military figure *and* his criticism of the family role in the colonial Indian wars, what image could the father have succeeded in portraying for the son? Both Warren Winslow (the dead sailor-cousin of World War II, to whom "The Quaker Graveyard in Nantucket" is dedicated) and Lowell's father indicate a demise of some heroic even if questionable military tradition present within the Lowell family ever since the colonial Indian wars.

There exists in Lowell a curious and illuminating tension between his rejection of the aggressive military figure and his fascination for such a personage, a tension that might be subsumed by his ability to imagine the hero who is reminiscent of military valor but whose energies are not simply put in the service of destruction. (This desire bares the psychological investment that Lowell has in one of his finest poems, "For the Union Dead.") Lowell's poetry presents the conflict of two cultural ideals—that of the general and that of the civic hero. This contradiction accounts for some of the interesting strains in his poetry.

One could imagine Lowell as a boy (a boy, say, who grew up and wrote "Falling Asleep over the Aeneid") secretly wishing to be the object of Napoleon's will:

My arms, that is my sword, the one I carried at Austerlitz. . . . My gold dressing case, the one that served me on the morning of Ulm, of Austerlitz, of Jena, of Eulau, of Friedland, of the Island of Lobau, of the Moskwa, of Montmirail. In view of this, I wish that it will be precious to my son.

(The passage is quoted by Hans Morgenthau in an article whose very title could be appropriated for a study of Lowell's war poetry: "From Napoleon to Armageddon.")[18] Lowell's drama has been that of the young man who rejected the father because the father had not sought a heroic or military role for himself. And this despite the fact that Lowell, more than most, has registered the disasters brought about by grandiose military postures in the last two hundred years. Lowell's paternal disappointment finally conveys a longing for a heroism that will be transformed from the aggressive military pose to something peaceful and noble. In the metamorphosis of Lowell's poetry, the statue of General Hooker gives way to the figures of Colonel Shaw and Major Myers and finally to those 1967 peace marchers who "look like green Union Army recruits for the first Bull Run. . . ." Statues move to life.

Given the family military background, evident in "91 Revere Street," we can appreciate the family feelings of treason that probably greeted Lowell's desire to be a conscientious objector during World War II (such feelings hinted at in the *Lord Weary's Castle* poem "Rebellion," with its hidden drama of the conscientious objector who uses violence against his own father). Even if we disagree with Lowell's position during World War II, we can appreciate the courage it must have taken for him to make that moral decision not to register for the Selective Service Act. We might also imagine his lonely but keen feeling that in being a conscientious objector he was really continuing a brave stance he admired in some of his military ancestors. As a conscientious objector, Lowell eventually did more to inform us about the nature of World War II than he would have done by simply being a combatant. In rejecting the Allies' excessive aerial destruction, he was the true man of courage in a time of war. A recently converted Catholic, he was the dedicated man seeking to convert the sword into the cross. In this transfer of courage from the military hero in battle to the man of conscience who is a hero of sorts by refusing the military role, Lowell's life and poetry reflect a shift in the sources of family and personal honor. This shift has national implications, for it asks us to recognize the honor and courage (those old military values) it takes for a young man to reject national conscription for unworthy acts of destruction.

Thus it is that Lowell finds himself undertaking a historical role, not by reaching for one, but by showing us most intimately the forces and frustrations that went into the making of him. In *Life Studies*, Lowell has dramatically verified Jean-Paul Sartre's observation that "at a certain moment, an individual, in his very deepest and most intimate conditioning, by the family, can fulfill a historical role."[19] By remaining loyal to the truth of personal and family experience, Robert Lowell emerges as a figure whose significance transcends that family. And in this way the Lowells have been returned to their public role.[20] In *Life Studies*, the art of describing family and personal intimacies comes to reveal issues central to the culture.

CHAPTER 6

The Intent of Imitations

Tradition . . . cannot be inherited, and if you want it you must obtain it by great labour. It involves in the first place, the historical sense . . . and the historical sense involves a perception, not only of the pastness of the past, but of its presence. . . .

—T. S. Eliot, "Tradition and the Individual Talent"

I *Approaches to* Imitations

IN the direct and honest introduction to *Imitations* (1961), Robert Lowell first asks us to hear the book as one voice; and no less than six times in the three pages of the introduction and acknowledgments he informs us of his recklessness with and his pillaging of the poets he imitates. It is not translation he is after, or not quite, but imitations, poems dependent and derivative, but also new and individual ones—much as Picasso imitated Velazquez, or Kurosawa imitated Shakespeare. Lowell himself claims that his method is not new, for an earlier example is found in Sir Thomas Wyatt's renditions of Petrarch. Jerome Mazzaro points to John Dryden's "Preface to Ovid's *Epistles*" as an earlier work in support of Lowell's approach in *Imitations*.[1] Lowell's book seems less and less an unparalleled assault on classic texts after we consider previous examples from various sources. Emerson's poem "Hamatreya" is a free rendering of a passage from the Vishna Parana in the first line of which he substitutes the names of the first settlers of Concord for Hindu sovereigns in the original. Yeats informs the reader that his poem "At the Abbey Theater" is "Imitated from Ronsard." Martin Buber acknowledges in a foreword that he has not translated but has retold *The Tales of Rabbi Nachman* "with full freedom, yet out of his spirit as it is present to me."[2]

In *Imitations*, Lowell works with important poets from Homer to Boris Pasternak, with the majority from the last two centuries and

93

with a concentration on Villon, Baudelaire, Montale, and Pasternak. Or, as Lowell says, "I have tried to write alive English and to do what my authors might have done if they were writing their poems now and in America." But, of course, they're not; Lowell is. In one sense, his statement is a traditional defense of a poet's aggrandizing of his sources, but his remark also reflects that contemporizing of the past, one characteristic which makes a culture modern.

For the most part, Lowell has chosen familiar poets or poems; he read in all of the languages he worked from, except Russian. The fact that he excluded Latin poets, whom he worked on previously and returned to later, but included Pasternak indicates that these efforts have much to do with Lowell's absorbing into English the tones and qualities of modern European poetry. To a great extent, the poets concentrated on are part of what we might loosely call "the modern temper"; indeed, a number of these poets have had a strong influence on modern British and American poetry.

In some ways the title *Imitations* is like *Life Studies:* the very titles are not as obscurely suggestive as some of Lowell's earlier ones; but they bring to mind sketching, portraying, or copying; a translation of life; a borrowing from other styles; a using of those styles for what one wants to say oneself. Also, the spirit of the *poète maudit,* one spirit of *Life Studies,* is registered in *Imitations* in terms of some earlier poets—Villon, Baudelaire, Rimbaud. The poems about the deaths of poets that Lowell imitates in this book also serve as connecting links between *Imitations* and *Life Studies.* "Villon's Epitaph," "Heine Dying in Paris," and both Hugo's and Mallarmé's "At Gautier's Grave," all, in their way, reinforce the third part of *Life Studies,* the part devoted to dead or dying writers who meant so much to Lowell.

The confessional impulse is also one of the ties between the two books. A passage from the imitation of Baudelaire's "My Beatrice" could serve as epigraph to *Life Studies:*

> "Let's stop and watch this creature at our leisure—
> all sighs and sweaty hair. We'll take his measure.
> It s a great pity that this mountebank
> and ghost of Hamlet strutting on his plank
> should think he's such an artist at his role
> he has to rip the lining from his soul
> and paralyze the butterflies and bees
> with a peepshow of his indecencies—

and even we, who gave him his education,
must listen to his schoolboy declamation."

(It is as if Lowell cleverly arranges for Baudelaire, and by implica-
tion for all of the other poets imitated in this volume, to examine
Lowell at the very moment he is exploiting them and their works.
Through the imitations, Lowell and these poets become contemporaries conscious of each other.) In addition to the passage from
"My Beatrice," there are a number of other passages from the
Baudelairian imitations, including parts of "To the Reader" and
"Voyage to Cithera," which reannounce the *Life Studies* effort to
get some unavoidable and measurable sense of self-disgust into the
poetry. This consciously ironic exposure of the soul is the modern
poet's birthright, along with an unrelenting self-awareness and the
display of the self in various poses.

The approach to imitations put forth by Daniel Hoffman in his
survey of Lowell's poetry from *Imitations* to *Near the Ocean*, an approach that I find intelligent and sympathetic, forms the basis of
this chapter. Hoffman observes that "In his *Imitations*, Lowell has
set out not merely to learn from or acknowledge the existence of
these poets and their traditions; he has undertaken to master those
traditions, as he interprets them. The way in to these traditions (or
any other) for a poet is not . . . primarily through scholarship and
literary history. The way in is through translation. This is how a
poet can put his imagination directly in touch with that of each of
his spiritual forbears in other languages. As he struggles with their
vision, their style, their problems, they become his doppelgangers in
their times, and he theirs in our time." Considering *Imitations* an
"exploration of modern Europe," Hoffman also sees the book as "a
long, fragmented poem of the self, struggling in its engagements
with history."[3] With imaginative accuracy Hoffman has described
the total effort of *Imitations* and its place in Lowell's career;
therefore, this chapter considers *Imitations* in the spirit of Hoffman's remarks. It should be recognized, however, that Lowell's
Imitations, perhaps like no other book by him, can legitimately be
viewed in more than one way. Those who approach the book in the
spirit of Hoffman's words see the work as an exciting confrontation
between the mind of a contemporary, vigorous poet and the poetic
life of modern Europe. Those, on the other hand, who see the book
only or principally as a form of translation in the usual sense are in-

clined to include *Imitations* in George Steiner's complaint about Lowell's deracinated *Phaedra:* "modesty is the very essence of translation. The greater the poet, the more loyal should be his servitude to the original."[4]

I find it useful, interesting, and valid to look at *Imitations* in the spirit of its offerings because, in the words of T. S. Eliot, "One of the surest of tests is the way in which a poet borrows. . . . The good poet welds his theft into a whole of feeling which is unique, utterly different from that from which it was torn. . . ."[5] To be sure, Eliot did not have in mind the kind of imitation in which Lowell has engaged; but the spirit behind Eliot's words validates Lowell's effort. The discussion in this chapter also finds support in Lowell's comment in the introduction to *Imitations* that "the excellence of a poet depends on the unique opportunities of his native language." Furthermore, Lowell's imitations are in the spirit of Ezra Pound's translations: the poet intends to fuse the original, foreign text with "the nervous system" (Lowell's phrase) of his own language and time. In his imitations, Lowell's work is in a "modern tradition" pioneered by Pound.

As verification of some success by Lowell, experts in the languages and poetry he has imitated, even in a language he did not know, have reported that, although Lowell has been free with syntax and imagery, "the result is new poems, astonishingly true to the tone and content of the original ones."[6] Brazen, unfair, and even egotistical as *Imitations* may seem (in the hands of a lesser poet, such endeavors are sure suicide of pride and ambition), is not Lowell simply displaying the imagination necessary when the poet connects tradition to his individual talent? Moreover, Lowell's imitations of other poets have, as already indicated, a bearing on his own themes and art. Through a dramatic use of other writers in terms of his own concerns and experiences, Lowell affirms that the writers in *Imitations* sustain him just as Ford, Santayana, Schwartz, and Crane did in *Life Studies*.

II *Military Motifs, the Theme of War*

Imitations begins with Homer. The very first lines of *Imitations*, the opening of the *Iliad*, indicate, as Hoffman's eye detected, a Lowell change from the usual translation of the epic's invocation:

> Sing for me, Muse, the mania of Achilles
> that cast a thousand sorrows on the Greeks

> and threw so many huge souls into hell,
> heroes who spilled their lives as food for dogs
> and darting birds. God's will was working out,
> from that time when first fell apart fighting
> Atrides, king of men, and that god, Achilles. . . .

Lowell does not choose one of the usual words, "rage," "wrath," or "anger," to describe Achilles' state of mind but the clinical term "mania," suggesting a personality disorder as well as an intellectual or ideological obsession. In this way, Achilles is connected to what concerns Lowell. Also, these opening lines suggest a rendering of the Greek epic into the alliterative rhythms of Old English, as if Lowell wishes to incorporate the first great Western poem into the tradition of poetry written in English: "the excellence of a poet depends on the unique opportunities of his native language." Thus Achilles has the qualities of a "modern" hero while the very sounds of the poem echo older poetry in English, especially old poems about battles.

Lowell's emphasis upon the obsession of Achilles is also evident at the end of his Homeric imitations. After killing Lykaon, Achilles gives vent to his anger at the Trojans (Book XXI):

> "Die, Trojans—you must die till I reach Troy—
> you'll run in front, I'll scythe you down behind,
> nor will the azure Skamander save your lives,
> whirling and silver, though you kill your bulls
> and sheep, and throw a thousand one-hoofed horse,
> still living, in the ripples. You must die,
> and die and die and die, until the blood
> of Hellas and Patroklos is avenged,
> killed by the running ships when I was gone."

The repetition of "die" and "kill," an overemphasis when compared with other translations, yet in keeping with Achilles' "mania," transforms military heroism into the undisguised fact of public, national murder. The killing appears to be more obsessive than it is in the original work, resembling the kind of "overkill" characteristic of twentieth-century wars. That triple rendering of the phrase "and die" may also be Lowell's effort to conjure a Shakespearian credence and emphasis in this crucial and influential poem about war. In any case, the rendering of Homer's lines is in keeping with the sense of cultural doom and the military motif in *Imitations*. In addition to this passage from Homer, poems by Victor Hugo, Rimbaud, Valéry, Rilke, and Montale treat of war, death, and the military.

Moreover, Lowell continues his preoccupation with the military leader as butcher, but also as a fascinating figure.[7] As previously noted, the military figure has struck deeply in Lowell's imagination, in the way Ahab must have obsessed Melville, or Satan Milton. Lowell once, oddly, felt compelled to observe that "Macbeth must have tons of Shakespeare in him."[8] Along with his fascination for Napoleon, Lowell repeats his interest in the French disaster in Russia, found in "Napoleon Crosses the Berezina" in *Lord Weary's Castle,* and now in Victor Hugo's "Russia 1812." One might almost expect Hippolytus, disdainful of his father's military life-style but strangely captured by his own disdain, to spend his time writing war poetry like this. From Homer's Achilles to Hugo's Napoleon to Rimbaud's "great captain" to Montale's Hitler, Lowell accumulates a terrifying vision of the military hero in Western culture and in its poetry.

Fittingly, Achilles' military mania is the basis of the poet's invocation to the muse, and that invocation opens this book. If, as Lowell quickly says in his introduction, the book "should be first read as a sequence, one voice running through many personalities, contrasts and repetitions," it is soon evident that this "one voice" continues the military obsession through some of the poems and poets imitated. The very next poem in the book, "Three Letters to Anaktoria," an imitation of Sappho, touches on the war theme. Later on, the conclusion of Hugo's "Russia 1812" expands a passage from Lowell's opening imitation of Homer. During "the mania of Achilles," the poet insists, "God's will was working out." At the end of Hugo's poem, terrified Napoleon considers his defeated and dying army:

> "God of armies, is this the end?" he cried.
> And then at last the expiation came,
> as he heard some one call him by his name,
> some one half-lost in shadow, who said, "No,
> Napoleon." Napoleon understood,
> restless, bareheaded, leaden, as he stood
> before his butchered legions in the snow.

God's will has, indeed, been working out; and it still is, from Homer's to Hugo's time and on to the moment when the poet describes "Boyleston Street [where] a commercial photograph/shows Hiroshima boiling."

Through the military theme in *Imitations*, Lowell is trying to handle, in the largest terms, the theme that has haunted his own work from its beginnings. For example, the dead Ghibeline in "The Soldier" (from *Lord Weary's Castle*), who is thrown into the River Styx, where good and bad angels fight over his soul, and the drowned Warren Winslow (from "The Quaker Graveyard in Nantucket") are one with Homer's Lykaon, who is hurled into the Skamander to be fought over by the fish. And once again referring back to Hugo's poem about Napoleon's retreat, we notice that the line "Yesterday the Grand Army, today its dregs" and the phrase "ice rimes the gray mustache" echo passages from "For the Union Dead" and "Christmas Eve Under Hooker's Statue," respectively. Also, two imitations dealing with war that are in *Lord Weary's Castle* are reimitated for this book: "France" is lengthened to "Villon's Epitaph," and Rimbaud's "War" becomes "Evil."

Other reconstructions of this all-pervasive military motif can be found in *Imitations*. The Mary who was identified with military obsessions in *Land of Unlikeness* and who was ineffectively offered as a way past the violence in such early poems as "The Dead in Europe" and "The Quaker Graveyard in Nantucket" is now replaced by Valéry's "Helen," who begins her sonnet by claiming Mary's color: "I am the blue!" And Helen concludes, perversely echoing Homer's opening lines of the *Iliad*, that all the military adventurers who "sang about their shady wars" now, along with the gods, "reach out their carved, indulgent arms to me!" Even the word "arms" changes from the gesture of a Marian supplication to the motion of violence, for Helen is the inspiration of poets whose art means consciousness of war.

The military motif is so important to Lowell in this volume that he goes out of his way in the opening line of his imitation of Villon's "Ballad for the Dead Ladies" to change the names of two of the ladies so that a military suggestion can be made. The last two women in Villon's passage—"Dictes moy ou, n'en quel pays, / Est Flora la belle Rommaine, / Archipiades, ne Thais,"—become, in Lowell's version, Andromeda and Helen. Villon's two women of beauty and grace (during the Middle Ages, Archipiada was thought to be a woman) are replaced by two women whose famous beauty caused battles and the deaths of warriors. However, for the opening

of his imitation of Baudelaire's "The Swan," Lowell retains the
reference to Andromache, wife of the soldier Hector.

Through *Imitations*, Lowell is indeed putting himself in touch
with artistic and cultural traditions, insisting that they help him
bear what he is witnessing. The solitary consciousness could not survive the military vision that haunts the life and the poetry of
Western culture; that consciousness needs to beg, borrow, and steal
from earlier writers, who had the same or a similar nightmare, in
order to survive, to continue writing. War is an old theme of
Lowell's, his long concern he can never escape; his are like the
thoughts of Prometheus, who ponders man's violence while he is
chained to his rock.

III   *Villon: The Compassionate Self*

The various poets bring special tasks, sympathies, insights, and
chances which point up the diverse explorations of Lowell's imitations. Villon, the wily, riotous outcast capable of extensive sympathies, gives Lowell the opportunity of conveying through an un-
abashed "I" a range of compassion. There is a common and divine
humanity in Lowell's imitations of Villon's religious exclamations
that are not felt in the furious appeals and pleas of Lowell's early
religious poetry.

"Villon's Prayer for His Mother to Say to the Virgin" is a return
effort by Lowell, for Lowell usurped a passage from this poem for
the last part of the elegy on his grandfather's death, "A Prayer for
My Grandfather to Our Lady." A comparison of the two versions is
illuminating. The last part of the prayer from the poem in *Lord
Weary's Castle* reads

> "On Copley Square, I saw you hold the door
> To Trinity, the costly Church, and saw
> The painted Paradise of harps and lutes
> Sink like Atlantis in the Devil's jaw
> And knock the Devil's teeth out by the roots;
> But when I strike for shore
> I find no painted idols to adore:
> Hell is burned out, heaven's harp-strings are slack.
> Mother, run to the chalice, and bring back
> Blood on your finger-tips for Lazarus who was poor."

And, in the later imitation—

> at Mass each Sunday, I have seen
> a painted paradise with lutes
> and harps, a hell that boils the damned:
> one gives me joy, the other doubts.
> Oh let me have your joy, my Queen,
> bountiful, honest and serene,
> by whom no sinner is condemned—
> in this faith let me live and die.

What was originally the prayer of a medieval illiterate woman, which the poet expropriated for his grandfather, has been returned to its source. Rhetorically distracted from his religious effort in the poem to Arthur Winslow, Lowell now allows the old woman to speak for herself, to recite her own prayer. Obviously, Lowell has lowered the rhetorical pressure, if not eliminated it entirely in this case. Such "simple" lines as "one gives me joy, the other doubts" and the refrain "in this faith let me live and die," are more convincing than the first version with its exaggerated appeal to Mary..

If Mary is anything like the reader, she must find it hard to consider the appeal of Villon's mother in *Imitations* as merely the poet's mannerisms. The lines made up for his grandfather's deliverance in *Lord Weary's Castle* foment the suspicion that the skill the poetry evinces is more important to Lowell than the actual prayer to Mary. The changes that Lowell has made in this prayer confirm the comment he once made that "looking back at *Lord Weary's Castle* . . . I see it as out of the mainstream, a rather repellent, odd, symbolic Catholic piece of work."[9] By way of the European poets in *Imitations*, Lowell is really revisiting himself.

Through Villon's poems, Lowell can develop the "I" in his poetry and try out shorter lines and compact stanzas—and such lines and stanzas influence the poetry to come in *For the Union Dead* and *Near the Ocean*. If the opening of "The Great Testament" is compared with the openings of "Memories of West Street and Lepke" and of "Christmas Eve Under Hooker's Statue," to work back from *Imitations* to Lowell's first important book, it is evident that the Villon testament is closer to the style of the *Life Studies* poem, as is much of *Imitations*. Moreover, the comparison reveals how Lowell is relaxing the *Lord Weary's Castle* style at the same time that he is

compressing the informalities of *Life Studies*, steering a path
between the formality of one and the informality of the other:

> I am thirty this year,
> near Christmas, the dead season,
> when wolves live off the wind,
> and the poor peasants fear
> the icy firmament.
> Sound in body and mind,
> I write my Testament,
> but the ink has frozen.
> ("The Great Testament")

> Only teaching on Tuesdays, book-worming
> in pajamas fresh from the washer each morning,
> I hog a whole house on Boston's
> "hardly passionate Marlborough Street,"
> where even the man
> scavenging filth in the back alley trash cans,
> has two children, a beach wagon, a helpmate,
> and is a "young Republican."
> I have a nine months' daughter,
> young enough to be my granddaughter.
> Like the sun she rises in her flame-flamingo infants' wear.
> ("Memories of West Street and Lepke")

> Tonight a blackout. Twenty years ago
> I hung my stocking on the tree, and hell's
> Serpent entwined the apple in the toe
> To sting the child with knowledge. Hooker's heels
> Kicking at nothing in the shifting snow,
> A cannon and a cairn of cannon balls
> Rusting before the blackened Statehouse, know
> How the long horn of plenty broke like glass
> In Hooker's gauntlets. Once I came from Mass. . . .
> ("Christmas Eve Under Hooker's Statue")

Each opening, successful in the poem and in the book in which it
appears, registers the temper of the poet at the time of the poem.
But one of the features of *Imitations*, which can be appreciated by
looking at this stanza from Villon as it is placed in the context of
Lowell's previous work, is Lowell's effort to regroup his highly conscious sense of traditional form by modifying that expansionist,
radical self and the open world he had already put into *Life Studies*.

Villon, in effect, offers Lowell the opportunity to "economize" the sympathetic, self-indulgent "I" he had evoked in *Life Studies*, yet not quite return to the oddly distant, astringent persona of *Lord Weary's Castle*. William Carlos Williams, who not only wrote an introduction to Villon's poetry but also wrote poems that influenced Lowell in considering the sympathetic magic of the poet's "I," encouraged Lowell to write poetry whose art lay in an uncontrived and forthright acceptance of life's immediacies. Through Villon, Lowell also finds ways of absorbing Williams—and to him he dedicates his imitation of Villon's "The Great Testament."

IV   *The Theme of Infinity*

The Leopardi poems begin a special note in the book—as first found in the title of a poem by Leopardi, "The Infinite." The infinitude that is interestingly and mysteriously explored is one that leaves the poet's mind isolated, within a world of nothing, within a vacuum that is also the place of the mind's strange and mysterious nourishment. The mind is captivated by the thought of itself flourishing within a larger sense of nothing, or within a sense of its own annihilation.

In the Leopardi imitations Lowell begins this strange exploration of consciousness. The narrator remembers a hill, some nearby hedges, and then recalls the time

> When I would sit there lost in deliberation,
> I reasoned most on the interminable spaces
> beyond all hills, on their antediluvian resignation
> and silence that passes
> beyond man's possibility.
> Here for a little while my heart is quiet inside me;
> and when the wind lifts roughing through the trees,
> I set about comparing my silence to those voices,
> and I think about the eternal, the dead seasons,
> things here at hand and alive,
> and all their reasons and choices.
> It's sweet to destroy my mind
> and go down
> and wreck in this sea where I drown.

The mind in this poem has not quite reached an absolute beyond but moves toward it. This note can be picked up here and there in

the book: the final nothingness of Basel in Hebel's "Sic Transit";
the French soldiers lost in the vast solitude of their retreat from
Moscow in Hugo's "Russia 1812." At Gautier's grave, Hugo's dead
friends' "fixed eyes draw me to infinity." In Baudelaire's "The
Abyss," the narrator is haunted by the infinite at every window, and
in "The Voyage" that same "infinite is rocked by the fixed sea." In
Rimbaud's "Nostalgia," "the river's spotted mirror steamed / off to
the bare sky's perfect, burning sphere." Rilke sees his father's hands
in a picture "reach out toward nothing . . . , grasp distance and
disappear." In Saba's "Winter Noon," "a sky-blue balloon drifting / through the blue of the winter noon" causes the narrator to
lose his happiness as he traces the balloon, like some part of his soul,
"dipping and lifting" into space. In Montale's poem "Dora
Markus," the woman of the title is told, "you point out the other
shore, / invisible, your true country"; and Rimbaud's "The
Drunken Boat" indicates other and similar directions. The book's
last poem, Rilke's "Pigeons," declares "Over non-existence arches
the all-being."

This quest for infinitude is yet another example of the irony that
a highly self-conscious mind may simultaneously wish to exploit in
order to escape the specificities of unrelieved consciousness. In
writing about Whitman's "Out of the Cradle Endlessly Rocking,"
Leo Spitzer speculated whether "powerful personalities crave death
as a liberation from the burden of their own identity. . . ."[10] If we
substitute "infinity" for "death," we sense what is involved in this
quest for infinity throughout *Imitations*. (Incidentally, Spitzer's
observation also helps explain the powerful concern with death in
the two Jonathan Edwards poems in *Lord Weary's Castle*.)

The urge for self-annihilation—for the end of identity—so often
felt in Lowell's poetry, increasingly encourages through these
writers in *Imitations* some fertile void where—in being destroyed,
or in being "voided"—the mind finds itself reborn, or transformed.
The infinitude of self, and of one's dreams, presents a wider world
of possible being than the world of recognized, ordinary reality. The
poetry is reaching for that wider world. Indeed, the ordinary reality
the poetry suggests, is itself dying into some infinitude, incapable,
perhaps, of taking itself at face value.

In the fascination for infinitude, Lowell explores and dramatizes
that moment when self-consciousness would void all that it knows
and struggles under in order to be reborn into a new world.
Consciousness is, now, not merely an endless registering of the

world; it almost seems to be born anew, bereft of its ancient and tiresome burdens. Europe, poetry, awareness—each is tired of itself. Lowell goes to the "tradition" in order to spring loose from that tradition. The poetry advocates a consciousness beyond the one that only sees the world as serving up consciousness to its own suicide. The suggestiveness of infinitude in Symbolist poetry is present in this collection of European poems.

The ordinary, recognizable reality—the one culturally given and agreed upon—has become a tyranny from which the mind must be freed; that reality must be not merely predictable but converted into something life-rendering. This kind of attitude, or this kind of awareness, can be observed in a culture (and it has been with ours for almost two centuries now) when its poets (the antennae of the race, we have been told) register the quest for a new reality or another "order"—for the commonly accepted one has gone to seed.[11] The poetic tradition is thereby the right one to the very extent it can be re-created, restructured and, by its very fertile nature, encourages the poet and the reader to do so.

The concern for infinity in *Imitations* is Lowell's effort, through other poets and their poems, to extend the possibilities of what the mind might find in life if it releases itself from the ordinary circumstances of its existence. At the same time, the hope is that the sense of infinity will finally enable the consciousness to return to a new reality, a new order. It is as if Lowell sets in motion the poets of *Imitations* not to work up the authorized tradition in modern European poetry but to use his knowledge of that tradition in order to let his mind discover other or new possibilities of image-making. *Life Studies*, on the other hand, reveals the release and understanding a man may find by bravely submitting himself to the situations and the things of this world—to the given reality.

Lowell's long-time interest in Montale may be due to the Italian poet's ability to bring forth an image as if his poem produces it from some wide possibilities of a consciousness deeply housed in the poem. Montale's poems, at least in Lowell's imitations, seem to take place in a void. Even when the scene is specific, the narrator is speaking to another person usually not present and far away. Or, as in the case of "The Chess Player," the player addressed is near; but the narrator is far away, or he seems to be speaking from a distance, some step removed from the player himself. Often it isn't clear if a man is speaking to another man, to a woman, or the other way around.

This quality of the Montale imitations is related to the theme of infinity. Out of this distance between the voice in the poem and the character being addressed, the poet finds his mind discovering and working with imagery that emerges or rises from that image which, for all of its suddenness, is relevant; but curiously from afar. Some of Montale's poems in the book encourage a sense of infinity within an ordinary reality so that almost anything might rise out of the consciousness, might trick the sensibility into new realms, into making discoveries.

V   The Quest Theme and Uses of Baudelaire

Lowell's imitations of Baudelaire contain some of the most significant attitudes and uses of language found in the book; and they are a crucial part of Lowell's development. Baudelaire supplies at least one important motif or concern: the theme of voyaging out (a theme also strongly present in Montale's poetry). Baudelaire's "The Voyage" handles the concept of sailing to new territories with neither the purple hopes of Tennyson's "Ulysses" nor the frenetic "let's go, let's go"—at least these are not the only attitudes of the poem. "The Voyage" offers the disappointments, the final tracing of one's own shadow; but the need to seek is still present, with no illusions or assurances. Lowell's imitation of Baudelaire's "The Voyage" is rooted in restlessness. An observation by the sociologist Emile Durkheim relates to the poem and Lowell's infinity theme: "It is everlastingly repeated that it is man's nature to be eternally dissatisfied, constantly to advance, without relief or rest, toward an indefinite goal. The longing for infinity is daily represented as a mark of moral distinction, whereas it can only appear within unregulated consciences which elevate to a rule the lack of rule from which they suffer."[12] From more than one point of view, Lowell imitates poems that bear upon contemporary difficulties and attitudes.

The different "kinds" of language, even different "styles," of this Baudelaire poem, bridge Lowell's volumes and offer many possibilities of direction. Some of the following lines are reminiscent of the language of Lowell's earlier volumes—those running, whipped up lines containing horrible knowledge:

> Strange sport! where destination has no place
> or name, and may be anywhere we choose—
> where man, committed to his endless race,
> runs like a madman diving for repose!

> Our soul is a three-master seeking port:
> a voice from starboard shouts, "We're at the dock!"
> Another, more elated, cries from port,
> "Here's dancing, gin and girls!" Balls! it's a rock!

Other lines remind us of, say, Philip Larkin's poetry, and of a flippantly serious, saddened informality that also appears in *Life Studies*. These two tones also appear in the opening of Villon's "The Great Testament," which suggests a merging of "Christmas Eve Under Hooker's Statue" and "Memories of West Street and Lepke." This mixed style—or cross between hardness and informality, between firmness and the almost flippant sense of pain—can be discerned throughout *Imitations*: "she had the true blue look that lied"; the woman "disintegrating in a slowly dirtying slip"; "as cool delinquents watch a madman clown." These hard-struck insights with a tenderness alongside them bring in more tones than the earlier poetry of Lowell or different tones. His language became increasingly capable of conveying different kinds of experience, of giving play to more phases of personality. It suggests an extension of possibilities, of no less accuracy, but perhaps more compassion.

Baudelaire's "The Swan"—not the only poem in the book about the death of a city, of a culture—offers one good example of how Lowell works his imitations:

> Paris changes; nothing in my melancholy
> stirs . . . new mansards, *arrondisements* razed *en bloc*,
> glass, scaffolding, slum wards—all allegory!
> My memories are heavier than rock!

To use French like that in a poem originally in French and about Paris is obviously to talk about New York, or Boston, or whatever might be the reader's favorite city of urban renewal, the city he loves and resents. Lowell's Boston is one with Dostoevsky's Saint Petersburg, Dreiser's Chicago, and O'Casey's Dublin. From *Lord Weary's Castle* to *Life Studies* to *Imitations* and beyond, Lowell's Boston has been subject to the Christian and the secular imagination. Lowell is one of our major poets of the city, and in "The Swan," "Death from Cancer," and "Where the Rainbow Ends," as well as in "For the Union Dead," the city is a place of heroic revery and present despair.

In the poetry of Lowell, the city is social reality, a larger sphere of being, with which we must come to terms imaginatively. The Hart Crane of *Life Studies*, lost in the city, yet holding to his integrity, is

somewhere in the end of "The Swan": "I think of Paris raising the
white flag, / drowned sailors, fallen girls . . . and many more!" In
Lowell, the urban dread that informs some of the poems from
Baudelaire's *Les Fleurs du Mal* mixes with something of Whitman,
Crane, and William Carlos Williams, and with the belief that the
modern spirit will define itself through what its imagination makes
of the city.

VI   *Nature in the Pasternak Imitations*

Pasternak, Lowell has said, gave him special problems, and these
imitations also present difficulties for the reader; indeed, Pasternak
is the most puzzling of the poets here. Pasternak's poems, at least in
Lowell's versions, are reminiscent of the famous photograph of the
Russian poet sitting at a table, strong-faced, sympathetic, yet silent-
ly maneuvering behind all that lovely cut glass on the tablecloth.
Pasternak's poems sometimes seem to be strategies of temporary
removal from metropolitan life. His nature poems seem to be ineffectual flights from the city and from a city nervousness, perhaps
the way Lowell might have looked from Boston to Char-de-sa, the
name of his grandfather's farm. Pasternak's nature seems to be
viewed as by a city man on his weekends: nature seems part of
society, a part of a man's life with other men, but it also lies outside
the city life, despite its connection with an urban consciousness.
(This kind of nature Lowell presents later on in "Central Park" and
"Spring" in *Near the Ocean*.)

Pasternak's nature is usually depicted at the end of summer, or in
the fall, the time to return to the city. If the poems contain a longing, it is one not far removed from a human setting, from society in
some sense or other. Lowell's version of Pasternak's nature, unlike
Dylan Thomas's or Theodore Roethke's, is one that the city mind
knows most deeply. In Pasternak's poetry, nature is the means by
which the complicated consciousness registers its complications.
Nature is not an escape from the beleaguered consciousness as
much as it is a means of reregistering that consciousness or of reex-
pressing it on another plane. Nature offers freedom, yet it is the
freedom granted to an urban mind. Some of this quality appears in
two stanzas from "Sparrow Hills":

> Here the city's trolley tracks give out.
> Further, you must put up with peeled pine. The
>   trolley poles are detached.

Further, it's Sunday. Boughs screwed loose for the
  picnic bonfire,
playing tag in your bra.

"The world is always like this," say the woods,
as they mix the midday glare, Whitsunday and walking.
All's planned with checkerberry couches, inspired with
  clearings—
the piebald clouds spill down on us like a country woman's
  house-dress.

Much of the scene is connected to a life other than nature's, and the last line suggests some final, overall domesticity to the scene. "The world is always like this," say the woods—that is, nature is just itself, and this message is stated because the mind in the poem does not usually conceive of nature as being just itself, and it must be reminded of the fact.

Indeed, the very "statement" by the woods is undercut by the fact that, in the mind of the narrator, nature is not just itself since it mixes with "the midday glare, Whitsunday and walking." Nature is really man's consciousness of nature. Lowell's imitations of Pasternak suggest that nature is not a place of escape from life as much as a place where the person in the poem gathers some energy and self-understanding in order to participate again in ordinary social intercourse. Through his versions of Pasternak, Lowell places in the book a sensibility somewhat in opposition to the longing for infinity as he strategically returns to some of the burdens of awareness.

In "Hamlet in Russia, A Soliloquy," if I read aright this intriguing and puzzling poem, the narrator thinks of escaping social and artistic obligations by imagining himself on a lake, far away from the stage of social and artistic obligations. He imagines himself out there in nature just before he is to receive his cue to go in front of the audience and perform. The poem is only the respite of his imagination, a self-induced respite that gives him a perspective on what he does when he accepts his role, takes his cue, and performs before an audience. The exploration of Pasternak's Hamlet is related to that self-analyzing Hamlet who hears others berate him in Baudelaire's "My Beatrice."

Lowell's imitations of Pasternak express the poet's urge to seek an extension of his consciousness in nature—a nature that returns him to himself, to his "city life," and finally to his consciousness of himself as a person writing poetry. *Imitations* enables Lowell both to go beyond himself and to recover his most deeply possessed attitudes, his familiar modes of examining life. *Imitations* (like *Life Studies*) is an appealing book in the way Lowell's urge for expansion of self is tied to an old, unremitting sense of himself. This dual state of identity is the personal level of his poetic engagement between "the unique opportunities of his native language" and his heritage.

Finally, Pasternak is an appropriate poet for ·Lowell to imitate because Pasternak himself translated Georgian poetry into Russian, although he did not know the original language of the poems and worked from literal renditions supplied by their authors. Lowell's imitations of Pasternak thereby have a special dispensation derived from a similar task undertaken by the Russian poet as he too translated, presumably with some freedom, from an unknown to a known language.[13]

VII   *Rilke's "Pigeons" and an Overall View of* Imitations

Imitations concludes with Lowell's version of Rilke's "Pigeons." In itself, the poem is a summary of what Lowell has been trying to do in the entire book. It is a poem about going beyond one's usual territory, and the risks that entails—the risks, the gains, and the losses. The conclusion of "Pigeons" evokes the urge of the poet not only to transcend his familiar home but also to return to it. "Mania," the word for the intent of Achilles at the beginning of the book, becomes the word the poet bequeathes to his own ineluctable commitment at the end of the book. The conclusion of "Pigeons" indicates how a sudden sense of infinity and a sudden image from "out there" can appear in the poet's consciousness and can mysteriously heighten the freedom, or the flight, of the poem.

After muttering about "The same old flights, the same old homecomings," and after considering that some pigeons get "clear of the pigeonhouse" while others never leave, the voice in the poem reminds himself that

> . . . only by suffering the rat-race in the arena
> can the heart learn to beat.
>
> Think of Leonidas perhaps and the hoplites,
> glittering with liberation,
> as they combed one another's golden Botticellian hair
> at Thermopylae, friends and lovers, the bride and the
>   bridegroom—
> and moved into position to die.

Over non-existence arches the all-being—
thence the ball thrown almost out of bounds
stings the hand with the momentum of its drop—
body and gravity,
miraculously multiplied by its mania to return.

Both the instructions in the middle stanza and the conclusion bring
to mind "Memories of West Street and Lepke": the roof of the
jailhouse which reminded Lowell of his school soccer court; the
flight into freedom of conscience that led the poet to the jail; the
fellow prisoners (like fellow poets) who shared their presence and
skills with him. In writing *Imitations,* Lowell has flown his "house"
and has also shown the "mania to return." As in "The Exile's
Return," the poet returns, but with greater consciousness of what
his home is and who is occupying it.

The essential view of *Imitations* in this discussion is that the book
is an extension of Lowell: it is a work in which Lowell tries out
Lowell. In 1960, upon being honored at the Boston Arts Festival,
Lowell wrote, "When I finished *Life Studies,* I was left hanging on
a question mark. I am still hanging there. I don't know whether it is
a death-rope or a lifeline."[14] *Imitations* indicates how a poet can
fashion a lifeline—sometimes out of somebody else's death-rope.
These imitations come to "filter and fiber" Lowell's own poetry;
they have an effect on his "original" work, just as the imitation of
Juvenal in *Near the Ocean* influences the first poem in that book,
"Waking Early Sunday Morning."

As pointed out at the beginning of this discussion, *Imitations* may
be read in other ways; but this chapter concentrated on one way of
looking at the book. From this point of view *Imitations* is a certain
kind of poetic aggrandizement. In cultural terms *Imitations* asserts
the idea that our heritage is everywhere. Our heritage is anything
we find usable, "translatable," anything capable of being imitated.
Literary tradition is anything that opens up our world to us, or us to
the world. Everything is up for possession; all is conceivably conver-
tible to our own terms, to our own familiarities and perplexities.
There are grave and obvious dangers to this view—a mindless
modernizing of the past, an insufferable and narrow contemporary
consciousness, a terrible nationalism of the "modern moment."
These dangers are everpresent, but Pound's cry "Make it
new"—one of the cries of modern poetry—means, in some sense,
making the past what in truth it was not. There is
potential hubris in this attitude. Lowell no doubt has opened a Pan-

dora's box, yet "A virus . . . digs in and multiplies on our lost
blood." Lowell's book can be seen as a literary version of André
Malraux's idea of the availability of all artistic tradition. The
museum without walls becomes the poem imitated beyond its
origins and initial contexts.

In *The Revolt of the Masses*, Ortega y Gasset explains that the essence of the modern situation is man's being cut off from the past,
or his inclination to see the past only in terms of the present.
Imitations stems in affirmative ways from this situation because
Lowell's poems show us that part of the modern sensibility is the
feeling that the entire past culture is potentially available for contemporary reworking. The past is not our heritage unless it is
"pillaged" out of some deep necessity for us to come in contact with
it. In the words of T. S. Eliot, tradition only means a live past if we
use it, if we labor for it. Or, as Pound once movingly put it:

> To have gathered from the air a live tradition
> or from a fine old eye the unconquered flame
> This is not vanity.
>   Here error is all in the not done,
> all in the diffidence that faltered. . . .

Lowell's career lies at the heart of our cultural situation. His career
can be viewed as a writer's effort to exploit the difficulties and the
opportunities of that situation. His poetry may be read as not only
voicing the modern hurt, the modern temper, but as dramatizing it
and placing it in the largest world we can inhabit. *Imitations* is an
effort to write a poetry that will invoke that world.

CHAPTER 7

Self-Introspection and For the Union Dead

The drama of this stage of human development seems to be the drama of disease, of self-revenge . . . . self-awareness tends to reveal us to ourselves as monsters. This is undoubtedly a political phenomenon, an action taken against personal impulse or against the personal demand for adequate space and scope. The individual is obliged, or put under pressure, to define 'power' as it is defined in politics, and to work out the personal conse- quences of this for himself. Thus he is provoked to take revenge upon himself, a revenge of derision, contempt, denial of transcendence. This last, his denial, is based upon former conceptions of human life or on images of man at present impossible to maintain.

—Saul Bellow, *Herzog*

A LTHOUGH the two titles jar against each other, *For the Union Dead* (1964) proceeds from *Life Studies* (1959); a seemingly endless self-investigation continues. *For the Union Dead* is a poor sequel to *Life Studies* because it is less successful in its ex- plorations. *Life Studies* is a volume in which the confessional poetry was new, vigorous, and exciting—a consciousness discovering itself. Furthermore, whereas *Life Studies* artfully structured and paced the self-explorations, *For the Union Dead* is overburdened by a relentless self-turmoil. The book does show some signs of organizing the bitter demands of memory and self-analysis, but the reader too often feels deluged by the poet's insistent, unhappy recall. The best poems in the book are usually those in which Lowell can relate his painful self to another person or to a larger situation.

As with many of Lowell's books, the title is a key to the poetry. Like the title of his next work, *The Old Glory*, *For the Union Dead* registers some intense skepticism about the national ethos. Yet the vaguely awkward syntax of "Union Dead" protects the book from a smug negativism, a casual despair, a pat pessimism. The wording of

113

the title unexpectedly quivers. At the same time that *For the Union Dead* commemorates the death of some unifying experience, it creates an unexpected pulse in our minds. *For the Union Dead,* an organizing force for many different poems, is itself the title of the final and most important poem of the book, a poem about the failure of the culture to create a union between a city's presence and the moral passion of individual consciousness.

The title also refers to the past marriage of the poet, to past relationships with another woman, and to relatives he knew as a child, who are dead or dying, but whom the poet has never been able to release from his mind. They may be dead, but they are indissolubly connected to him. Even poems about his present marriage indicate the complexities of union. The poem "The Flaw" imagines both husband and wife dead. By the end of the book, the poem "Night Sweat" tries to offset and yet continues the bothersome union felt in the initial poems about marriage.

In addition, the title refers to some of the elegies of the book. In "Alfred Corning Clark" Lowell movingly and honestly mourns the death of an old friend. In "The Scream" a child thinks of her mother who has been taken away; in "Lady Raleigh's Lament" the wife thinks of her executed husband; in "Epigram" (which could serve as epigraph to the book) the poem honors the hoplites "who moved into position to die." Even such rewritten poems as "The Public Garden" and "Beyond the Alps" refer to the title; the first is about the dying union of two lovers; the second, about the forsaking of Rome's unities for "Paris, our black classic, breaking up / like killer kings on an Etruscan cup." *For the Union Dead* mourns, among others, a Civil War hero, a playboy, Sir Walter Raleigh, Caligula, the hoplites, and Harriet Winslow. Moreover, the title also applies to the two fine poems about Hawthorne and Jonathan Edwards in the middle of the book. Lowell is attached to these dead writers through their aloofness, their shy but concentrated awareness, their dedication to their own consciousness.

I   *The Opening Poems*

The book has a loose structure which the reader vaguely feels as he goes through it. The organization is makeshift and should not be overemphasized, but to the extent that it exists it is worth using in approaching the poetry. The first three poems are about former relationships. "Water" is about a relationship to an unnamed woman and "The Old Flame" is about a former marriage, while "Middle Age" is a brief, intense, painful poem about the poet's inability to escape his dead father. The first two poems attest that some dead unions provide live ghosts in the mind. These opening poems also indicate Lowell's particular interest in the short four- and five-line stanza, an interest which culminates in the final, title poem. The opening poem, "Water," also adumbrates the obsessive animal imagery that dominates the volume (in this regard, too, it is a continuation of *Life Studies*). It is as if some persistent self-denigration and turmoil reducing him and his situation to animal terms forces Lowell to appropriate increasingly the consciousness of a Lemuel Gulliver on his second and fourth voyages. The animal imagery (especially in such poems as "Skunk Hour," and "For the Union Dead") also conveys a wish on Lowell's part to make contact with some vibrant force that animates will and character.

The fourth poem in the book, "The Scream," is also about a past family relationship; but here the voice is that of a child who mournfully remembers her mother who has died, or has gone insane, or has simply left the child. (There is also the secondary possibility that it is the child who goes insane.) At the end, the child bravely but pathetically tries to suffer through her situation. "The Scream," which is like some of Randall Jarrell's poems about the plight of childhood, is a touching statement about the child as orphan; and the poem is written from within a chiild's sense of her own helpless bravery.

The next six poems, from "The Mouth of the Hudson" to "Eye and Tooth," usually spoken by the author's "I," are more testimonies to the despair of childhood. All in all, the reader is likely to agree with the ending of the last of these poems, when the author complains, "I am tired. Everyone's tired of my turmoil." Too often the poems seem nervous fragments left over from *Life Studies*. These poems show us that the poem that springs from a painful memory does not necessarily offer the poet a release. Indeed, the overwrought memory can be a stumbling block in the way of recovery from the past. Memory can be freedom, but it can also be oppression. If remembering the past allows a person to understand and assuage that past, it is also true that one can become fascinated and obsessed with such memories, which then undercut his ability to release himself from the past. However, the mind terrorized by its memory does seem to be for Lowell a last frontier of sorts, a place where the mind can still define itself in lively terms.

One of the interesting qualities of some of the poems is the imagery that Lowell creates in order to express the perplexed, frightened mind. In "The Mouth of the Hudson," a man watches "the wild ice / ticking seaward down the Hudson, / like the blank sides of a jig-saw puzzle." In "Fall 1961" images follow one another like a procession of states of horror. Lowell's brief, incisive images, even those that have appeared previously in his poetry, take hold of the reader's mind. "Fall 1961" (the time of the Cuban missile crisis) unifies political and personal fears.

"Alfred Corning Clark" is about a dead playboy friend, a failure, a wastrel, a poor little rich boy. The effort of the poet is to find some meaning in his friend's life. At first, it seems that Lowell can hardly do anything but list the idiosyncrasies of that life and talk about the secret chess games the two schoolboys played. But Lowell is aware, *in the poem*, that the poem must be more than such remembrances because his own sense of loss is greater than his mere listing of the details of the late friend's stylish dilettantism. Lowell ends by registering the fondness he felt for the dead man's "triumphant diffidence" and "refusal of exertion." The attraction of failure, of an ultimate betrayal of life's energy, is what connects the poet to his friend, or what the poet strangely honors in this personal obituary.

Although the failure of Lowell's father also haunted him, the poet feels more pity for the school friend than for his father. The father's failure is unforgiven and is felt as a moral and personal waste, whereas the friend's similar fate is understood, identified with, almost catered to, and found to have meaning. Alfred Corning Clark signaled in Lowell's mind the enticement of nothingness, the final victory of nothing. What is appealing about the poem is Lowell's ability to assign to the death and vacant life of his friend that strange nobility of "triumphant diffidence" and "refusal of exertion." It is the odd honor of withdrawal that Lowell praises here. The poem is in honor of a certain kind of strategic retreat that Emily Dickinson would have understood was worthy of the poet's quiet praise.

The poems that follow are either like "The Public Garden" and "Lady Raleigh's Lament," which deal with a dead and dying union of man and woman, or like "Child's Song" and "Myopia: a Night," which "celebrate" the locked-in consciousness of the poet or that of the character speaking the poem. The imagery, as well as the situation, is predictable: "The barbed hooks fester. The lines snap tight"; "the compass needle dead on terror"; ". . . I hear / the lonely metal breathe / and gurgle like the sick." Not until we read the poem on Hawthorne do we come to a work that includes these ideas but that escapes Lowell's near self-parodies.

II *"Hawthorne" and "Jonathan Edward"*

"Hawthorne" opens with a description of a street like the one young Robin might have walked down in the beginning of *My Kinsman, Major Molineux* and of a group of houses that resemble Lowell's description of his own house in "91 Revere Street":

> Follow its lazy main street lounging
> from the alms house to Gallows Hill
> along a flat, unvaried surface
> covered with wooden houses
> aged by yellow drain
> like the unhealthy hair of an old dog.
> You'll walk to no purpose
> in Hawthorne's Salem.

This scene is also in keeping with the setting of some earlier poems in the book: the Maine lobster town and the slab of rock in "Water," or the dismal urban landscape in "The Mouth of the Hudson," or the "Burnished, burned-out" atmosphere of "The Public Garden." Whether Hawthorne himself or the reader walks this city of Salem, the place traps the mind.

Then Lowell thinks of Hawthorne trying to keep warm during his duties as a customs officer despite "the merciless march of professional feet." Something about Hawthorne withstands the scene, the work, and his fellow New England writers. He appeals to us as they do not, as Lowell presents a picture of one kind of union dead: "Look at the faces— / Longfellow, Lowell, Holmes and Whittier! / Study the grizzled silver of their beards." The recital of the names of these dead writers with the repeated initial accent suggests a rigidity of rhythm. Once again Lowell is forced to reject an old member of the family for an outside sympathy. Hawthorne (no gray poet) differs from the others, and in his difference he appeals to Lowell and to us as an artist of military-like intent:

> Hawthorne's picture,
> however, has a blond mustache
> and golden General Custer scalp.

He looks like a Civil War officer.
He shines in the firelight. His hard
survivor's smile is touched with fire.

Hawthorne's survival is predicated on his ability to retain a force
of consciousness despite the inertia of his environment and of his
time. Or, as many of the poems from *For the Union Dead* would
have it, a man, in order to survive, honors his turmoil. The idea is
paradoxically stressed in the last stanza of the poem where
Hawthorne is imagined as

bent down, brooding, brooding,
eyes fixed on some chip,
some stone, some common plant,
the commonest thing,
as if it were the clue.
The disturbed eyes rise,
furtive, foiled, dissatisfied
from meditation on the true
and insignificant.

Here Lowell is less describing Hawthorne than presenting a certain
kind of artist: one whose power lies in his ability to concentrate on
the immediate facts of experience that escape any large meaning
but that haunt the imagination precisely because of that escape.
Lowell's Nathaniel Hawthorne is but Alfred Corning Clark taken
fire with his sense of his own mind's voiding itself through its
strategies of awareness. This mind's final honor and heroism is its
ability to imagine its inevitable helplessness, and in that
helplessness lies a secret exertion of consciousness. The subject of
the book's final poem, Colonel Robert Gould Shaw, shows that
there lies in a public hero the power to know life and thus to choose
a meaningful death.

The poem "Hawthorne" effectively drops from the street scene
to the picture of the novelist and his contemporaries, dropping
further to the writer bent and brooding until the poem finally
penetrates his dissatisfied eyes and mind. Ultimately, Lowell
presents a picture of a man who must live with his seething and dissatisfied consciousness, something that troubles Lowell throughout
the book; but this poem succeeds in a way most of the others do not
because it is more than a work of moiling introspection. Through
Hawthorne, Lowell is able to project and dramatize his own situa-

tion; through Hawthorne, Lowell can bear his consciousness. As in *Life Studies* and in *Imitations,* the union with dead writers has the effect of sustaining life.

The poem that follows, "Jonathan Edwards in Western Massachusetts," is a longer work set in quatrains. Edwards serves as the man who keeps his faith in his own ideas and in his own purposes despite the fact that the world leaves him far behind. Lowell addresses Edwards in that tone of appropriated intimacy with an older, respected man—one which he also displays in the *Life Studies* poems for Ford Madox Ford and George Santayana. These men have all "failed," or their isolation has a heroic quality to it; and Lowell respects their presence at the same time that he seems to take liberties in approaching them. Lowell appreciates the Edwards who is loyal to his own views, to his writing, and to his distrustful shyness of others and of social obligations (qualities Hawthorne also possesses). Edwards is finally loyal to himself, and the poet makes a pilgrimage to Northampton and to Edward's spirit in order to register his identification with him.

At the end of the poem, when Edwards emphasizes the defects that should prevent him from becoming president of Princeton, and his disinclination to leave "those studies / that have swallowed up my mind," there exists a union between an early American writer and the kind of mind Lowell has a deep sympathy for. It may well be that this kind of mind is too self-consciously diffident, yet it can also be idiosyncratically heroic when Lowell discovers it in a Hawthorne, in an Edwards, or especially in a Robert Gould Shaw. In *For the Union Dead* Lowell carries on some of his liveliest "conversations" with the dead.

III   *"Caligula" and "The Severed Head"*

The three poems that follow, "Tenth Muse," "The Neo-Classical Urn," and "Caligula," house within their classical references the contemporary turmoil of the writer. Yet they do little more than tiresomely reregister those turmoils, for "The Neo-Classical Urn" describes the boyhood pranks and maliciousness found in *Life Studies.* "Caligula" is easily the most interesting of the poems because it is addressed to both Lowell himself and to the Roman emperor whose name, shortened to "Cal," became a boyhood nickname for Lowell that survived. Lowell was not sure why he took the name "Cal," or what he saw of himself in the emperor to make

him do so. Obviously, in specific details Lowell's life was not
Caligula's, yet there was something about the Roman's fate that
came to haunt Lowell.

After an initial success as emperor, Caligula became ill. Upon
recovering, he changed, becoming mad and licentious; he even
built a temple to himself as Jupiter and appointed priests to attend
to his worship before he was assassinated. Caligula's urge to throttle
the Romans parallels the description Lowell gives of himself as a
boy imprisoning turtles in "The Neo-Classical Urn." Caligula's self-
glorification can be seen as some strange extension of Lowell's in-
vestigation and dramatizing of himself in his poetry. Looking at the
face of Caligula on an old Roman medal, Lowell thinks of himself
and of his own "lowest depth of possibility." In addressing
Calig ıla, Lowell addresses himself: "yours the lawlessness / of
someth ing simple that has lost its law, / my namesake, and the last
Caligula "

The fear of some self-destructive pattern after an early career of
promise, the pattern of Caligula's life, haunts the poet in this poem.
This fear is also present in the poem to Jonathan Edwards and in
many other poems in the book. If there is a union between Caligula
and Lowell, it is a union that the poet is afraid suggests the death of
an "orderly" personality after an illness. But, as so often, Lowell
really cherishes or secretly nourishes the "lawlessness" of a
Caligula; it is as if there lies in the frightful turmoil of a Caligula
some force of self-destruction that Lowell fears yet wishes for. In
the poem he relives Caligula's last night. Caligula might have been
one of the "thoroughbred mental cases" from the *Life Studies*
poem "Waking in the Blue."

The next poem, "The Severed Head," is one of the most puzzling
and intriguing in the book, or in all of Lowell's poetry. Reminiscent
of Edgar Allan Poe, the poem describes a hellish moment when the
speaker meets some ghost of himself, some doppelgänger, in the cell
of consciousness. It is far from being the only poem in *For the
Union Dead* in which the speaker, or the poet, meets his double;
such a meeting also occurs in "Dropping South: Brazil," and in
effect, in the poems to Hawthorne, Edwards, and Caligula, as well
as in the poem "Middle Age," in which the poet complains that he
meets his father, who is his own age.

Almost a terror-stricken extension of "Falling Asleep over the
Aeneid," "The Severed Head" opens with the speaker's drowsing
over the Bible. He imagines himself locked in his room, where he

was left meditating on a chandelier that the early evening shadows metamorphose "into a gryphon climbing upward." Then,

> a man came toward me with a manuscript,
> scratching in last revisions with a pen
> that left no markings on the page, yet dripped
> a red ink dribble on us, as he pressed
> the little strip of plastic tubing clipped
> to feed it from his heart.

A weird scene, it is fascinatingly precise. The speaker of the poem is threatened before the man appears and is doubly threatened upon his arrival. The man is in strange disarray, yet he is very close to the speaker as he caresses his hand and assumes a deep intimacy. The man then tears up his manuscript and speaks for the first and only time:

> "Sometimes I ask myself, if I exist,"
> he grumbled, and I saw a sheet of glass
> had fallen inches from us, and just missed
> halving our bodies, and behind it grass-
> green water flushed the glass, and fast fish stirred
> and panted, ocean butterflies. A mass
> of shadows followed them like moths, and blurred
> tentacles, thirsting for a drop of life,
> panted with calm inertia.

After this strange character leaves, the speaker reads and thinks about the heroine Jael who (in Judges, chapters 4 and 5) destroys Sisera, the enemy of her people, under the pretext of giving him food and shelter. At the end of the poem, the poet seems to be neither Jael nor Sisera but a consciousness caught somewhere within their murderous and duplicitous relationship.

"The Severed Head," thus, is not an easy poem; it leaves us with fascinating passages rather than with an understanding of its entirety. But we can hazard interpretations: the poem is about a poet who writes confessional poetry and feels himself immured by his obsessions and his imagination. The doppelgänger in the poem betrays this incestuous interest in self (the ghost draws blood from himself in order to write); at the same time, he carries the urge of the speaker (or poet) to escape the pure rage of self-knowledge by creating a double of himself. Lowell said that he rewrote painfully and often, and the descriptions of the man's possessing the manuscript suggest some final obsession of rewriting, a writer's obsession about a revision that finally destroys the work itself. "The Severed Head" is a powerful if obscure poem in which the poet nearly offers up his own murder to himself, which is one way of describing confessional poetry. The person in the poem is so self-questioning that he too is almost severed.

Often in his poetry Lowell uses an image of a face or a life separated from the outside world by glass. (See such poems as "The First Sunday in Lent," "A Mad Negro Soldier Confined at Munich," "For Sale," "Waking in the Blue," "Fall 1961.") A student of mine, Mrs. Jeanette Connors, offers the interpretation that this repeated image symbolizes the poet's urge to spy on life; at the same time, he fears that he will lose touch with things, that he will see everything and feel nothing, that he will be a witness but not an actor. "Oh to see and also to be in touch" might be Lowell's cry. It might also be the cry of Hawthorne, Josiah Hawley, and the lobotomized Lepke. (*Notebook*, later *History*, can be viewed as Lowell's hectic, all-out effort to make contact with events, with others, with the active surface of life.)

"The Severed Head" is related to an earlier poem in *For the Union Dead*, "Florence," the conclusion of which shows the head of Medusa swinging "like a lantern in the victor's hand." In "Florence" Lowell indicates sympathy for the enemies beheaded by Perseus, David, and Judith. (Their beheadings are extensions of Jael's hammerings.) Lowell repeats "Pity the monster! Pity the monster!" "The Severed Head," like "Florence," conveys Lowell's fascination for the victory over the "monster" and his sympathy for the monster itself. (Lowell writes in a poem from *Notebook 1967 - 68*, "I am a worshipper of myth and monster.") "The Severed Head" is a continuation of a theme in *Life Studies*, the poet's paradoxical fear of being cured and of destroying the "monster." Lowell's poetry displays the situation in which the patient finds his illness, his obsessions, more invigorating than the normality of health, or more interesting than a victory over destructive forces in the self. Such a mind may create a union with these forces at the expense of its health and life, but such a union is also desired by the poet—and herein lies a special obsession of Lowell's poetry: implicitly and sadly, the poetry favors an inner disturbance that in its strange way protects a person from the dull cure of a pedestrian life or from some public disorder. One reason the final poem, "For the

Union Dead," is the book's most appealing one is that it succeeds in elucidating and dramatizing a public situation by way of the poet's inner turmoil. Mere confessional turmoil in a poem does not necessarily lead to such success.

The title "The Severed Head" and the fact that the poem is in *terza rima* also evoke Dante's description (in the twenty-eighth canto of *The Inferno*) of Bertrand de Born's carrying his severed head as a lantern. Another apt if weird image of the pain and process of confessional poetry, Bertrand de Born is subject to his particular punishment in hell because he was a sower of discord between kinsmen, especially between father and son. Discord between father and son, as well as the sowing of it, is one of the sources of Lowell's poetry.

"The Severed Head" explains and explores the confessional impulse in Lowell's work. But that effort also risks a frightful and public mutilation of self, and Lowell knew this, and this awareness in turn became the subject of a poem. It was always painful to think of Lowell's developing further this kind of self-consciousness.

IV   *Some Short Poems and "New York 1962: Fragment"*

The following four poems of the book all contain place names and allow Lowell to extend the geography of some ultimate dissolution that he feels, a decay that extends from Washington to Buenos Aires, from Europe to South America. "Beyond the Alps," "July in Washington," "Buenos Aires," "Dropping South: Brazil" display dictatorships, petty governments, political oppression, bureaucracies, tyrannies in the governments of these lands where the poet happens to find himself. Even an escape from this situation in one country seems only to force one to discover it elsewhere. (Another kind of "union dead"!) This terrible, relentless contact combines the state of the poet throughout the book and his sense of his world. Finally, these four poems of place names prepare the way for the final poem about contemporary Boston.

The next four poems, which conclude the book, except for the final and title poem, "For the Union Dead," are about the poet's family. "Soft Wood" is dedicated to and is about his relative Harriet Winslow, whose house in Maine the poet and his family inhabit. She is old and ill; he is her heir. The other three poems are about the poet and his wife. "The Flaw" imagines both of them dead; and in "Night Sweat," as in other marriage poems by Lowell, the poet appeals to his wife to save him from himself. Of the four poems, by far the most interesting and most difficult is "New York 1962: Fragment," dedicated to the poet's wife, which begins

> This might be nature—twenty stories high,
> two water tanks, tanned shingle, corsetted
> by stapled pasture wire, while bed to bed,
> we two, one cell here, lie
> gazing into the ether's crystal ball,
> sky and a sky, and sky, and sky, till death—
> my heart stops . . .
> This might be heaven.

The husband and wife's union is expressed in terms of an urban landscape which houses the mind the way nature once did. The opening of the poem captures the urban imagination, much as an Antonioni movie can describe a city landscape as if it were a new kind of nature. The water tanks are strapped "by stapled pasture wire," a phrase combining a sense of freedom and restriction. Nature and space are seemingly available to the lovers at the opening of the poem. But the water tanks are also strange and powerful reminders that, while the man and woman seem to be, like two posing lovers, gazing into the infinite, they cannot escape some gross, inevitable sign of city life and of their own situation. That situation might be heaven, but it is not.

What is interesting and striking about the poem as a love poem is that the couple, so close to each other, reach some false mutual freedom and consolation. The idyllically preserved region where the man and the woman serve each other within nature's beneficent and protecting scope might be the classical love situation, but this couple achieves a bond and release through consciousness of an urban world. Their intense relationship is inseparable from the harsh intrusion of the urban world that mockingly suggests images of a freer, pastoral world. Love's intimacy and "overflow" depend on an ungainly urban image in order to advance its constricted sense of itself. The poem opens with a mock apotheosis and concludes with the lovers trapped by the reality "here below." One of the limitations of Lowell's "love poetry" is that it turns out in the end to be another excuse for the poet to acknowledge his own trapped awareness. Love is no release in Lowell's poetry—at least not marital love.

V *"For the Union Dead"*

The final and title poem of *For the Union Dead* is the climax of the book and one of Lowell's finest poems. Its imagery and concerns are related to the poems that precede it, but in achievement it surpasses them all. In a sense, this final poem binds up the wounds of the book. In quatrains, the poem culminates Lowell's excursions into this form and his growing interest in the stanza that combines short and long lines, or in the poem that combines stanzas of long lines with stanzas of short lines. The quatrain, Lowell feels, makes "For the Union Dead" a formal poem, though just why that is so he isn't sure.[1] He has remarked that what he likes in any good Roman poet (and "For the Union Dead" is his Roman poem) is his "block-like formality."[2] Through his own quatrains, more like little boulders than blocks. Lowell arranges his facts, his impressions, which threaten all classical formalities. The rough quatrains allow him to shape the aggressions of the scene before him, yet not make them falsely succumb to a rigid or a formal pattern. These quatrains enable Lowell to make contact with the American scene just as that "block-like formality" must have helped the Roman poet to organize his ideas about his own time. Lowell said that he has always admired the fruitful ways by which Williams Carlos Williams could enter the quotidian world of America, something he found difficult to emulate.[3]

"For the Union Dead" is a public poem, and not only its title but its Latin epigraph indicates the "role" of the poem. More accurately, the poem is a personal statement that melds with public concerns. The epigraph reads: "Relinquunt Omnia Servare Rem Publicam"—"They gave up everything to serve the republic." The epigraph is a modification of Charles W. Eliot's inscription on the frieze in Boston Common dedicated to Colonel Robert Gould Shaw, who led the first Negro regiment from Boston in the Civil War and who was killed at Fort Wagner in 1863. The relief, which shows Shaw leading his soldiers to the war, was made by Augustus St. Gaudens and was dedicated in 1897. On the monument, the Latin statement is in the third person singular, "he"; but Lowell changed the wording to "they," thereby including the Negroes with Shaw and making the statement ironically relevant to the construction of an underground garage adjacent to the statue, which the poem also describes.

Dividing the poem into four sections enables us to discuss it con-
veniently. Its opening part is the first six stanzas:

>The old South Boston Aquarium stands
>in a Sahara of snow now. Its broken windows are boarded.
>The bronze weathervane cod has lost half its scales.
>The airy tanks are dry.
>
>Once my nose crawled like a snail on the glass;
>my hand tingled
>to burst the bubbles
>drifting from the noses of the cowed, compliant fish.
>
>My hand draws back. I often sigh still
>for the dark downward and vegetating kingdom
>of the fish and reptile. One morning last March,
>I pressed against the new barbed and galvanized
>
>fence on the Boston Common. Behind their cage,
>yellow dinosaur steamshovels were grunting
>as they cropped up tons of mush and grass
>to gouge their underworld garage.
>
>Parking spaces luxuriate like civic
>sandpiles in the heart of Boston.
>A girdle of orange, Puritan-pumpkin colored girders
>braces the tingling Statehouse,
>
>shaking over the excavations, as it faces Colonel Shaw
>and his bell-cheeked Negro infantry
>on St. Gaudens' shaking Civil War relief,
>propped by a plank splint against the garage's earthquake.

The public scene is related to the private mind in the poem, but this
mind does not obsessively come to dominate the scene as it does in
some of the previous poems. Though the poem affirms a
relationship between the scene and the inner turmoil of the poet,
the end of the sixth stanza shows us how the poet can find some of
his most suggestive lines simply by being receptive to the images of
the world.

Lowell has said that until "For the Union Dead" was written,
"I'd stopped writing a poem as impersonal as that." But he also has
said that he always wanted to write a Northern Civil War poem,
and "Finally at 43 I did."[4] He found the poem a difficult challenge,

especially as it was written shortly after he had been writing the intense personal poems included in *Life Studies*. "For the Union Dead" struck him as being more like some of his early poems. The jagged yet self-contained quatrains are stepping stones that Lowell fashioned for himself between his newer work and some qualities of his earlier work that he wanted to retain or reformulate. Indeed, logic of style and of content dictated Lowell's choice of "For the Union Dead" as the concluding poem of the original paperback edition of *Life Studies*.

The imagery of a dessicated life, found elsewhere in *For the Union Dead*, opens the poem. When the "I" is brought into the poem in the second stanza, the larger setting has already been presented, or enough of it to place the personal voice within this larger situation. Memory, which plays an intrusive role throughout the book, is present here as well; but here it also serves as a window overlooking some communal situation, a memory befitting the private consciousness of Shaw as he moved into a public act of self-sacrifice.

The opening stanza organizes and establishes the tone and ideas in the poem. In the first line, most of the accents appear in words of one syllable or in the first syllable of a word. At one point there are three accents in a row, and half of the line is capitalized. This heavily accented opening line is not an especially felicitous one to read aloud; it presents a heavy beat that threatens to be oppressive. This oppression (identified with a destroyed public edifice) is one of the forces the poem is aware of, impresses us with; it is a factor the reader must consider and withstand.

The first sentence concludes in the middle of the second line at the same time the last word of the first line, "stands," alliteratively foreshadows the first half of that second line. This alliterative "foreshadowing" helps Lowell construct the stanza. The alliteration connects the lines to one another and assists in formulating the sentences, each of which may or may not take up a line by itself. The last half of the second line has a double alliteration of *b*s and *d*s. The *b* is picked up by the second word in the third line, which then goes into its own double alliteration of *l*s and *s*s in the last five words.

The third line, like the opening line, is heavily accented, and again the accents insistently fall on words of one syllable or on the first syllable of a word. Thus we can begin to see how in this loose but ingenious way Lowell can put together his unrhymed quatrains. The "primitive" but in this case sophisticated techniques of alliteration and heavy accentuation suggest the urban scene insisting on its presence. The very way the last half of the stanza finally settles into one sentence for each line may also quietly suggest that some restrictive experience is at work here.

The fourth line is the shortest one of the quatrain; in iambic trimeter, it is the only "regular" line in the stanza and, in its sounds, the lightest. Its assonance comes across as a lighter version of the alliteration in the previous lines. The fourth line serves to lift the reader slightly from the scene and into the next stanza in which Lowell reminisces about the time when he was at the scene as a child. (One of the reasons Walden meant a great deal to Thoreau as an adult was that he had visited the pond as a child. Part of his joy in being at Walden was due to his ability to recover an un-adulterated pleasure he had as a child. Conversely, for Lowell the adult experience only ironically intensifies the experiences of the child.)

So far we can see how deftly Lowell is working with the quatrain, nearly each one end-stopped, and giving the poem a structure comparable to the block-like but interesting formality he admires in Roman poets. Once correctly achieved, the form convinces us it is appropriate; but we can appreciate the difficulties Lowell must have encountered in arranging the poem this way. All too easily the poem could have slipped this kind of arrangement and run away with itself or become "stiff quatrains shovelled out four-square" (from "Waking Early Sunday Morning").

The second and third stanzas present the water scene of darkness and mysteriousness that any reader of Lowell's poetry soon recognizes. He has long been fascinated by that "dark downward and vegetating kingdom" (at least ever since he wrote about those "Sea-monsters, upward angel, downward fish" in "The Quaker Graveyard in Nantucket"). But the urge to enter the depths of nature's possibilities is not unduly emphasized here; there is no in-dulgence of the poet's private turmoil. This long-time fascination takes its proper and not overdone place in the poem, just as the poem utilizes but does not overextend the book's insistent connec-tion of people with disagreeable animals. One reason that the third stanza suddenly shifts from the reminiscence to the current scene at the torn-down aquarium is that Lowell is insisting on breaking off the self-reminiscing turmoil in order to bring the poem back to the scene of the construction of an underground garage, with the nearby famous statue of Shaw having to be supported. Also the fish and reptile of the third stanza relate to the fourth stanza's description of the machine-animal moving behind its cage.

This entire opening section, especially the fourth, fifth, and sixth stanzas, shows how Lowell can effectively select details from what the husky world presents (homage to William Carlos Williams) in order to further his sense of that world. The "yellow dinosaur steamshovels," the "Puritan-pumpkin colored girders," the image of a hero "propped by a plank splint," as well as the newly strung barbed wire: all originally come from the scene itself—the world out there; and these images richly convey the poet's sense of the scene. The suggestion of a concentration camp world; the long-time Lowell concerns for the Puritan heritage; the obsessive, denigrating animal imagery; the fascination for the military hero—all these concerns movingly and convincingly appear as Lowell looks at his world, shrewdly connecting it to his own inclinations and reminiscences.

"For the Union Dead" in its own way is a culmination of many poems from *Lord Weary's Castle* which are concerned with "The Exile's Return," or with the state of the colonial heritage in this century as in "Salem," "Concord," "Children of Light," or "Where the Rainbow Ends." The scene of urban reconstruction contrasts with the once-heroic image of Shaw leading his troops. The frieze celebrating Shaw barely survives in the present as the "underworld garage" threatens to usurp Shaw's significance by connecting him with some mass, contemporary graveyard. Though Shaw was buried in a common plot with the soldiers he commanded (as the poem indicates later on), this bronze image of the hero fragilely represents a heroism of choice and fate, immediately sensed, that the poet cannot locate in the other activities described in the poem.

The next four stanzas compose the second part of the poem:

> Two months after marching through Boston,
> half the regiment was dead;
> at the dedication,
> William James could almost hear the bronze Negroes breathe.
>
> Their monument sticks like a fishbone
> in the city's throat.
> Its Colonel is as lean
> as a compass-needle.

He has an angry wrenlike vigilance,
a greyhound's gentle tautness;
he seems to wince at pleasure,
and suffocate for privacy.

He is out of bounds now. He rejoices in man's lovely,
peculiar power to choose life and die—
when he leads his black soldiers to death,
he cannot bend his back.

Colonel Shaw is the kind of hero we would expect Lowell's poetry
to celebrate, especially because some of Shaw's qualities parallel
Lowell's images of himself, as well as his descriptions of Hawthorne
and Edwards. This part of the poem insists on presenting Shaw, and
the numerous clauses beginning with "he" register this insistence.
Shaw is a hero not because he gained a military victory (which he
did not, any way) but because his military act exposes man's ability
to live his values and to choose a meaningful life (and death). In
juxtaposing the civic-military courage of Colonel Shaw during the
Civil War and a contemporary urban dismay, Lowell offers a new
sense of the hero in his poetry.

A man's relationship to military authority is an important theme
for Lowell from "The Exile's Return" to "Memories of West Street
and Lepke," from the characters in *The Old Glory* to *Prometheus
Bound*. But, for the first time in Lowell's poetry, there appears a
military leader whose significance is not in terms of the strident
realities of power but whose value lies in what William James, in
dedicating the statue, called Shaw's civic and "lonely kind of
courage . . . to risk his worldly fortunes all alone in resisting an
enthroned abuse."[5] The Lowell of "Memories of West Street and
Lepke" would be expected to support the conscientious image of
Shaw, but what is most interesting in terms of the history of
Lowell's poetry is that in Shaw he has at long last found a soldier, a
military hero, whose stature creates a military, a civic, and a noble
image of man.

Lowell was vaguely struggling for such a figure in his prose portrayal of Major Mordecai Myers in *Life Studies*, and the descriptions of his ex-naval officer father represent the negative side of the
search—what he must have missed in his father. Lowell wanted so
long to write a Northern Civil War poem, and has expressed a
strong desire to have known his Civil War ancestor, "my military
cousin Charles Russell Lowell," who was also killed during the war

and who, incidentally, married the sister of Robert Gould Shaw. In addition, William James's brother, Garth, who volunteered for service in Shaw's regiment, was wounded at Fort Wagner. Thus for James in making his address at the dedication of the relief, and for Lowell in writing the poem about Shaw and his men, the occasion is a mixture of national, Bostonian, and familial or personal concerns. In Shaw, James, and Lowell, we witness the New England conscience at a fine point, and each man inspires the next.

As a hero, Shaw is an implicit indictment of his countrymen, past and present; his image still indicates the separation between the hero (or the writer who can imagine him) and the world at large, which seems to end up only making more and more ditches. Through Shaw, Lowell can celebrate the kind of courage he himself evinced as a conscientious objector during World War II (when he was almost the exact age of Shaw at Fort Wagner) and the kind of objection he encouraged among young men during the Vietnam war. But in the poem the conscientious hero is posed in the right kind of military terms, and this fact makes the hero's image in this poem one of the strongest in Lowell's poetry. Even though it is "propped by a plank splint," the image of Shaw is that of the civic-military hero that Lowell has always been seeking. In Lowell's poetry the moral equivalent of the military hero who is a butcher is the military hero whose greatness is his moral courage, a courage which should be honored for its rendering of life to the community. Thus it's not surprising that in his 1967 poem "The March," Lowell describes himself and his fellow peace marchers as stepping "off like green Union Army recruits." Both in the marching poems from *Notebook* and in "For the Union Dead" Lowell has transferred the negative qualities of militarism (felt in *Lord Weary's Castle* and in "Inauguration Day: January 1953") to a positive cultural role.

The next part of "For the Union Dead" both widens and intensifies its concerns. Briefly and quietly, Shaw's image is contrasted with the usual small-town commemoration of the Civil War dead: "wasp-wasted," those stone statues "doze over muskets / and muse through their sideburns." As in *Life Studies*, Lowell places in the poem common, even sentimental, references to a shared experience; and this part of the poem connects Shaw to these other soldiers from his war. They are dead, too, but his kind of death and sacrifice finally and significantly contrasts with theirs. The formal setting of their burial and commemoration—New England greens, graveyards of the Grand Army of the Republic, the same statues of "the abstract

Union Soldier"—contrasts, as do their assured, almost sleepy com-
munities, with the pose of Shaw and its urban context. His "angry
wrenlike vigilance" might storm the statues that doze and muse.
(Lowell might be expected to prefer a nervous Boston, even a
destructive renewal, to sleepy towns.) The last stanza of this section
reveals the price Shaw paid for identifying with his troops:

> Shaw's father wanted no monument
> except the ditch,
> where his son's body was thrown
> and lost with his "niggers."

Lowell picks up a word from this stanza and carries it over to the
concluding section of the poem:

> The ditch is nearer.
> There are no statues for the last war here;
> on Boyleston Street, a commercial photograph
> shows Hiroshima boiling
>
> over a Mosler Safe, the "Rock of Ages"
> that survived the blast. Space is nearer.
> When I crouch to my television set,
> the drained faces of Negro school-children rise like balloons.
>
> Colonel Shaw
> is riding on his bubble,
> he waits
> for the blessed break.
>
> The Aquarium is gone. Everywhere,
> giant finned cars nose forward like fish;
> a savage servility
> slides by on grease.

Perhaps Shaw's civic courage is nervously transferred to the faces
of the Negro children who are presumably braving antagonistic
white mobs in order to attend integrated schools. But then the
close-up "reality" of television results in distorting what people actually look like. At the same time Lowell does not deny the heroism
of those Negro school children, their distorted television presence
lacks the immediacy and the distinct impact of the figure of Shaw.
That historical immediacy of Shaw is registered as the poet seems
cut off from the contemporary reality by the very way it presents

itself. In any case, the adult heroic figure is absent here, and the ditch where Shaw was buried threatens to take us all, with nothing left to celebrate. The life and heroism of Colonel Shaw and what we can learn from him (and from the children) hardly speak to the kind of world described by the end of the poem, a world that has explicitly been in the poem from the beginning.

Here is revealed another meaning to the book's title, one referring to the dead heroes of the Union but also quietly acknowledging the separation between the heroism of a Shaw and the larger public efforts for garages and the like. Once, when Shaw and his troops marched down Boylston Street and through Boston on their way to the war, William Lloyd Garrison wept at the sight and Frederick Douglass and John Greenleaf Whittier were thrilled.[6] This, too, was a military moment on Boylston Street, yet one significantly different from the scene in the World War II photograph. Or are we forced to realize that the military might which so thrilled Douglass and the others was finally to lead to the commercial-military image, just as, through Lowell's heavy punning, "Boyleston" foreshadows "boiling"? (This is the kind of question that haunts Lowell's figure of Prometheus bound to his rock.)

The poem bares the fate the poet fears will overtake the society. The poet himself is perhaps only left with the craft of his poem to rely on as he sneaks in ironic puns and culminates that alliteration with which he began. By the end of the poem, which brings us back to the epigraph, the scene, and the imagery at the beginning, we are almost ready for the statue to collapse; in one sense, it already has. In the way the construction gouges up everything in its path; the Latin epigraph (itself modified by the poet) takes on the severest of ironies—all, indeed, is to be put to national or public use, even the city's once dignified sense of one of its finest sons. Lowell's poem measures the contemporary relationship between a public art and civic pride. At the same time, it tries to support that plank supporting the frieze near the ditch.

The Boston that destroyed the old aquarium and that barely allowed the Shaw monument to survive awkwardly nourished in its midst a poet who tellingly records the truth of that Boston. "For the Union Dead" is a poem in which Lowell movingly combines his personal turmoil with a larger and meaningful view of the world; the personal and the historical situations reflect each other. This poem documents Richard Poirier's observation that Lowell is our truest historian.[7] The poem also confirms that Lowell's great ambition was to have been in his time what a good Latin poet was to his. After hearing Lowell read the poem during a discussion of poetry, Robert Penn Warren responded, "Very fine. That's one of your best, I expect. One of your very best."[8] "For the Union Dead" graces the book it concludes and empowers with its title.

CHAPTER 8

Character and Theme in
The Old Glory

It is generally accepted that the central theme of drama is the collision of
social forces at their most extreme and acute point.

All those facts of life which find their appropriate reflection in drama can
only crystallize in answer to their inner requirements if the colliding forces
. . . are so constituted that their struggle concentrates itself in persons
whose individual and social-historical physiognomies are equally in
evidence.

—Georg Lukács, *The Historical Novel*

I   *The Trilogy*

LIKE the colors of the flag referred to in the overall title, that
flag which appears or is prefigured in all of the plays, the
themes and actions of Lowell's dramatic trilogy. *The Old Glory*
(1965), form one pattern. Dealing with the three previous centuries
of American history and based upon earlier works of American
literature—Nathaniel Hawthorne's stories "Endicott and the Red
Cross" and "My Kinsman, Major Molineux" and Herman
Melville's novella *Benito Cereno*—all three plays are concerned
with rebellion: the justice of the rebellion, the inevitable price paid
for it, and the succeeding effort to restore social order. Because of
this theme the plays demonstrate a nervous view of American experience, and they reflect the playwright's concern for the struggles
and demands of his own period. The plays take on the force of contemporary observation precisely because they carry within
themselves the authority and posture of three former centuries of
American experience.

In the trilogy, as in Lowell's version of *Prometheus Bound* (1967),

135

life seems to be a series of endless rebellions. These rebellions are both heroic and disturbing. The thoughts of Lowell's Prometheus underline the dilemmas of the trilogy: "We have struggled to where we are by living through a succession of tyrannies," Prometheus observes. A thoughtful rebel, he envisions "an infinity of former rulers of the gods, each the betrayer of his own father, each betrayed by his own son. It's the same dull and hideous old story. I fear something much deeper, something I cannot answer." A constant oppression in the name of freedom, the way that a moral ideal inevitably relies upon its own arsenal of violence, the way that something good continues to bear its opposite—these are the thoughts that finally cloud Prometheus's mind as he is chained to a rock somewhere in the wilderness of Asia. The burdens of Prometheus's perplexed understanding are one with the concerns of *The Old Glory*. The trilogy, however, unlike Lowell's imitation of Aeschylus, is steeped in the specific history of a specific nation.

In each of the plays from *The Old Glory*, an idealist, or a man who regards himself as noble-minded, suddenly finds himself in the midst of a rebellious situation in which his noble tendencies give way to violence, or his noble sentiments find themselves inadequate to the frightening, rebellious situation before him. The principal characters of the plays show us what a horrible thing moral ambition or righteousness can be. In all three of the plays, violence becomes the final defense, or implementation, of apparent ideals or principles. The high values are either freedom *or* social order. In all cases, these values are in conflict; and weapons impose one over the other. Through this trilogy, Lowell gives his fellow citizens their history plays.

The paradoxes of the plays are frightening, for the defender of social order stifles rebellion (the legitimate desire of the rebellious to secure their own identity) in the name of social responsibility or of his own freedom, one originally gained through some rebellion. At a certain point in confronting the disorder that escapes their authority, that seems to taunt them, Governor Endecott, of the first play, *Endecott and the Red Cross*, and Captain Delano, of the final play, *Benito Cereno*, feel beyond their depth; a dreamlike nervousness sets in and they only recover their grip through weapons. Order is really oppression, and rebellion is a form of discovery the representatives of order cannot live with. Yet, as in the case of Governor Endecott and his Puritan followers, rebellion may also be an oppression instituted by the newly rebelled, a form of death, a frustrated imitation of the order rebelled against. In both *Endecott and the Red Cross* and in *My Kinsman, Major Molineux*, those who revolt do so in the name of a liberty that itself comes to threaten innocent persons, revile the opponent, and turn its own supporters into servile followers.

Whatever Lowell's public opinions about the themes in these works, the plays themselves, especially *My Kinsman* and *Benito Cereno*, display the monster *demos* that lies within even the most justified rebellion against tyrannical masters. Lowell has honestly observed, paraphrasing T. S. Eliot, that in the poetry "you write what you have to write and in criticism you can say what you think you should believe in."[1] The plays evince a distrust not only of usual social authority but also of the revolt against such authority, historically inevitable and even desirable as that revolt may be. The plays, especially the last and major one, *Benito Cereno*, indicate that although rebellion of the masses is a modern sign (one of the acts built into the drama of history), and although we are drawn into sympathy with these forces, rebellions weave strange death masks of freedom. These masks are inherited from the oppressive force being opposed.

In the plays, the "destructive" rebellion (even when it succeeds) is the logical outgrowth of the opposed oppressive order. That oppressive order dictates the nature of its challenger or replacement, and the rebellious opposition ironically succumbs to an imitation of its oppressor. As a result, the rebellions in Lowell's plays undertake a frustrating, death-seeking role, whether they succeed or fail. Lowell cannot conceive of a rebellion without its fostering a guilt about replacing the old order or without its closely imitating this order. When the libertarian or rebellious forces become, if successful, the "new" social order, it too must be rebelled against as it becomes oppressive. This interpretation does not imply that the plays simply ask us to throw up our hands in the face of anarchic history; the playwright is fascinated with rebellion but also fears it. The plays express a sympathy for the paradox of human struggle in the name of freedom; but, behind the concern for rebellion and military force in all of Lowell's works, there lies a deep dismay over violence. If, as Leon Trotsky said, "Works of art are the embodiments of presentiments,"[2] Lowell's plays about the American past register his fears for the American future.

Lowell may be accused by some of being unable to conceive of a rebellion free from a death instinct, from the urge for failure, from an implicit rejection of its own ideals, and from an imitation of its opponent and the order it replaces. He may even be accused of being unable to escape a racial and class bias in viewing contemporary revolution and rebellion, or of simply projecting his own psychology as he writes about forces in the world. Lowell may seem to some the model of the intellectual whose sense of human paradox and whose personal and class identities force him to blunt the thrust of his own radical awareness.

The plays from *The Old Glory* may appear to be merely vehicles for ideas that might be considered commonplace, especially since the French and Russian revolutions; but their ideas are dramatically registered. Opposing forces dramatically come together. In *Endecott and the Red Cross*, the Puritan Endecott speaks of his temptation for the Cavalier way of life at the moment when he is about to suppress it in New England. In *My Kinsman, Major Molineux*, a man with a mask signifies rebellion when his face is entirely red, the color of the uniform of the British soldiers he is defying.

The most revealing connection between opposed forces occurs in *Benito Cereno*, a play based upon Melville's novella. Don Benito, the Spanish captain, and Babu, the rebel slave who secretly holds Benito hostage, are in an unspoken alliance to prevent Amasa Delano, the American captain, from perceiving the truth about the situation on board the ship. Or, as we shall see, Benito and Babu might be considered "allied" in order to convey covertly and dramatically the truth to Delano. It is as if the Spaniard and the African are simultaneously trying to protect the American from evil, yet exposing him to it. Or, even more ironically, Babu and Delano, the African and the American, the final antagonists, are firmly bound together at the end of the play:

Babu: Yankee Master understand me. The future is with us.
Delano: This is your future *[he shoots Babu]*.

They share the last point of understanding: they are the future opponents. Delano, who gives Babu his future, gives one to himself at the same time. Social order (oppression) and rebellion are locked in a historical marriage, and one depends upon the other.

The plays that form *The Old Glory* are part of the lexicon of American literature, and they call upon Americans to understand their hidden loyalties and tendencies. In both Endecott and Delano appears a disturbing swell of moral righteousness; both decent men, they are also the authority behind the triggers of military order and oppression. Their very commitment to ideals, or to what is decent and proper in their eyes, perverts their humanity. The inevitable irony about the military force behind human ideals, an ancient glorified relationship of weapons and morality, appears implicitly in the title of the trilogy. This paradox is bound up with American experience, certainly as it has been registered in its literature. Hawthorne in his tales about scientists and seekers of an absolute morality, Melville in his epic about Captain Ahab in *Moby Dick* and in his novel *Pierre*, and Henry James in his novels and stories about Americans abroad and at home describe the intriguing and sometimes disastrous limitations of American "idealists." Even Whitman, who celebrates the expansive ego, our gift to ourselves and to the world, warns about our aggressive, unleashed selves in the prose of "Democratic Vistas." *The Old Glory*, Lowell has remarked, is partly a tribute to America's past and partly pure irony. In his own view the theme of the trilogy "might be summed up in this paradox: we Americans might save the world or blow it up; perhaps we should do neither."[3] In this ironic awareness by our most important writers, a group which now includes Lowell, there is a troubling double sense of some "old glory."

The Old Glory plays enabled Lowell to work with historical and literary themes, to add new ones or to modulate the old ones, as he saw fit. One reason he insisted on imitating important past European poets and on basing these plays on older American material is that such sources allowed his imagination a workable freedom in terms of both tradition and the present. The established older margins disappear as they allow the new material taking shape within them to create its own structures and attitudes, though these are tempered by what went before. In writing his plays in verse, in basing them upon works by two earlier and great American writers, and in dealing with themes and conflicts important to American life and to the great works of dramatic literature, Lowell sought to offer plays that are part of "The Old Glory" and are attuned to the contemporary situation.

II   Benito Cereno

The final and longest play, *Benito Cereno*, is the one that ultimately demands the greatest attention. Although all the works of the trilogy are related in theme, technique, and intent, only the last one is a major work. However, we do sense the superiority of *Benito Cereno* partly because the other works prepare us for it, "play up" to it (just as the earlier parts of *Life Studies* lead up to the final superior poems).

It made a great deal of sense for Lowell to arrange the plays chronologically and in the order of their quality, for our sense of what is at stake in American history increases as we go from the seventeenth century and *Endecott and the Red Cross* to the nineteenth century and *Benito Cereno*. By the time we conclude the book, this impetus forces us to confront our own time and those historical forces that have shaped contemporary national difficulties. Arranged as they are, the plays move from a Puritan and colonial rebellion against Anglican and English rule to that historical moment when the Americans are those rebelled against or are those who find themselves in opposition to the rebels. The last play, *Benito Cereno*, takes place on Independence Day; but another people are now making their bid for freedom, and doing so against the Americans. The circle of events creates a new cycle in which one rebellion has led to another.

In the beginning of *Benito Cereno*, Captain Amasa Delano of the *President Adams* strikes our attention even before he speaks. In neat blue coat and white trousers, wearing a straw hat and smoking a corncob pipe, Delano conveys a mixture of authority and informality, a representative American pattern we are disposed to accept. Delano is where he is, or has his lines to command, because Thomas Morton, Governor Endecott, Colonel Greenough, and Major Molineux have previously existed on the dramatic and historical scene.

Delano, the subtlest of Babbitts, is the intelligence locked in the heart of all clichés; and we are strangely ill at ease with him because he seems to represent so many fine American qualities, which nevertheless add up to the most disturbing weakness of all—the inability to appreciate a reality beyond the terms of his own ameliorative Americanism. Lowell has created an important figure in Delano, a philosopher in the mode of Benjamin Franklin. Delano is a significant creation because his character represents that social-historical complexity which Georg Lukács has correctly observed must be found in the personality of a chief character of a drama.[4] Unhappily, how many of our favorite American terms can be used to describe Delano! We know him only too well. A man of will, he is also a man of applied moderation. He is inquisitive, tolerant, international-minded, an attentive guest of ports and cities around the world (he has learned to speak Spanish like a native, he claims); he is serious, pragmatic, open-minded, cheerful, intelligent, and a man who knows his job. Delano, seemingly the perfect ancestor of William James and William Carlos Williams, even has a touch of the poetic about him. In short, Amasa Delano is the great American liberal, the great white hope, the junior achiever sent out to command a ship, or to defend his country's interests across the seas.

Yet for all of the broadness, the display of civility, the easy intelligence, the indulgent peace-of-mind philosophy, his faith in the rational approach—indeed, because of all of these characteristics—there is something fundamentally shallow about Delano. He turns out to be stridently chauvinistic while he cloaks himself in the colors of internationalism, which really means making the world over into America's image. Delano, like Governor Endecott, feeds on a moral ambition and a human awareness which finally become a disguise for the tyranny of his own values and influence. Moral ambition and righteousness supposedly began the colonies and the nation, and they still haunt the country in the three plays of *The Old Glory*.

For all of Delano's apparent savoir faire and ability to accommodate himself to a new situation, his ultimate rigidity is frightening; and, as a result, Delano turns out to be least equipped for what will happen to him. In a shrewd and underplayed manner, Lowell's drama tells us that in Delano we perceive that liberal character and education that have played a role in developing all of us. The play lets us know that to the very extent we see a "better" part of ourselves in Delano and instinctively sympathize with him, we are vulnerable to our national and personal weaknesses because we automatically conceive of them as virtues.

Because of this deft portrait by Lowell, a dramatized insight, the play is a rich, challenging analysis of American character. Delano's packaged wisdom (hardly ever without its measure of intelligence) is difficult to reject completely or not appreciate at all. One of the functions of the play is that as an American in the audience begins to look at Delano, he begins to look at himself; and the play imaginatively helps him to discover himself in a more complex and richer way than is available to him, for example, on viewing Willy Loman, that dismally hackneyed representative American, in Arthur Miller's *Death of a Salesman*.

After the play opens with some small talk between Delano and his bosun, Perkins, and Delano's combined sophistication and narrowness are demonstrated, a strange ship is sighted. Delano looks through the telescope and contemplates the scene:

> I see an ocean undulating in long scoops of swells;
> it's set like the beheaded French Queen's high wig;
> the sleek surface is like waved lead,
> cooled and pressed in the smelter's mould.
> I see flights of hurried gray fowl,
> patches of fluffy fog.
> They skim low and fitfully above the decks,
> like swallows sabering flies before a storm.
> This gray boat foreshadows something wrong.

The imagery suggests the notes of rebellion, confusion, and apprehensiveness that dominate the play. What Delano thinks he sees is important throughout the play. But coming so abruptly after an opening chat between Delano and Perkins, during which Delano, with the casual and pompous wisdom of a Chamber of Commerce speaker, brags about his successful philosophy and his relaxed maturity, the passage has the label "poetic" on it. Its very success as a poetic passage, as a suddenly heightened moment, jerks the listener into remembering that this is a verse play. The passage points up one of the problems of writing a play in verse—how to avoid pulling the audience up short with the reminder that they are listening to poetry. Furthermore, despite the fact that Delano opens the play by pompously describing the American flag as "the most beautiful woman in South America," we are not quite ready to believe that he is a man who would indulge himself in such intense image-making upon scanning this new ship, strange though it be.

Yet this play has a marvelous ability to survive all sorts of criticism, and this passage illustrates the quality that makes it do so. For the heightened language does suggest, in ways prose might not so effectively or so quickly, the deep and sudden concern this strange ship causes in Delano, even before he himself is fully aware of the ship's situation. This passage is typical of the play in that even after we offer all the appropriate negative criticisms, the work strongly touches us. The play has a secret ability to make the critic perceive that even its "faults" can be viewed as intensifying its concerns, as we will see later when considering the reservations that W. D. Snodgrass had about the events in the middle of the play.

After taking a dour view of Perkins's Puritanism and declaring, "God save America from Americans!" Delano, who does not mind getting involved, decides to aid the stricken ship. Delano is a do-gooder, and the serpent wisdom of the play demands: who would really criticize the American captain for that? Yet the man who begins his involvement as the Good Samaritan ends in a situation beyond his understanding; and he becomes an oppressive force precisely because his "idealism" and his humanity prevent him from imagining a world beyond his assured sense of good-feeling and from conceiving one that had its own rhythms long before he came on the scene. Delano, Perkins, and a few American sailors board the *San Domingo*, which looks exactly like the American ship named after the Federalist President Adams, "except for litter and disorder," as the stage directions tell us; and these are not the only signs that the Americans are the heirs of the Spanish situation. In the name of order and assistance, the American Navy enters where the Spanish military used to be.

From the moment Delano spots the *San Domingo* (the name of a saint and a name of the devil), he is uneasy; and his uneasiness surreptitiously increases during his visit on the Spanish ship. Through the intriguing, unrelenting, and very old device of a play within a play, Lowell advances this queasy situation, not that we are directly told that what we are seeing is literally a hidden drama, and certainly Delano does not know that he is confronted by a contrived situation. The play is a "play" of events on board a strange-looking ship that has been taken over by slaves who *dramatize* the illusion that the ship is still under the role of its Spanish captain. Stage directions refer to a "charade" of the blacks, and the surviving Spanish sailors are directed to make "showy bows" to the American visitors and to display a "ritual and dumbshow of distress." Even a canvas is pulled "ceremoniously aside," and old men who take off their clothes turn out to be young men. This "playing" intensifies the longer the Americans remain on board. Later on there are mock ceremonies, "musical" instruments, props, and even a chorus. In addition, to keep Delano from getting bored, Babu, the leader of the revolt, and his fellow ex-slaves put on a series of scenes for the Yankee Master, on a revolving stage no less. This deliberate "playing," like the self-consciousness of so much modern drama, is felt all the time; sometimes it comes to the surface, sometimes lurks just below it.

Delano, of course, does not know that he has boarded a ship

which the rebellious slaves have taken over. And again, in implicit sympathy with Delano's ignorance, we are forced to ask, how *could* he know? The terrible answer seems to be that Delano's nature and his previous experience prevent him, except when faced with disaster (and perhaps not fully even then), from knowing and imagining the justice and possibility of such an occurrence.

From the beginning of their encounter the Spanish Captain Don Benito Cereno talks cryptically, and Delano's unlimited optimism unknowingly mocks Benito's situation. Such ironies suffuse the play, and Babu especially indulges in double statements. Delano does, too, but unknowingly. The disturbing, uncanny atmosphere is charged with this underground conversation, and Delano on one level or another is not completely immune to the situation. We see this doubt enter his mind as early as his initial reaction to the strange ship, and once on board the *San Domingo* he thinks, partly to himself and partly aloud to Perkins:

> The wind is dead. We drift away.
> We will be left alone all day,
> here in this absentee empire.
> Thank God, I know my Spanish!

The formal lines contain the confusion and the apprehensiveness at the same time that they play on our minds and subtly intensify what is disturbing. (For all his intelligence and ability, what *does* Delano know?) The poetry has a way of formulating what is disturbing Delano (and us) but at the same time making it elusive in the way the one- and two-syllable words of the above passage nervously drum at our ears, or a couplet may unaccountably appear in a verse pattern that usually avoids such a pairing of lines. The order that reveals disorder haunts this play.

Something *is* amiss, Delano feels, as a pattern emerges but should not be there. Angry at Benito, Delano quizzically mutters, "This absolute dictator of his ship / only gives orders through his slaves!" Delano puzzles, but every effort of his to look objectively at the situation, to consider rationally the scene on board the ship (like Robin's efforts to make sense of the rebellion taking shape before his eyes in *My Kinsman, Major Molineux*), falls apart. The one reality behind it all does not, for him, fall within rational possibilities. His social imagination fails, his sense of human possibilities is limited, and thus all his efforts for a rational, sensible view are doomed. Again reminding us of the second play, *My Kinsman, Major Molineux*, the conversations between Delano, Benito, and Babu are like the efforts of the Boston citizenry to "educate" Robin into a complex knowledge.

For a brief moment early in his encounter with Benito, Delano considers taking over the ship by force and thereby clearing matters up. But he returns to his rational efforts to understand what has happened to the ship, to comprehend the distress it suffers. Yet again and again he never is really satisfied with the inconsistencies in Benito's narrative; nor is he capable of the imaginative leap that would surmount them. The disarray on the ship—its lack of command, its litter, the constant presence of the slaves—just is not clear to Delano, even though in a general way he accedes to Benito's advice, "You must be patient, Captain Delano; / if we only see with our eyes, / sometimes we cannot see at all."

However, one aspect that Delano is sure he understands and sympathetically responds to is Babu's allegiance to and care for his captain. Delano waxes sentimental over Babu's fidelity, Benito's trust, their deep ties; and, enlightened American that he is, Delano exploits his appreciation of this foreign relationship—the finer, more cultured way *others* live—in order to moralize on the sad limitations of the American character and way of life. "The beauty of that relationship is unknown/in New England" muses Delano, who possesses the American mind educated to that level of self-criticism that prevents it from becoming a real critic of its world. Delano, a precursor of the American college graduate, glides between a pompous appreciation of foreign mores and a glib support of American superiority. He is, to repeat, the subtlest of Babbitts.

Disturbed by Benito's poor seamanship, which Delano attributes to "inexperience, sickness, impotence and aristocracy" (traits of a falling European empire), he will nevertheless completely refit the *San Domingo* (again a sign that the Spanish power is taken over by the American force, which however is not able to discern its future in the Spanish present). And Delano, the man of goodwill, even goes so far as to offer advice to Benito. Delano surmises that Benito is unwell because the Spanish captain has lost his best friend at sea, the co-owner of the *San Domingo*, Don Aranda, who used to whip the slaves cruelly, but whose skeleton, unknown to Delano, was

stripped of its flesh, wrapped in black cloth, and, thus camouflaged,
placed on the ship's deck The irony becomes grisly at this point:

Delano: Pardon me, Sir. You are young at sea.
         My experience tells me what your trouble is:
         this is the first body you have buried in the ocean.
         I had a friend like yours, a warm honest fellow,
         who would look you in the eye—
         we had to throw him to the sharks.
         Since then I've brought embalming gear on board.
         Each man of mine shall have a Christian grave on land.
         You wouldn't shake so, if Don Aranda were on board,
         I mean, if you'd preserved the body.
Benito: If he were on board this ship?
         If I had preserved his body?
Babu: Be patient, Master!
         We still have the figurehead.
Delano: You have the figurehead?
Babu: You see that thing wrapped up in black cloth?
         It's a figurehead Don Aranda bought us in Spain.
         It was hurt in the storm. It's very precious.
         Master takes comfort in it,
         He is going to give it to Don Aranda's widow.

The play begins to suggest that it is not freedom that Babu is really
after, or, more importantly, that he really does not consider it possible to attain freedom, but that taunting the white masters (or ex-
masters) is really the game. Of the three plays that make up *The
Old Glory*, only in this last one, involving slaves, does the rebellion
fail.

As if to shift but also to intensify the forms of irony and diversion,
Babu announces that it is time for "the pardon ceremony,"
whereupon there follows the mock inquisition of King Atufal, the
former African king of the Negroes. Atufal, the mock slave, is in
chains, symbolically no longer king. (Lowell maintains Melville's
awareness that, with the coming of the slave trade, a Babu replaces
an Atufal.) Atufal appears before Don Benito, literally the acting
authority. After Atufal refuses to ask pardon for his "sins black as
night," the absurd and courtly farce is over. As a false warden, Don
Benito's former powers are again mocked; and Babu, through this
mock situation, symbolically places himself over Atufal, while
Delano is further disconcerted by the social forms on board this
ship. Yet, at the same time, the American captain is increasingly im-

pressed by Babu's delicate relationship with his master: he sees the servant as "almost a wife." Babu tauntingly responds: "You say such beautiful things,/the United States must be a paradise for people like Babu." Delano, after a slight demur, does concede the superiority of his country. He briefly notes Babu's "feeling for symbols of power." But much earlier in the situation, having told Benito "your slave has a pretty way of talking," Delano still fails to connect his observations of Babu's talents and tendencies to a reality behind the intricate masking of relationships.

Shortly afterward, an old and dirty Spanish sailor crawls before Perkins and Delano, throws some knots toward them, and then whistles toward the disappearing Babu and Benito Cereno before he is taken away by some Negroes. The actions of the sailor are obvious warnings, but all Delano does is explode: "These blacks are too familiar! / We are never alone!" Delano's obtuse but frank outburst may be an awkward effort by Lowell to offset his and the audience's increasing feeling that all the play is doing at this point is indulging in the game of mystifying Delano; and, indeed, Lowell's tendency is to overdo these mystifying hints that Delano insists on missing. (Surely, the viewer feels, *he* would not miss them if he were in Delano's situation.) Ironically, Delano's frustration mounts when he confronts a situation that is seemingly logical. His frustration only increases when Benito for the first time engages in consecutive discourse, when he logically asks questions about the state of the American ship. When Benito is rational and orderly, the mystery only deepens. Why should he be so interested in the cargo, armor, and manpower of the *President Adams*, Delano cannot but wonder; and he harbors and then rejects, as he has from time to time, the notion that the *San Domingo* is a disguised pirate ship.

While Benito takes his siesta, Babu offers Delano some entertainment which consists of a series of scenes that Babu interprets for the "Yankee Master," who is annoyed at finding them absurd, unconnected, and unclear. A Spanish sailor dips naked white dolls in tar; a deaf Negro boy holds bottles to his ears; another sailor throws a knot at Delano; a black Virgin Mary appears; and King Atufal is displayed in chains and wearing a crown. Delano cannot make any sense of such a drama, and the play again coaxes us into sympathizing with the plight of this sincere man who *is* trying his best.

In a questioning but sympathetic review of *The Old Glory*, W. D. Snodgrass wondered whether the "entertainment" (and we may add all the episodes of knot-throwing by the sailors) really advances

the play. Snodgrass observed that the hints in the entertainment do
not tell the audience any more than they know already, do not explain why Delano will not understand what is happening, and only
perplex us as to Babu's motivation in throwing so many clues and
hints to Delano. Snodgrass also felt that the entertainment and the
fascination for clues deflect our interest from the characters'
relationships to one another.[5]

Snodgrass's objections are important, but, as suggested earlier,
the concern for clues may be seen from still other points of view
(just as the entire ostensible reality on board the *San Domingo* may
be seen as hiding another reality). For example, the scene of the
deaf boy's holding bottles to his ears is one even Babu cannot explain, though he is "director" of the show; he weakly and stupidly
suggests that the boy is listening to the ocean, or to his mother.
Delano is, of course, annoyed at failing to understand what is being
portrayed and poses some sensible questions: "If he's deaf, how can
he hear the ocean?/Anyway, he can't hear me./I pass, let's move
on." Surely, Delano is justified in feeling his frustration and in
wishing the show to move on. Yet the very confusion of the weird
encounter makes us wonder: "What *does* Delano understand?"
"How *can* he understand what he sees before him?" "What form
could the reality take so that it would make sense to him?" The deaf
boy is a strange, black version of Delano's own "dumbness"; he is
Delano's Pip, we might say. Although Snodgrass raises important
criticisms of the play, he also recognizes that if we allow Lowell's
"excesses" their freedom we discover some surprisingly effective
answers to our critical doubts as we move deeper into the play.

As we return to our earlier questioning of Babu's motivation in
offering hints to Delano, in actually flaunting the American's ignorance and confusion, we must confront some other questions
about his seeming "excesses." What is Babu's intent? Why *is* he so
interested in offering suggestive remarks and situations to Delano?
Wouldn't it be wiser for Babu not to be so tricky? How do such
tricks advance his cause, which is, presumably, to get Delano to
refit the ship and to sail it back to Africa for the slaves? Or is Babu's
dramatic but questionable strategy merely a reflection, in this instance, of the poet's failure to envision a successful rebellion? Objectively speaking, Babu needs Delano to remain in ignorance, at
least until he repairs the ship. Yet, from his first comments, Babu
secretly strives to show Delano what is really happening.

We cannot be certain, but, as suggested earlier, what we may be seeing is the fact that Babu's sense of victory and power includes an involved fooling of the white masters. The deception must be as clever as possible; that is part of the revenge even when, practically speaking, such revenge may spoil his plot. Here Babu, the slave leader, is potentially damaging his revolt through a desire for vengeance against, and manipulation of, his former masters. This desire logically follows from his situation as a slave, but it may also undercut his bid for freedom. Babu in his rebellion is less assured of success than he is of simply frustrating the arrangements and the moral assuredness of the white masters. Thus Babu, caught in the reins of his own frustration (does he really have the power and vantage point to carry off a successful revolt?) senses his doom and that of his people; and the rebellion comes to be its own despairing end.

Rebellion in this case (separating it from the successful rebellions of the first two plays) is only the final and complete harassment. Real victory and freedom are just too much to expect under these circumstances, and the desire to rebel is the secret urge for defeat of the entire ship and the system that keeps it afloat. The frustrated rebellion is historically and psychologically believable. Unhappily, the doomed revolt may be the only means of self-discovery and self-assertion available to the ex-slaves under the circumstances. The play leaves us with the questions, aspirations, and fears of our own time, as we are witnesses of what has gone into the making of our era. This slave rebellion on board the *San Domingo*, even more than the struggle so described by Robin in *My Kinsman, Major Molineux*, reminds us of "Hell revolting on its jailers."

Even if we suspect that Lowell has reduced the effectiveness of *Benito Cereno* through the excessive "entertainments," this very suspicion leads us to think that the real subject is the poet's fear that, given the terms of the oppression, the rebellion can only lead to the tragic self-destruction of the rebels. The play, let us be clear, does not display a complex sense of slavery's tragic rebellion at the expense of a human sympathy for that rebellion. Behind the complex awareness, or along with it, is a strong sympathy for the plight of the rebels, a sympathy profoundly registered by the end of the play

As for Delano's confusions, given his background and upbringing, how *could* he understand and appreciate this relationship between oppression and the rebellion against it? How *could* Delano recognize and appreciate the rebellious mode of the ex-slaves? Perhaps, if Delano had read the two previous plays in the volume

150 ROBERT LOWELL

about earlier American history, about the relationship between rebels and masters, he would understand what is happening to him.

In the more than one hundred years since Melville's novella *Benito Cereno* (in which Babu's cunning is not so central to events as it is in Lowell's play), the white writer has come to possess a greater appreciation of the skill and demeanor of the Negro. Even if that skill is still usually seen from the outside and is still uneasily felt as destructive or violent, it becomes increasingly respected for itself. We are reaching the point where some writer, with the talent of a Melville or a Lowell, will give us the story of Benito Cereno from the point of view of the slaves. Such a writer might enlarge the situation in Melville's and Lowell's versions and bring to the fore all those secret discussions Babu must have been having with Cereno, Atufal, and the other Negroes. But Lowell's version, even *because* of its "limitations," is part of the process of American awareness. The Benito Cereno matter may become to American literature what the Trojan War was to Greek writers from Homer to Euripides, and what the Arthurian legend was to medieval writers.

If, as Snodgrass suggests, the long middle stretch of the play is dull, or merely goes on aimlessly, it is also true, as Snodgrass himself best puts it: "Later, however, when the ending comes down with such rockslide force, one cannot be sure. I, at least, can't tell how much of the final power was developed during passages which seemed dull at the time."[6] Even if, in accordance with Snodgrass's tentative doubts, the long middle stretch threatens to deny the autonomy of the characters and to become merely a "play" for Lowell's fears and doubts, Lowell after the entertainment scene movingly portrays the two captains who speak from their deepest selves. Perkins happily reports to Delano that he sees "a speck on the blue sea"; the American whaleboat with supplies is on the way. But Delano is dazed by what has been happening to him:

> A speck? My eyes are speckled.
> I seem to have been dreaming. What's solid?
>
> *[Touches the ornate railing; a piece falls onto the deck]*
>
> This ship is nothing, Perkins!
> I dreamed someone was trying to kill me!
> How could he? Jack-of-the-beach,
> they used to call me on the Duxbury shore.
> Carrying a duck-satchel in my hand, I used to paddle

> along the waterfront from a hulk to school.
> I didn't learn much there. I was always shooting duck
> or gathering huckleberries along the marsh with Cousin Nat!
> I like nothing better than breaking myself on the surf.
> I used to track the seagulls down the five-mile stretch
>   of beach for eggs.
> How can I be killed now at the ends of the earth
> by this insane Spaniard?
> Who could want to murder Amasa Delano?
> My conscience is clean. God is good.
> What am I doing on board this nigger-pirate ship?

During Delano's reminiscences, Don Benito has returned to the deck. Coming up behind Delano without the American's realizing it, Benito speaks, after Delano has referred to him as a walking ghost:

> I am the ghost of myself, Captain.
> Excuse me, I heard you talking about dreams and childhood.
> I was a child, too, once, I have dreams about it.
>
> Delano: [*Starting*]
>   I'm sorry.
>   This jumping's just a nervous habit.
>   I thought you were part of my dreams.
>
> Benito: I was taking my siesta,
>   I dreamed I was a boy back in Lima.
>   I was with my brothers and sisters,
>   and we were dressed for the festival of Corpus Christi
>   like people at our Bourbon court.
>   We were simple children, but something went wrong;
>   little black men came on us with beetle backs.
>   They had caterpillar heads and munched away on our
>   fine clothes.
>   They made us lick their horned and varnished insect
>   legs.
>   Our faces turned brown from their spit,
>   we looked like bugs, but nothing could save our lives!

Delano, who does not really consider the specifics of Benito's dream, exclaims, "Ha, ha, Captain. We are like two dreams meeting head-on." We do not learn what Babu dreams, or what his childhood was like.

These are appealing confessions by the two captains, especially
the one by Delano (what pity we feel for him at the same time that
we are shockingly aware of his limitations). The conversation is a
masterful moment when it seems that Lowell just lets the characters
speak for themselves. By means of what George Steiner calls
dramatic "altruism," Lowell enables the characters to create from
within themselves their genuine personalities. Simply, but movingly, the verse heightens the rhythms we have been hearing all along.
We recognize these voices as belonging to the characters, even
though for a moment the verse intensifies these voices. However,
there are times when Delano's remarks seem closer to being
Lowell's than those of the character he is creating. For example, we
have Delano's uncharacteristic observations: "Real life is a simple
monotonous thing" and "When a country loses heart, it's easier to
live." Or are these insights a kind of nervous honesty we also cannot
deny to Delano? Are these remarks again ways in which the play is
informing us that we just cannot separate Delano entirely from
some blind wisdom?

After the reminiscences by the two captains comes the famous
shaving scene, an episode which Lowell takes from Melville; and it
is the prime scene of role playing. This moment most dramatically
portrays the real master as the apparent servant and the real servant
as the apparent master. The apparent servant, Babu, holds a razor
to the face of the apparent master, Cereno, just as he has been
holding a knife to the Spaniard's back throughout the conversations
with Delano; but, even when in full view, how could one see the
truth? The scene epitomizes the secret power relationship of the entire situation.

In the shaving scene, Babu accidentally cuts Benito; and later on
the slave rushes onto the deck claiming before the American captain
that his Spanish master has cut him in revenge. Perhaps, as we sense
the play's potential dangers of lethargy, the shaving scene is meant
to alert us to additional intricacies. Delano is certainly further impressed even if he is, as always, confused. On board this ship even
shaving is like high mass, he was led to remark earlier, impressed as
he is by Babu's skill in dispensing toiletries.

After the whaleboat arrives, the American food is distributed, but
not without an unseemly incident, one swiftly patched up before
the Negroes lose their temper and storm Delano, who hits a Negro
who in the rush for food accidentally knocked him down. (The tension is building; it gets increasingly difficult to hold things back.)

Delano is then invited to dinner with Benito. They have their usual ghostly conversation, but Delano's conversation with Babu is at once clearer and deeper. Delano, who has brought American cider to the dinner, causes Babu to observe: "New wine in new bottles, / that's the American spirit, Yankee Master. / They say all men are created equal in North America." In mock imitation of his opponent, Babu deliberately utters words that might have been spoken by Delano himself. Delano responds, "We prefer merit to birth, boy"—a line whose irony, syntax, rhythm, and crushing spondaic ending it took centuries of American speech and experience to create. In the rest of the conversation Babu often says "Yankee Master," while Delano repeats "boy." In choosing their words, the characters play and assign their roles to one another.

When at the end of the dinner Delano again voices his disturbance over Benito's story, the Spanish captain tells the American that "only the unfortunate can understand misfortune." Delano, not one to ponder such baleful possibilities, prefers to conclude the meal with the positive toast: "*A good master deserves good servants!*" In the play, unlike Melville's novella, as Snodgrass points out, Bosun Perkins, not Delano, makes discoveries about the odd situations aboard the ship and reports his findings to his captain, who then offers his own unsatisfactory explanations but really plans to sound out Benito on these disturbing matters.

From here on that "rockslide" begins; and, as Delano accuses Benito of running a pirate ship and orders Perkins to remove the cloth covering Don Aranda's skeleton, Babu suddenly, gleefully, and ferociously agrees. Like some uncovered Iago, his public countenance changes at this point as he removes his mask and shocks the audience with his true self. Watching a good actor like Roscoe Lee Browne, who played Babu in the American Place Theatre production, the audience is physically shocked by Babu's alteration; the white man is suddenly confronted by the real black man behind the servile mask. (Again, in an unwilling identification with Delano, the white audience is shocked even though it has obviously "known" all along that Babu is in disguise. The role of Babu affords a Negro actor a wonderfully controlled opportunity of leaping against his supposedly understanding audience, just as Babu himself suddenly turns against Delano.) After some momentary confusion in which Babu and Perkins assist each other in ripping off the cover, while Benito weakly tries to prevent them (the two contestants agree to bring the situation to a head), Atufal and Babu

confront Delano. And, at this point, the ironic symbols pour forth.
The white bones of Don Aranda signifying the new leader are displayed. The figure of death is finally exposed while Babu shouts a
Fourth of July parody of an American marching song, "This is the
day of Jubilee, / I am raising the flag of freedom!"

Freedom, rebellion, and death are entwined as Benito and
Perkins are forced to kiss the mouth of Don Aranda's skull, the
mouth of freedom. The earlier notion that the slave rebellion is
sired to its doom by the system it is rebelling against is sealed into
the rhetoric at this point as the Negroes chant in front of the
skeleton, "He is white because his bones are white!"—a distorted
echo of their earlier chant in front of Atufal when he was challenged
by Benito to repent: "Your sins are as black as night, King Atufal!"

The only thing that saves Amasa Delano from kissing the skull, or
from his freedom to choose death instead, is the pistol he takes out.
Then the American Navy cruelly becomes the play's version of call-
ing in the marines, as Lowell gives the best and most frightening
reinterpretation of the *deus ex machina* ever seen in an American
play. Out of the litter of the dead Negroes, Babu arises; and he
possesses the symbols of power, a crown and a rod (Benito's cane)
and the world (a silver ball), the last two impotently held by Benito
when Atufal was made to stand before him. Like an angry,
frustrated god, Babu destroys the silver ball. Then we witness Babu
and Delano's final conversation, which bears citing again, before
Delano shoots him:

> Babu: Yankee Master understand me. The future is with us.
> Delano: This is your future.

This strong ending is shocking to see on stage. Babu and Delano
are certainly locked into the future, standing there amid all the
dead bodies, with only Delano's convenient military might
separating him from defeat. His victory is purely military—the final
basis of the social order he represents. Snodgrass reveals the
significance of the play when he concludes that, despite Babu's
committing of evil, "here is a theme profound enough for tragedy;
the establishment of order in the state and the psyche at the cost of
killing off the energetic and rebellious forces. Amasa Delano dares
not consider the justice of Babu's claims, the brilliance of his
savagery. What else but failure of this kind leaves us in the
doldrums of mediocrity?"[7] The play leaves us in the midst of our
reality or heightens our sense of it.

During the 1960s the phrase "Angry Arts" became a term for dramatic performances of all sorts protesting America's interference in Vietnam and the blindness of many of its domestic and foreign policies. But Lowell's play (compassionate art), which makes a protest on the deepest level, forces us to recognize what may be our terrible future and makes us wonder what other fates are possible, what other endings to our play history holds in the wings, when many of the available guns in the last scene will not be those from the *President Adams*. Finally, the lone Negro woman's terrible moan, which director Jonathan Miller added to the play at its conclusion, encompasses all the persons and bodies on the crowded stage. It is a moan echoed in the audience, echoed by Prometheus chained to a rock, echoed down the years of our history.

CHAPTER 9

Prometheus Bound: *The Intellectual in Spite of Himself*

. . . within that impatient [Promethean] spirit lurks one final danger for the years during which we must watch the approach of an unwanted future. This is the danger that can be glimpsed in our deep consciousness, when we take stock of things as they now are: the wish that the drama run its full tragic course, bringing man, like a Greek hero, to the fearful end that he has, however unwittingly, arranged for himself. For it is not only with dismay that Promethean man regards the future. It is also with a kind of anger. If after so much effort so little has been accomplished; if before such vast challenges so little is apt to be done—then let the drama proceed to its finale, let mankind suffer the evil it deserves.

—Robert Heilbroner, *The Human Prospect*

ROBERT Lowell's play *Prometheus Bound* raises the question: Knowing what he knows now, suffering as he suffers now, would Prometheus rebel again?

Since Prometheus is tied to himself and could not forego his role of eternal rebel without being what he is, the answer is that he would. Prometheus and the rock "have come together." It may or may not be wise for Prometheus to persist in his provocative role, but he would continue if he could, and he does so from the rock. Unable to forge a renewed coalition with Zeus, Prometheus will persist in differing with that maximum leader.

It is doubtful if Lowell's Prometheus wants any role other than the one he is now sentenced to by the father-God he helped to create. Even though at times Prometheus sounds as if he has had too much of this role, he cannot be other than himself. He is tied to himself, which is why he wasn't chained to a rock in some of the stage performances of the play. He wants no other role but that of the punished provocator, no matter what his tentative speculations

156

and feverish imaginings at the top of the world. He can have no other role because he is not willing to make the necessary compromises. He is as firm as the rock to which he is imaginatively bound.

Lowell's Prometheus has bound himself. Prometheus is his own opponent. Prometheus is the intellectual unhappy with himself. Prometheus helps create a ruler and then remains aloof from the powerful world he has assisted into being. He is the opponent of "the old order" who remains the testy critic of any social system, including "the new order" he has helped bring about.

Near the end of Lowell's play ("derived from Aeschylus," we are advised, not a translation), Hermes approaches Prometheus to announce the final torture. Prometheus mistakenly images that Zeus is coming to visit him and once again to join forces with him to delay some universal holocaust. Prometheus *is* fascinated by the marriage of intellect and power, part of his desire to see his ideas at work in the world. Quickly, Prometheus realizes that he is indulging an illusion, that Zeus will no longer count on his support. (Prometheus's ideas were to Zeus only the means of gaining power and of holding on to it.) Zeus will keep Prometheus hanging. The former ally will no longer be invited to assist the political ruler whom he tried to educate into a just use of power. No longer Zeus's braintrust, Prometheus is banished to his isolated post of intellectual observation.

Shortly before the arrival of Hermes, God's youthful agent, Prometheus explains to three seabirds the nature of his earlier quest. He found the world a hunting ground for man's mind. He could put the universe to work for men.

Prometheus thus typifies Renaissance explorers, Enlightenment encyclopedists, industrial inventors, Comtean sociologists, and atomic scientists. Prometheus thought he examined the world to some purpose. Even as he is chained to the rock, he is thrilled by his former exploration of the world. He trembles when he recalls those past pursuits. Prometheus's body itself responds to ideas. Lowell has made Prometheus into an intellectual—for him to possess an idea is to have power, the power of understanding, and his body responds to such a possession by the mind.

Prometheus recalls that with his help man was able to transform his life and transform the planet on which he lived. Prometheus was all change, and all change was for the good. Though now chained and suffering, Prometheus still feels that vision. There is a lilt in his voice when he recalls those ideas.

He remembers assisting man by helping Zeus bring order into the universe after the elemental, slipshod authoritarianism of Cronus. (What Prometheus could not foresee was the bureaucratic totalitarianism of Zeus.) Then Prometheus believed, "There's a mind in things." Then he discovered that the earth "was a map of cures" and man could be taught to read the signs along the way. Then he was excited because his "mind was in no way walled in or useless," and others joined him in this search. Then he also felt, "Something could be done!"

At the same time that Prometheus recites his old ambitions, he finds himself examining the weakness of his former position. Now he denies a larger order; now he is susceptible to the idea that "The nothingness of our beginning is hard at work to bury us."

The thoughts of Prometheus have evolved. Once, Prometheus tells us,

I used to see unending circles of light, gentle, supple, airy, living, and forever widening. But now I see a thunderhead, a false face, blackened, crisp, all-powerful. In the forehead, sensitive blue veins are still trickling, as they harden. Blood turns to metal.

In the face of Zeus Prometheus sees a superior order, a superior chaos. The radical, or ex-radical, is enthralled by the face of the tyrant.

Prometheus will have eternity to reflect upon his commitment to change, meaning, and purpose. Prometheus questions his pursuits at the same time that he reinvokes his original passion:

I think I should have been more loyal to the idiocy of things, or bolder, or more careless. Yet I had no choice, such was the gravity and devotion that drew me on. Now I stand fixed and nailed to a narrow frame, to a rock, but I cannot unwish a single minute I clung, transfixed and trembling, to the great frame of being—awed, absorbed, and stunned! Even here, something stirs in my heart. I feel hunger and passion tingle through my outstretched hand. Around some bend, under some moving stone, behind some thought, it if were ever the right thought, I will find my key. No not just another of Nature's million petty clues, but a key, *my key, the* key, the one that must be there, because it can't be there—a face still friendly to chaos.

"Awed, absorbed and stunned," Prometheus is the thinker who

reassesses his role without exactly reneging upon it, like the author of "Memories of West Street and Lepke." Still half-yearning for absolute solutions, Prometheus also distrusts his "idealism."

Prometheus is one of a number of impressive "idealists" (or absolutists) in American literature. Imagine a Captain Ahab who is resigned to leaving Moby Dick alone, though he may still dream of conquering the whale, and you have a sense of the condition of Lowell's Prometheus.

Prometheus has also achieved a new stage of awareness as he realizes that Zeus himself will fall, as all rulers fall, "each the betrayer of his own father, each betrayed by his own son. It's the same dull and hideous old story." Prometheus then curiously adds: "I fear something much deeper, something I cannot answer." In replying to one of the seabirds who asks him what he fears, Prometheus at first doesn't seem to answer the question and explain his fear. He begins by talking about slowing the pace of earthly development. Then he says that he fears fire. "Fire will be the first absolute power, and the last to rule." He fears the very fire he stole from the gods and gave to man. Prometheus fears his own energies. This is a new element in his thought.

Prometheus fears that man's ability to direct the universe will lead him to destroy it. He comes to fear man's need for purpose and meaning. Within Prometheus, the grand rebel, also lurks the half-desire to be part of the drift of things because purposiveness can be destructive. He wishes to escape the unrelenting mind, the insistent will. He is weary and distrustful of meaning, and that too is the meaning of Lowell's Prometheus.

It isn't that Prometheus really advocates rest and mere obedience to the drift of things over sublime ambition. Rather, he now questions his former commitments. He wouldn't unwish a single thing, yet he now questions all.

Lowell's play is about the revolutionary's conservative and private fear that improving the social order and making nature work for men will result in the restriction of life. The play is also about the unregulated, infinite quest of the "radical ethos." These are the fears haunting the open-minded, suffering Prometheus.

In *Prometheus Bound* Lowell questions the very direction of the culture that intellectuals have helped bring about, not just an aspect of that culture, but its fundamental purposiveness. Prometheus is the type of scientist or intellectual who continues his work at the same time that he harbors the fear that his work promotes the

burdens purposiveness and moral ambition have laid heavily upon
mankind. Lowell appropriately warns us at the end of his introductory note to the play, "These confusions and insights are in the
archaic plot . . . and are irreconcilable with reason only if one
wants to translate the old myth into marching orders." Well put.
Lowell's Prometheus does not take shelter in authoritarian ideology
or burn books in the name of total liberation. His problems remain,
however. He will never know transcendence now, except through
apocalyptic conclusions.

Prometheus persists in his inquiries, for what has replaced his
original radical faith in the improvement of mankind is his dedication to his own intelligence. (And that too is an isolating factor in
his life.) His is an intelligence that now perceives how limited all
systems are. In Lowell's Prometheus we view the intellectual entering upon a new phase, as he proves the need for change, even helping to bring it about, though dominated by a sense of the eventual
decay and disappearance of what he approves and struggles for.
Prometheus has become the radical without the romantic vision of
"a new world." For Prometheus, the freedom of man must be extended, but toward no goal superior to the ideal of the moment, the
ideal man chooses to read out of, or into, history. Reform has replaced transcendence. How to continue to work for reform and not
submit to passiveness or determinism or cynicism is another burden
of Prometheus.

Unable to wander away, though free to think, Prometheus has
also become a conservative within the radical tradition. The ultimate questioner and defender of man's needs, he has learned to
question his own commitments. Prometheus is the intellectual examining his own intellectual history, the rebel pondering his
rebellion.

But even in the beginning, there was doubt. Even in the heyday
of his adventure, Prometheus felt that his accumulation of
knowledge never would deliver the final clue, the final piece to
complete the picture—"*the* key," as he put it. Prometheus
suspected his own quest even when thrilled by it:

I imagined that each new thought was another upward step on my circling
road. To no purpose perhaps. No step reached a landing, no piece of knowledge ever quite turned into wisdom. Zeus gave up. In the end he knew that
nothing would satisfy his famished appetite.

Prometheus never fully committed himself to Zeus's regime of strength. In answer to Hermes' advice that he submit to the political reality principle represented by the gods, Prometheus says, "I would be more desperate than I am, if I trusted the savagery and hollowness at the core of power." Prometheus does evince a saving skepticism of political power, even of the power he helped to create and toward which he still has yearnings. Finally, Prometheus was independent of all commitments, except for a loyalty to his own mind—his magnificent isolation.

Prometheus exemplifies the intellectual and scholar who loves questions more than answers because he only finds answers in order to ask more questions. He enjoys answers, and does indeed seek them, but he adores questions and is passionate about answers that insist upon the rephrasing of questions. The intellectual needs to be troubled, not certain. Being troubled—this is his "happiness," or his excitement. This is his sense of the world. His desire to probe promotes his ability to see things that announce themselves as having to be understood. Prometheus is his own quest. This is the humanly heroic part of him.

Prometheus was compelled to pursue an infinity that he himself created with each advance of what he knew. Though this way led to inevitable frustration, Prometheus could not do otherwise. The world was there to be questioned. Intellectuality was a form of ravishment of the earth, a kind of engagement, at a distance, to society. This is the way the world revealed itself to him. It's his quasi-love affair with the world. It's also his burden.

There is a difference between the Promethean and the Faustian urge. The Promethean mind wants intellectual understanding, intellectual power. The Faustian mind wants, above all, earthly power—which may include wealth, sexual love, psychological and political domination. This is why, to stick to American literature for the moment, Melville's Ahab is in the Promethean mold, but Hawthorne's Chillingworth and Theodore Dreiser's Cowperwood are in the Faustian mold. The Promethean mold is superior to the Faustian because its final wish is not for power or fame but perception. However, even the Promethean wish, as we see in the case of Ahab, can lead to Caesarism.

As much as he assists man, Prometheus is also an opponent of all of man's conditions as they exist. For all of Prometheus's effort on behalf of man, there is something aloof about his intellectual grandeur. Yet Prometheus may also find he has a need to live with man as he is, not only as he might become. Prometheus shows signs of becoming weary of his probing, his restlessness, his search for meaning.

Lowell's Prometheus has a touch of Jonathan Edwards about him: "Hope lives in doubt. / Faith is trying to do without / faith." He is banished to his stone just as Edwards exiled himself to western Massachusetts. Both Lowell's Edwards and Prometheus parallel the situation of Henry Adams as described by Jay Martin in *Harvests of Change:*

Politically or spiritually the sensitive individual, Adams concludes, preserves himself only by rejecting the subtle—but no less real and decisive—compromises that modern faith requires. But such rejection leads only to public powerlessness. The self is preserved only by losing its influence, and ends in inertia.[1]

Lowell's Prometheus and Edwards are half in love with that inertia. It is their disturbing appeal to us as our intellects are fascinated and tired by the winds of events. Each day for us the new news; every day for Prometheus another sphere to map and exploit, more signals to read and convert to man's vocabulary. Lowell's Prometheus and Jonathan Edwards, as well as Henry Adams, and Lowell himself, show signs of an infatuation with the idea of the world cracking and disappearing. They endure, but they are tired. Perhaps what they wish is that their lonely role will disappear. But, really, so far as they know, it won't, and in part they don't want that. The dangerous drama lies in that secret wish of the tired and even courageous intellectual to have as his final passion the only meaning left—the final logic of destruction. "No, not just another of Nature's million petty clues, but a key, *my key, the* key, the one that must be there, because it can't be there—a face still friendly to chaos." The "idealism" of that passage is inextricably tied to some foreboding apocalypticism, a sense of the end of the world which was evident even in the earliest of Lowell's poetry. Sublime ambition is admired and criticized in Lowell's works—it is one of his "American themes."

An important difference between Prometheus and Governor Endecott and Captain Amasa Delano (from the trilogy *The Old Glory)* is that although each is "idealistic" in his way, Prometheus refuses to "solve" his problem. (Prometheus, as already observed, harbors desires for final solutions, but tries not to submit to them.) Prometheus will not join with power as a means of quieting ultimate fears within him. Both Endecott and Delano experience a curious, nervous moment when they begin to realize how futile or confusing their lives are. But they cannot persist in exploring this moment; they soon insist on regaining control above the confusion and loneliness. Finally, Endecott and Delano will spring from such an unnerving interlude into murder in defense of their social system. Weapons, political power, and ideological crusades are more dependable than the loneliness of one's thoughts. So conclude, instinctively, Endecott and Delano. They lack the "inwardness" or the passion for inaction of Prometheus at the end. The finest virtue of Endecott at the end of his drama is that he realizes (perhaps more in the tones of Lowell than anybody else) how others have paid for his ambition.

To his credit, Prometheus is the rebel who will not use crime and tyranny in order to bring down the gods or the previous regime. To borrow some terms from Albert Camus's *The Rebel*, Lowell's Prometheus refuses to turn into a Caesar. This is his value to us even if we notice some inclination on his part to be reunited with Zeus. Lowell's Prometheus chooses to remain the heretic rather than become the oppressor. Prometheus remains the rebel and does not convert to godhood. He chooses the human condition rather than a divine authoritarianism.

In the end it is Prometheus's knowledge that places him above the Zeus who tortures him. For Prometheus sees that the gods themselves are not immune from decay and fall: Zeus is finally powerless to prevent his own downfall. And here we recognize the superior power of Prometheus, superior in its recognition of limits even to gods. This is Prometheus's great insight: gods, like men, peak and decay. This understanding alone, perhaps, redeems his suffering. It is an insight born of political impotence. Prometheus has reached the rare point of understanding the experience he is witnessing, the experience in which he participates through the torture of his own body.

Even while chained to the rock and about to be the endless meal of the eagle sent by Zeus, Prometheus knows that the gods are also subject to the restlessness, decay, and death that occur to men. It is by being shorn of influence that Prometheus comes to perceive the limits of power, the end of all authority. Zeus's cronies and frightened supporters identify eternity with Zeus. But Zeus is finally not beyond the losses and failures that Prometheus and man must undergo. The weakness of the gods is Prometheus's perception, a bequest of his own weakness. His intelligence sees deeply precisely because it is not tied to public power. Impotence and insight are connected. (Thus the parallel to Jonathan Edwards and Henry Adams.) To the extent Prometheus can live with the insight that gods too will die, he is wiser than the other gods. It would take a god sympathetic to man to realize that gods themselves do not live forever. Almost like a Boston Lowell, Prometheus turned his back on his prestigious associates to identify with ideas of another order and was given a sentence for his betrayal, out of which he achieved insight and created his drama. In this way Prometheus becomes superior to Zeus.

Every system thinks it is permanent or tries to be. In *Endecott and the Red Cross*, Mr. Blackstone, who represents the Anglican Church in colonial America, thinks aloud, "In a year or two, our new order will be the law of the land." Meanwhile, Governor Endecott imagines his new system. Each one thinks he institutes a superior system forever. But we see that one system replaces another, the earlier one containing the seeds of what follows. The fear that haunts Lowell's plays is that each system is a tyranny of its own, a tyranny that may finally paralyze the mind of a Prometheus. This is the conservative "bias" that lurks within the revolutionary themes of Lowell's plays with its concern for "violence cracking on violence." "All tyrants must die as this man died," is a cry repeated at the end of *My Kinsman, Major Molineux* as one authority replaces another. The American imperium begins to replace the sagging decadent Spanish system in *Benito Cereno* as Babu, the leader of the rebelling slaves, points to the skeleton of his former cruel master, Don Aranda, as the lesson for tyrants. *Benito Cereno* is the culmination of the trilogy *The Old Glory*. The slaves aboard the Spanish ship make their bid for freedom against both the Spaniards (the dying empire) and the visiting Americans (the rising empire) on July 4th. (That date is a Lowell addition to Melville's plot.) The African slaves are simply continuing "the old glory" as they replace the Americans in the revolutionary role and the Americans replace the Spaniards in their role.[2]

Life for Prometheus is a series of endless rebellions, struggles for improvement, that lead only, perhaps, to the need for future rebellions or improvements. This is the never-ending turn of the democratic wheel. The urge for reform is justified and appropriate. But the Renaissance-Enlightenment-Democratic Necessity gives man no rest and removes his sense of a reliable moral center as his freedom increases. The question is whether Prometheus will be able to live with his frustrating insights, his disappointments, or indulge an extravagant, histrionic pleasure as he realizes, "Soon my voice will be lost in the sound of breakage." Prometheus must learn to survive himself, to swim through his own insights.

At the end of the play Prometheus's voice sounds close to the tone of "The Dead in Europe," the next to last poem of *Lord Weary's Castle,* in which European victims of World War II bombings make a reiterative appeal to Mary to rescue them from the jellied fire, for "Our sacred earth in our day was our curse." Prometheus at the end cries, "I am burning in my own fire." "Oh Earth, my holy Mother, look, you will see us suffer." An inclination to find a release in the apocalyptic logic of this conclusion is one of the conditions against which Prometheus must struggle. And this is so precisely because in both *Lord Weary's Castle* and *Prometheus Bound* the appeal for mercy is unheard. Some twenty years after Lowell's first book his work still displayed an attraction for the conclusion of Revelations. Once again Lowell's incisive, haunting remembrance from World War II comes to mind. ". . . I have never gotten over the horrors of American bombing." At the end of *Prometheus Bound* that remembrance now has a severe ecological edge to it.

The dark side of Prometheus's rebel vision is the sense of an ending—the ending not only of a particular class or culture or historical moment but of the earth itself. This is what makes *Prometheus Bound* one of the unhappiest plays ever written. Lowell's *Prometheus Bound* doesn't have the vaudeville-like antics of Samuel Beckett's plays which enable their characters to *perform* their pessimism. In Lowell's play there is only man-god's intelligence, the change and destruction that Prometheus sees. It is a sad play, a play even beyond the pleasures one can also feel in sadness. The only joy in it is Prometheus's recalling of the tingling of his body when he had new ideas. Prometheus is one of those characters for whom his misery is his grandeur. (Some poets do see the gift of the Muse as the remembering of the pain of life, as Lowell admits to at the end of his "Afterthought" in *Notebook.*)

Chained to himself, Lowell's Prometheus cannot go elsewhere. At the end, no one will come to soothe him, and he cannot leave his role, even if part of him wants to. The play releases the voice of ineffectual compassion at the end. Like a great deal of Lowell's poetry, the play insists on its extremist situation and thus is sometimes overbearing and repetitious.

Lowell's Prometheus is his own captive audience. There is no drama, but much thought. This is why the play doesn't dramatize but mediates, speechifies. The play's weakness is ponderous mutterings, profundities thrown out carelessly. Since it is a play, we expect something to happen; we expect character to unfold. But nothing happens and the main character is locked into what he already knows. Prometheus sees (and perhaps desires) the end of all drama. We appreciate Prometheus's suffering at the end, but we also wonder if his final fear of "the sound of breakage" masks a wish for the release that end will bring. Prometheus's final struggle lies less with tyrants than with himself.

CHAPTER 10

Final Volumes

I don't see how Henry, pried
open for all the world to see, survived.

What he has now to say is a long
wonder the world can bear & be.

—John Berryman, from the
first of 77 *Dream Songs*

I *The 1973 Books*

TO read through the three books of 1973—*History, For Lizzie and Harriet* (poems that once were a part of *Notebook*, now separated), and *The Dolphin* (the truly new book, yet an emotional carry-over from the other two)— is to be disappointed. Of course, no one will fail to be instructed as he moves through the many poems of *History* which have enough private and historical references to keep him busy through many readings. In a hundred years (or perhaps in only a few decades) some scholar will receive a grant to issue an annotated *History*. The book sometimes feels like Lowell's effort to unload his impressive knowledge and draw freely from his friends, associates, and fellow-writers. (Have we ever had a more *knowing* American poet?) Yet after two sonnets to a page for 183 pages, the poet's knowledge and sensibility are lost in the rockslide of history, now *History*. *History* is in large part an outgrowth of *Notebook 1967 - 68* (1969) and its revised and expanded edition, *Notebook* (1970), volumes which throw together sonnets about the poet's own life and sonnet musings on history.

Lowell's fourteen-liners are like fishnets that capture everything, the fisherman refusing to throw back anything. Maybe in America, as I said, we have never had a poet who seemed to know as much as Lowell does about history. And probably we have never had a poet

167

who has spent as much time as Lowell in plotting the breakup of his
marriage and then remarriage. (Of course, less is revealed than we
might imagine or fear at first glance.) The feeling we get, however,
is that anything may and does end up in the poetry—a passage from
a book; a letter from a wife, now ex-wife; a political moment; a
daughter's dream. From one point of view, Lowell's openness to his
life and thought and his making it all potentially available to his
poetry are touching. But in poetic effect what results are surrealistic
minutiae   and   accumulated   disconnections,   sometimes   affect-
ing—without the kind of incremental awareness of *Life Studies*.
The once high tide of Lowell's art now "Mutters to its hurt self,
mutters and ebbs," to quote *Lord Weary's Castle* against *History*.

No more dependable than the rest of us, the poet must struggle
simply to see himself through. Occasionally, we are surprised by
Lowell's ability to find a sudden pleasure of insight or memory in
his troubles—like a luminous gray in an overcast sky. But the
measure is gone, gone because of some terrible reiteration. A critic
Lowell quotes against himself refers to "the seedy grandiloquence
of *Notebook*." There is also the reiterated muddling of *For Lizzie
and Harriet* and *The Dolphin*. The disappointment a reader feels in
Lowell's volumes of 1973 is a negative confirmation of the power
once felt in his poetry. To be disappointed is to have expectations
because we have had satisfactions. Critical disappointment will best
express itself against the recognition of what has been achieved
previously by the poet.

In the beginning, with *Lord Weary's Castle*, Lowell used a
fierce style forcibly enjoined to Catholic-Calvinist inclinations,
often placed in a Boston or New England context, in order to frame
his sense of experience. The poems of that book still sometimes
strike one as magnificently opaque, drilled in terror, a judgment
come to World War II New England in harsh rhythms and stubborn
sounds. Yet after *History, For Lizzie and Harriet*, and *The Dolphin*,
that book looks unexpectedly gratifying. Its poems still possess the
formal power to disturb. Religious or political allegiances don't
matter as the poems of *Lord Weary's Castle* pull the reader into
their world. Then in *The Mills of the Kavanaughs*, Lowell had some
success in describing the lives of others, especially that of an old
man (a fictional relative) who fell asleep while reading the *Aeneid*
and that of a reactionary but active nun who enjoyed hunting,
"Mother Marie Therese." New England and relatives appeared unexpectedly more interesting than ever in *Life Studies*, the book
which remains the great accomplishment of Lowell's career. Lowell

managed an openness to life, and to his own vulnerabilities, that enhances and is enhanced by his poetry. *Life Studies* is a book to experience and admire. In that book Robert Lowell added a new character to American literature—himself. The tremors of *Life Studies* are finely sounded—a life bared, a life redeemed. Like a great nineteenth-century Russian novel, it seems beyond our ability to exhaust it. *Imitations* and *The Old Glory* are different ways in which Lowell relies on past writers to provide him with the framework for poems and plays of his own. In those poems and plays he is in touch with his own "great tradition."

The sonnets of *Lord Weary's Castle* and *Life Studies* are crisply achieved, even when in the later book they appear loose and irregular. By the time of *History, For Lizzie and Harriet*, and *The Dolphin* one feels all too painfully the fear Lowell once expressed that "it really is very hard for me to write a sonnet and not have padding and clumsiness it it."[1] Lowell now began to resemble Saul Bellow's description of Moses Herzog who "sometimes imagined he was an industry that manufactured personal history."[2]

A change has occurred. Whereas formerly Lowell had a family, a city, or even a religious belief in terms of which he could define himself—the questionable inheritor, the idiosyncratic convert—he was now only left with himself. And Lowell was the kind of poet, the kind of sensibility if you will, who needed these "external arrangements" against which to measure himself. In one of the poems from *The Dolphin* his second wife, soon ex-wife, warns him, "You can't carry your talent with you like a suitcase." Putting aside her personal efforts reflected in that warning, the advice does fit in with Lowell's career. And Lowell must quote her out of some fear and recognition he finds in her words.

The family—the family of Lowells and Winslows—is gone now. The world is the poet's own, with a vengeance. In their place is Lowell's own immediate family, breaking up and held together by letters and transatlantic telephone calls or a brief return visit to New York around Christmas time. Then there is remarriage and resettling in England. Lowell begins to look like an odd kind of refugee—Boston, New York, London—each time fleeing the presence of one family or another. The exile's wanderings and returns haunt several of his books.

One advantage that Lowell has lost since *Life Studies* is this family setting by means of which he defined himself at the same time that he reacted against it or used its "inheritance" for his own purposes. The family (like the presence of Hawthorne and Melville behind *The Old Glory*) set the boundaries which were expanded or "imitated" but which served as a source of inspiration, a guideline to follow or depart from. Lowell seized the occasion to move beyond that family. (Of course, there is always that family of writers, their genius and predicaments, of which Lowell makes us feel that he is a part in *History*. We also sense that family of writers even closer to home, in the friends he writes about and the women he marries.)

In the three volumes of 1973 both poet and poetry seem to be at loose ends. Lowell perhaps was at a point comparable to that he had reached after *Lord Weary's Castle* and *The Mills of the Kavanaughs,* but before he struck the rich element of *Life Studies*. What came out in *History* (and in its accompanying two volumes) is a half-realization of an intriguing remark Lowell made to Alfred Alvarez in an interview in 1965:

. . . I have a feeling that . . . we are free to say what we want to, and somehow what we want to say is the confusion and sadness and incoherence of the human condition . . . I don't know why the arts say this so strongly. It may be a more miserable time, more than others, with the world liable to blow up. We're in some transition domestically: I mean one's family life and everything else. There are new moral possibilities, new moral coherence. It's a very confused moment. And for some reason it's almost a dogma with us: we'll show that confusion.[3]

That urge affected his late style.

In *The Poetic Art of Robert Lowell,* Marjorie Perloff has shown that Lowell's style of clausal modification (of adjectival series, for example, put to useful effect in *Life Studies*) has by the time of *Notebook* been reduced to a mannerism. Now modifiers don't modify anything or anyone, or they are gratuitously compiled.[4] A once discriminating technique has become habit or a way of padding sonnets. The disconnected adjectival series or unrelated adjectival phrases reflect Lowell's situation as he is disengaged from that family or home-urban-American historical context that formerly created for him the necessary ground of his struggle. His stylistic weakness resulted from that situation the poet was warned against by his soon-to-be ex-second wife: "You can't carry your talent with you like a suitcase."

Lowell can produce an inspired line in many of these poems, but how many consist of fourteen passable lines in sequence? These books seem to be hoping that turmoil will reveal something significant—some keys if not *the* key—if one only persists in writing about unresolvable tendencies and mixed feelings. Too often we feel in these poems "the unreliable touch of the all." And yet how harsh dare any reader be when the poet himself poignantly asks: "Can I be forgiven the life-waste of my lifework?" Lowell is not easy on himself.

If *History* feels like a drudgery of fourteen-liners, each page having to be filled with twenty-eight lines and two poems, the poetry of *For Lizzie and Harriet* and *The Dolphin* is saturated with the poet's life, with apparent self-revelations. Even if we aren't bothered by the exposure of the ex-wife's feelings through the quoting of her letters, and even if we feel that Lowell makes himself more vulnerable and open to criticism than any of the other characters, the poems don't seem to go anywhere. The momentary sheen or the dark-soaked truths of one, two, or three lines give off the impression that the poems were completed only to retain such lines, to expose this confusion or that uncertainty, with a kind of fragmentary insight or illuminating glint. It is the art of writing lines rather than poems. Lowell's picture of himself never does get hung straight. Deficiency will have to serve here. We had something more in the best of Lowell's preceding work.

The former attraction of the poet is now "vanquished by his mysterious carelessness" as "failure keeps snapping up transcendence," again to quote Lowell against himself.

Some of the best poems in *History* are not in the mode of self-revelation. In "Stalin," for instance, Lowell is not merely filling out a fourteen-liner but relates the form to its concerns. The poem begins with an impression from nature that is converted to a political concern. The poet notices that, subject to the play of winds, stems

> . . . creak like manmade things;
> a hedge of vines and bushes—three or four
> kinds, grape-leaf, elephant-ear and alder,
> an arabesque, imperfect and alive,
> a hundred hues of green, the darkest shades
> fall short of black, the whitest leaf-back short of white.
> The state, if we could see behind the wall,
> is woven of perishable vegetation.
> Stalin? What shot him clawing up the tree of power—
> millions plowed under with the crops they grew,
> his intimates dying like the spider-bridegroom?

The large stomach could only chew success. What raised him
was an unusual lust to break the icon,
joke cruelly, seriously, and be himself.

Lowell's earlier descriptions of Charles V, Caligula, and Hannibal
achieve a frightening culmination in this poem about Stalin, the
political leader who is even more realized than nature. We move
with interest through the poem from the first part with its sense of a
curious, disparate nature to a Melvillean image (suddenly entering
the poet's mind) that the state, too, if we could only look at it, is imperfect and perishable. But then after this middle, apparently summarizing couplet, the poet disturbingly thinks of Stalin in terms of
these preceding ideas, and man's self-perfection suddenly looms as
the harshest sight in the world, contrary to the variety and im-
perfection of nature. The poem assumes such a relentless political
consciousness that even a sensitivity to nature turns out to reinforce
that political awareness.

Lowell has no equal among American poets in his treatment of
political themes, his "Stalin" being one of the most interesting
sonnets in American poetry: the form helps the troubled awareness
achieve itself. "Stalin" separates into a sestet, a couplet, and a
sestet, with the final section breaking down to a question and echoing answer of three lines each. The concluding and "settled epitome
of truth the sonnet tradition calls for" (to quote the critic Alan
Williamson) [5] is shifted to the middle couplet, only to be jarred and
contested by the concluding sestet. Lowell thus distorts the sonnet
tradition for his own nervous, unsettling purposes. The sonnet is
changed to organic form and Lowell in the process lends support to
the thesis that whereas the sonnet evolved as a form in English
poetry, it is subject to sudden wrenchings in American poetry. With
a skill unusual in *History* Lowell breaks the sonnet form in order to
reinvigorate it.

Four times in *Life Studies* he distinctively shapes the sonnet form
to his own ends. (See "Beyond the Alps," "Inauguration Day:
January 1953," "Words for Hart Crane," " 'To Speak of Woe That
Is In Marriage.' ") No plodding or mere filler-effects are in these
sonnets strategically dispersed among the pages of *Life Studies*, ad-
vancing, through variation of form, the themes and concerns of the
book. *History* rarely parallels or extends the skill of *Life Studies*.

I would settle for one Lowell book, with or without plotting,
which would contain simply the best of the many poems in the
History, For Lizzie and Harriet, and *The Dolphin* volumes. I would

be satisfied with one small book containing "Stalin" as well as such poems as "Robert Frost," "William Carlos Williams," "Two Walls," "The Well," "The March I," "Rembrandt," "Hell," and finally "The Dolphin," a poem which deserves some consideration.

In this poem of fourteen lines plus one, Lowell speaks of the Dolphin that guides him by surprise. The Dolphin doesn't seem to be the old, familiar, plotting muse but a kind of wandering miracle of life which has led the poet past his own expectations, his own plans, even beyond his confusions. The Dolphin is also an image for the surrealistic tendencies in Lowell's late poetry as well as the sudden "jumps" in the poems from one thought to another, as, say, the jump from nature to the state in "Stalin." For once, the sea monsters of Lowell's poetry are replaced by a pleasant sea animal. Even the eel, a repellent image from Lowell's earlier poetry, has something worthwhile about it in this poem. One also guesses that the Dolphin reflects the poet's feeling for his third wife, or for the new situation of which she is a part. The dolphin image, present a few times elsewhere in the book, represents for Lowell half a willingness to live with himself.

In "The Dolphin" Lowell apologizes for his life, but also refers to a force that has moved him through his life:

> When I was troubled in mind, you made for my body
> caught in its hangman's-knot of sinking lines,
> that glassy bowing and scraping of my will. . . .
> I have sat and listened to too many
> words of the collaborating muse,
> and plotted perhaps too freely with my life,
> not avoiding injury to others,
> not avoiding injury to myself—
> to ask compassion . . . this book, half fiction,
> an eelnet made by man for the eel fighting—
>
> my eyes have seen what my hand did.

By the time we reach this last poem we know the pain the poet's current situation has brought to him as well as to others. We cannot be sure that the impact of "The Dolphin" is not due, in part, to the marital and personal situations presented in earlier poems from all three books. The culminating effect of "The Dolphin" is also achieved through a kind of purging of all the particulars that have burdened many of the previous poems. It is as if the final poem from these three books (its placement does not mean, of course, that it was necessarily written last) is Lowell's effort to recognize and yet move beyond what all of those other poems said. "The Dolphin" serves as a culmination of the previous poems in the way "Skunk Hour" does at the end of *Life Studies,* with the further impression that "The Dolphin" is a somewhat removed retrospect, a brief, surprising leap from dangerous waters.

II Day by Day

Robert Lowell's last book of poems, *Day by Day* (1977), appeared the year of his death. Divided into three parts (with an appendix of three translations), *Day by Day* is an accretion of poems principally concerned with the themes of aging and dying. Many of the poems are a looking-back to earlier periods (often childhood) of the poet's life, underscoring a remark Lowell offered in what must have been one of his last pieces of prose writing: "From year to year, things remembered from the past change almost more than the present."[6] That remark suggests that time of life when the past occupies a person's mind more than the present—when one feels oneself getting old. Lowell's last poems force us to feel that in his death we lost a poet whose work was more and more concerned with that very subject.

The three parts of *Day by Day,* written in unrhymed free verse, show Lowell concerned with memory and aging. Part One, the briefest, opens with "Ulysses and Circe," one of the best poems in the book. It is Lowell's last version of "The Exile's Return" motif, the poem opening *Lord Weary's Castle.* After twenty years of war and wandering (including an unhappy sojourn with Circe), Ulysses returns home to Penelope, to a final act of slaughter, and to the knowledge that he will make one more voyage. A resignation sets in:

> Young,
> he made strategic choices;
> in middle age he accepts
> his unlikely life to come. . . .

The exile of the opening and closing poems of *Lord Weary's Castle* has metamorphosed to the Ulysses of Lowell's final book whose facing of his situation is devoid of literary and religious support. These last efforts in unrhymed free verse suggest that the bare accents of

life have replaced the heavier strategies of earlier lines. (Compare
the passage above to the conclusions of the first and last poems of
Lord Weary's Castle):

> . . . but already lily-stands
> Burgeon the risen Rhineland, and a rough
> Cathedral lifts its eye. Pleasant enough,
> *Voi ch'entrate*, and your life is in your hands.
> ("The Exile's Return")

> . . . What can the dove of Jesus give
> You now but wisdom, exile? Stand and live,
> The dove has brought an olive branch to eat.
> ("Where the Rainbow Ends")

Lowell neatly envelops *Day by Day* with this theme of the exile
by ending the book with a translation from Propertius, the letter of
Arethusa to her soldier-husband Lycotas. She anxiously wishes him
to return home from his wanderings and battles. Thus the opening
and closing poems of *Day by Day* deal with soldiers away from their
wives and the ensuing problems of domestic reunification after
years of military excursions on the part of the husband. The
problem of return after heady experiences abroad (conveyed
through translations or reworkings of classical material) objectifies
Lowell's return(s) to home and family after his own turbulent experiences. Much of the rest of the book is concerned with Lowell's
own returns to the geographies and memories of earlier families and
friends. Not quite settled with himself, Lowell still evinces a desire
to live with his own misalliances.

Much of the second part of *Day by Day* is taken up with Lowell's
urge to define his relationship to old friends, other writers, former
wives. The shadow of death and bad dreams hangs over the book,
particularly in this second section. Even the latest marriage, mention of which appears in the third section, is soon crowded out by
the fear of not being able to continue one's life. Lowell's revisitings
of old friends, old haunts (including streets and homes where he
grew up) give the reader the overall impression of the poet making
his last visitations before he is taken away permanently. Rotting, going up in smoke, sleeping alone, the sense of life passing—all these
fears,from which even the new marriage cannot save the poet,
dominate the last section of the book. The only "reliable" experience seems to be still another breakdown, still another period in

a mental hospital. (Lowell's sense of humor, not the hallmark of his
poetry, shows signs of being invigorated when he describes his
periods of breakdown and rest in hospitals, perhaps because such an
experience gives him the leisure to toy with a passivity and dullness
he otherwise fears will possess him.)

The art of poetry, Lowell has warned his readers more than once,
does not cure mental or physical illness. Yet "the unshakeable terror
that made me write" releases for the poet "the grace of accuracy."
The gift of life and the burden of life are both reflected in the title
Day by Day.

Putting aside some moments of joy in the poems, the tone of
voice dominating *Day by Day* is resignation. It's as if Lowell is more
than half-resigned to his own demise. In the process he seeks a style
that is different from the plottings of his other recent books. It is a
voice that in its best moments combines the poet's perennial despair
with descriptions of aging, whose power he both honors and fears.

This acceptance of one's situation can be felt in many parts of the
book, but two passages seem to me to convey the pathos of this
situation. In the last part of the opening poem, Ulysses is described
as returning to the world he left twenty years previously, now
changed, like himself:

> He has seen the known world,
> the meanness and beacons of men;
> the full heat of his pilgrimage
> assumes the weight
> and gravity of being alive.

A poem in Part Three, "Return in March," in a section dealing with
Lowell's own return to Boston, takes further this acceptance of self
and fate:

> Tannish buds and green buds,
> hidden yesterday, pioneers today.
> The Georgian thirties' Harvard houses
> have shed their brashness in forty years;
> architecture suffers decline with dignity
> and requisitions its atmosphere—
> our hope is in things that spring.
>
> Tonight in the middle of melting Boston,
> a black chimney tapers, and points a ladder
> of white smoke into the blue-black sky.

The grace of being alive and the responsibility for being what one has experienced are infused by the sad, unrelenting awareness of some eventual demise, not too far away. And it all seems part of a given world that the poet neither controls nor protests against. On the contrary, he seems to accept life's terms, with perhaps even a willingness to float beyond that life. Lowell's unrhymed free verse is a stylistic equivalent of the willingness to accept what life has offered up and then the final relinquishing of will to what life makes of us. No more plottings. *Day by Day* suggests a welcome tiredness.

III   *Conclusion*

This last section is like a coda in which I will summarize and briefly touch upon the main accomplishments of Lowell's work. The goal will be an overall view of Lowell's themes, achievement, and development, though I will concentrate on those books which in my view remain his best work.

Shaped under the recently ended World War II, *Lord Weary's Castle* shelters the harassed spirit seeking redemption from its sense of destruction. Appearing in 1946 and winner of the Pulitzer Prize for Poetry, Lowell's first major book presents the work of a renegade religious convert who writes about his relationship to New England and to his family and its traditions. He also sees the recently concluded war as having a terrible effect on the sensibility of the victors. The problem of recovery after war is one of the themes of the book.

The very first poem of the book, "The Exile's Return," registers that note—the effort to recover after war. A stranger returning home, the exile sees the destruction about him and the need to rebuild his life after war. Though a German exile returning home, the exile in the poem is an Odysseus returning home after war. The poem offers ironic possibilities of homecoming for the modern spirit that knows itself as a refugee, that knows itself as a consciousness in exile. Such was (and remained) the situation for Lowell amid his world, whether it was the world of his region, of his religious beliefs, of his family, or of his world at war.

Three important observations have to be made about Lowell's war poetry in *Lord Weary's Castle*. (Of course it is an obsessive theme detectable in almost all of his books).

The first is that Lowell's war poetry was the only body of religious poetry that was written in response to World War II and that attempted to explain the violence which everyone witnessed. In Lowell's poetry, war becomes the immoral equivalent of religion, a weird mirror-image of Christianity; yet in its very perversion of Christian experience, the war affirms the significance of the energies disciplined and conveyed in Christianity. It might be said that Lowell's poetry demonstrates a "wartime" Christianity, one which, as portrayed on the title page of his first volume, cannot conceive of the cross without a horrendous gargoyle clutching it. It is as if the cross captures the imagination because the mind can never relinquish its knowledge of the sword but must prepare and suppose a redeeming transformation of that awful knowledge.

Second, though the past military leaders portrayed in *Lord Weary's Castle* do not display luster or brilliance or engage in a great moral cause (the poems present them as butchers), Lowell displays a fascinating split between a rejection of the military figure on the one hand and a secret admiration for him on the other hand. In this split we sense Lowell trying to exorcise the destructive military role while retaining the military capacity for energy and heroism.

The third and shrewdest achievement of Lowell's war poetry is that Lowell's very alienation from the purposes of that war enabled him to perceive the hardening of sensibility that was occurring in Americans because of their victory. The war, the poetry of *Lord Weary's Castle* attests, was creating a callousness in the American consciousness. The Americans were not able to comprehend the extent of the violence their military prowess was unleashing on the world:

> Sailors, who pitch this portent at the sea
> Where dreadnoughts shall confess
> Its hell-bent deity,
> When you are powerless
> To sand-bag this Atlantic bulwark, faced
> By the earth-shaker, green, unwearied, chaste
> In his steel scales: ask for no Orphean lute
> To pluck life back. The guns of the steeled fleet
> Recoil and then repeat
> The hoarse salute.

It matters not that Lowell at the time did not seem fully to comprehend the threat of Naziism. Or perhaps it does matter, because this very critical view of the official purposes of the war enabled him to perceive what violence was visiting upon the consciousness of its participants regardless of officially stated and meritorious reasons for going to battle. No other body of poems emanating from World War II registers the impact of that war's violence on individual sensibility and culture in the way that *Lord Weary's Castle* does.

In title, technique, and concerns, *Lord Weary's Castle* was Lowell's brilliant and strained effort to bring his talent to bear upon contemporary experience. "The armor of convention" (Lowell's phrase for Milton's poetry)[7] of Lowell's first major book reveals not some frozen traditional bent on Lowell's part but a deeply felt need to encase his sensibility for fear of being torn apart by what he perceives.

On looking back, we can see that *Lord Weary's Castle* is Lowell's striking yet strained effort to make his skill and knowledge open up and enhance his world, a world the poetry also implies could not be helped too much anyway. But if he were to continue writing after *Lord Weary's Castle,* Lowell would eventually have to move onto a work like *Life Studies,* where life refuses to accommodate itself to prearranged and traditional constructions.

Whereas *Lord Weary's Castle* largely gives the impression of having been written in one voice, *The Mills of the Kavanaughs* shows Lowell bringing other people into his poetry. The world is not reduced to the fierce Catholic-Calvinist mood that dominated *Lord Weary's Castle. The Mills of the Kavanaughs* shows some shifts occurring in Lowell's poetry: shifts from religious dependencies to secular perspectives, from lyric to monologue or dialogue, from the poet's deliberations to characters contemplating their own fates.

Some of Lowell's characters now talk for themselves. Lowell's interest in presenting characters with their own voices can be seen even in *Lord Weary's Castle,* especially in "Katherine's Dream" (part III of "Between the Porch and the Altar"). This tendency is extended to the title poem "The Mills of the Kavanaughs" (and other poems from that book) and appears again in "A Mad Negro Soldier Confined at Munich" in *Life Studies.* Here Lowell is allowing the characters in his poetry to confront their fate in their own voices and less and less with the fierce consolations of religious belief. Lowell then, like one of his own characters, begins to confront himself. Mental breakdown is also a theme which appears in *The Mills of the Kavanaughs* (though again with early signs in "The Death of the Sheriff" from *Lord Weary's Castle).* It is, of course, one of the major concerns of *Life Studies.*

The relationship of the family past to the present appears in all three of his early books. In *The Mills of the Kavanaughs* the dilemmas of the inheritance of family history is portrayed well in "Falling Asleep over the Aeneid." At the end of that poem the old man wakes from his dream of the *Aeneid* and recalls the funeral of his uncle, a Civil War hero. He still recalls standing near the bier of his uncle, and at the end of the poem he ponders the `relationship between the family-national tradition and the kind of behavior he can expect from himself:

> . . . It is I, I hold
> His sword to keep from falling, for the dust
> On the stuffed birds is breathless, for the bust
> Of young Augustus weighs on Vergil's shelf:
> It scowls into my glasses at itself.

The alliteration and couplets continue from *Lord Weary's Castle* though the fierce style of the previous book can be seen as giving way a bit as the speaker is trying to figure out just what his family and national past mean to him. Breakups, uncertainties, and questioned attachments pervade *The Mills of the Kavanaughs*.

Life Studies remains Robert Lowell's greatest book. It is a book of poems that reads like a novel (with its narrative element, the influence of prose, portrayal of characters, social and family settings) yet maintains the formal intensities of poetry. The entire book leads up to its magnificent last poem, "Skunk Hour," with its seemingly artless yet carefully arranged stanzas. *Life Studies* is the book in which Lowell seems to be saying (to borrow a line from Yeat's "Ego Dominus Tuus"), "And I would find myself and not an image." It is the book in which Lowell rejects the pedigree he was brought up to prize. Or better to say that in *Life Studies* he allows for a pedigree to emerge from the writers of his own time (and slightly earlier) whom he finds are his true ancestors.

By the end of the book Lowell (or the "I") is standing alone, identifying with a family of skunks eating leftovers. No other book by Lowell captures so deftly and so sympathetically, so wryly and so casually, the physical facts of people's lives. The comic and stubborn furniture of the soul resides in this poetry. The household elements refuse merely to be part of a given scene or to be fierce props for the drama of God's wrath in New England or amid Calvinist interpersonal relationships. Possessions shimmer with the psyche of their possessor. They quiver with the nuance of social encounters that remind the reader of similar items, of different activities, of other owners of like things elsewhere in the book. The poems casually yet intensively reflect each other throughout. The world tumbles through the book. It is all strangely and pleasurably of one piece, of one life—the life we read in all of its disparateness yet come to share, the life we study. How the generous, spreading details of *Life Studies* contrast with the gnarled, clinkered, jammed (though fascinating) particulars of *Lord Weary's Castle!*

Lowell's willingness to raid his own life, culminating in "Skunk Hour" (actually the first written of the "Life Studies" poems), made the book possible—the casually intense Chekhovian mode, the random memories in seemingly negligent lines, the apparent offhanded sound repetitions; the seemingly accidental, clumsy rhymes. Those tones and techniques organize remembrances in almost unnoticed yet persistent ways. How ingeniously Lowell's style conveys the demise of hierarchies, formal inheritances, and traditional ways of ordering experience.

At the end of *Life Studies*, the poet, like the mother skunk, will poke for what keeps him going. "The rich air" the poet breathes is half-echoed in "the ostrich tail" of the skunk. *Life Studies* has a playful, perverse courage about it, potent in its way. In the book's final poem the poet-character has portrayed and made contact with a disturbing yet nourishing force. In its ability to find poetic equivalents of that playful perverse courage, "Skunk Hour" is Lowell's greatest single poem, unless one wants to give that kudos to "For the Union Dead."

Of Lowell's several plays, *Benito Cereno*, the last play in *The Old Glory*, is the one that is bound to be playable in the future. In it Lowell has succeeded in dramatizing the figure of Captain Amasa Delano, a significant American type, the "do-gooder." Optimistically and naively, Delano comes to the aid of a drifting Spanish ship suffering from a revolt of its slave-cargo, a revolt, however, hidden from Delano. Proud of his spontaneous international good-Samaritanism on the high seas, Delano's involvement reflects also his urge to impose American benevolence on others who need economic assistance. Much of his proferred good will is nullified, however, by his failure to comprehend the events that occurred on that ship *before* his arrival. Delano's casual sophistication and self-assurance lead him to a misreading of the complex situation he has entered, a situation that ultimately will not succumb to positive thinking, technical expertise, veneer of tolerance, and magnified sense of purpose.

Poignantly, Delano's very commitment to his own brand of
progressivism hides from him the dangers of his condescending
view of the black slaves, who simultaneously play up to and mock
his attitudinizing toward them. His self-assurance turns out to be
his weakness. The dilemmas of American character are exposed in
each play of the trilogy, culminating in this last one, in which
America has become a nation itself and begins to throw its weight
around the world, confident it will assist the needy beyond the
American shores.

We come to see Delano as the American who realizes that in the
last analysis he will not survive and save his system merely through
an apparent open-mindedness and ostensible benignity. The last
test for Delano in the play comes down to weapons. (The conclusion
of the play is half a shoot-out). We know that this is only one
dramatic moment (occurring around 1803) permitting Amasa
Delano and the crew of the *President Adams* to sail away in safety.
Robert Lowell's version of Herman Melville's novella *Benito
Cereno* is part of a continuum of American experiences, part of the
play of our history.

Even for those readers for whom Lowell's earlier work remains
his work that dominates the imagination, his entire career is a compelling plot. Essentially, the career of his poetry is that of shifting to
various styles in an effort to respond to the issues and concerns that
dominated his consciousness at the time he was writing. The history
of that poetry also reveals an urge to make his art new so as to force
him not to rely on worn attitudes and worn forms which would prevent him from responding freshly to his world and to his own experiences.

Influenced by both T.S. Eliot and William Carlos Williams, having studied with Allen Tate and having stepped off with Norman
Mailer in a peace march, having majored in Classics as an undergraduate and having through his family felt the impact of
American history, having undergone both Catholicism and
agnosticism, Lowell combined the desire for a meaningful tradition
with an urge to exploit his contemporaneity. He appeals to us in
both ways. At his best—for example in "The Quaker Graveyard in
Nantucket," "Falling Asleep over the Aeneid," "Words for Hart
Crane," "For the Union Dead," *Benito Cereno*, the closing stanzas
of "Waking Early Sunday Morning"—we sense the vital interplay
of the past and the present; one helps the other to endure. Lowell
has given us poems that make us feel the tremors of national and

personal experience. His poems show us that even America is not exempt from history and that engagement involves past and present. Thus, in the opening poems of *Life Studies*, the settings of Rome, Paris, Manhattan, and Munich claim for us the role of ancient tourists who know these cities again because of recent wars.

For all of the earlier excesses of rhetoric, for all of the overdone introspection of some of the poems, for all of the fascination with historical catastrophe, Lowell had been engaged in writing a body of poetry that offers a sense of his own time and his own place combined with a sense of earlier experience. World War II merges with Jehoshaphat; Vergil's *Aeneid* shadows the death of a Civil War hero; Grandfather Winslow is compared with his colonial and Revolutionary ancestors; the spirits of Napoleon and Caesar hover over our wars; Catullus, Shelley, and Hart Crane share their fates; Hawthorne's Salem reminds us of 91 Revere Street; Melville's character, Babu, a slave in revolt, returns, somewhat altered, to vie with Amasa Delano (also changed from Melville's original story) over who should occupy the center of the stage; America and Rome pursue empire. And in the midst of these currents and illuminations, we also sense the persona of Robert Lowell working his way toward appraisal of private and social concerns. As we share the perplexities and engagements within Lowell's poetry, we also evaluate ourselves with a sense of all that history and all that inner life enveloping us.

Of the poetry of his generation, Lowell's remains the most ambitious, the poetry that tried to make connections between issues at large and the poet's personal obsessions. When he succeeds, Lowell reminds us how great was his gift. He was the one poet of his generation who made us feel that the powers of English poetry were being revivified in an American context. Lowell's word was steeped in his own time, in the dilemmas of his own character, and in those traditions which by challenging and making his own he extended.

CHAPTER 11

Epilogue: Looking for Robert Lowell in Boston

ONE day in late August, 1968, I wandered around Boston looking for Robert Lowell. He himself had moved to New York earlier in the decade and that summer was shuttling between a Yeatsian ancestral home in Maine and the Democratic National Convention in Chicago, where Eugene McCarthy was losing the presidential nomination. *Lord Weary's Castle* was already being dismantled to *Notebook,* which in turn was to be recast into *History.* While "the real Robert Lowell" had gone elsewhere, I was walking around Boston looking for versions of Boston, and versions of Lowell, that entered his early poetry.

The elevated expressway that took me into Boston reminded me of the West Side Highway in Manhattan that I had travelled many times. I turned off the last of the roads leading in from the Cape Cod cottage that I rented with a summer grant from my university to write a book on Lowell. Since I wanted to have a better grasp of the presence of Boston in Lowell's poetry, I had academic reasons for my stroll. I hoped through this leisurely tour to make a kind of physical contact with Lowell's poetry, to soak up his Boston. I also wondered if the tour would help clarify the reasons his poetry had attracted me over the years. Looking for Lowell was also looking for the reasons he moved me. It's almost as if our relationship on the page were not enough. I parked my gray Rambler station wagon in the garage and made my first walking stop at Trinity Church in Copley Square.

A wide, open area pleasantly led up to the porch of the church whose "architecture is a free rendering of the Eleventh Century French Romanesque" according to a fact sheet available for the tourist. Trinity Church still looked pleasant enough and not too small for Copley Square as it does now, one of the detrimental effects attributable to the new skyscraper that I saw when I revisited Boston in 1973.

I opened the door of the church and entered a lobby where there were racks of religious pamphlets and a guest book to sign. Then I opened the door to the sanctuary. I was looking for a stained glass window where I would see what Lowell says he saw in "A Prayer for My Grandfather to Our Lady," the last section of his poem "In Memory of Arthur Winslow":

> "On Copley Square, I saw you hold the door
> To Trinity, the costly Church, and saw
> The painted Paradise of harps and lutes
> Sink like Atlantis in the Devil's jaw
> And knock the Devil's teeth out by the roots. . . ."

There was no such scene over the front door. Was the poem referring to some painted scene within? I walked down the main aisle, staring up at the stained glass window. But I found no scene that corresponded with the one described in the poem. I walked outside to check. No, only huge slabs of red stone. Where, in Copley Square, in Trinity Church, in Boston, did Lowell see this scene of Paradise sinking into Hell?

Perhaps to another reader, more alert and shrewd than I was, the answer was obvious. I was reading the lines literally. But even now when I look at that last part of the poem I feel that Lowell actually saw this scene above his grandfather's head. What I had missed at the time, however, was that what Lowell "saw" was a scene he had imagined (i.e. imitated) from "Villon's Prayer for His Mother to Say to the Virgin":

> . . . I have seen
> a painted paradise with lutes
> and harps, a hell that boils the damned:
> one gives me joy, the other doubts.

As it turned out, Villon's poem and mother had not been transferred to Boston without some changes. Nor had Boston remained the same. Lowell had taken liberties. The Boston of Lowell's poetry was both here and elsewhere.

Leaving Copley Square, I walked along Boylston Street. (Why, I wondered, does Lowell spell it Boyleston in "For the Union Dead"?) I knew enough background of "For the Union Dead"

(which would also this day lead me to the Boston relief com-
memorating Colonel Robert Gould Shaw and his soldiers) to know
that this was the thoroughfare down which Shaw on May 28, 1863,
led his black troops of the 54th Infantry Regiment on their way to
the Civil War and death at Fort Wagner, South Carolina, in July,
less than two months later.

From Boyleston Street (to use Lowell's spelling), I walked over to
Marlborough Street, the Jamesian "hardly passionate Marlborough
Street" to which Lowell refers in "Memories of West Street and
Lepke." It is a street that might be in London, with its gas lamps
converted to electricity, the comforting trees, and the large parlor
rooms that one imagined behind the three- or four-story flat facades
in gray, brown, or white stone. Everything was well preserved.
Even the newer lampposts, arching over the streets, seemed to fit
here. Marlborough Street looked subdued and kept up. Things
seemed in order. The only irregular note was a girl in a swim suit
sun-bathing on top of a little roof formed by a first-floor room that
bellied out from the otherwise flat facade. She looked down on me
curiously as I was passing by. When she lay down again, I could just
see the angle of her bent knee. She became my imagined descendant of the woman who sings and welcomes the young Robin
visiting Boston for the first time and looking for his uncle in *My
Kinsman, Major Molineux:* "Soldiers, sailors. / Whigs and Tories,
saints and sinners, / I'm your refuge from despair." Of course, she
did not sing.

Lowell had first lived on Marlborough Street with his parents.
Later he had written *Life Studies* there. After a three-month stay at
a mental hospital, he returned to Marlborough Street and his wife
and young daughter. There he had encountered and proved false
his fear of being unable to write again.

The street and some of its buildings stayed with me. A few years
later when Richard Eberhart reminisced with me about the rich
time for poetry he experienced while living in Boston during the
late 1940s and early 1950s—the Boston of Lowell, Archibald
MacLeish, the Poets' Theatre in Cambridge, Richard Wilbur, F. O.
Matthiessen, the visitations of Dylan Thomas—I automatically
thought of Lowell's Marlborough Street. While Eberhart was
reminiscing, a representative house from that street immediately
rose in my mind. It had large windows and wide front steps. It sym-
bolized to me all that Eberhart was talking about. That real yet imagined house on Marlborough Street was the scene of "Home After

Three Months Away" and "Memories of West Street and Lepke,"
the house where Lowell, despite his fears, had not gone stale. The
house on Marlborough Street, some house I had half-arbitrarily
picked out and reconstructed in memory, was an image of poetry
for me as I listened to Eberhart recall his time in Boston. That
"hardly passionate Marlborough Street" had gone far beyond
Lowell's Jamesian, disclaiming phrase.

Marlborough Street led to the Public Garden, the place where
David seduces Bathsheba in one of Lowell's early poems, a poem
which he rewrote, retitled, and included in *For the Union Dead*. In
both poems the woman (in the first version called Bathsheba)
returns to the park where David first won her over, but in the second version she is some urban, nameless descendant of the attractive biblical woman, who points out to her lover

> the shedding park-bound mallards, how they keep
> circling and diving in the lanternlight,
> searching for something hidden in the muck.

While she feels guilt or the end of a passion, "the jaded flock/of
swanboats paddles to its dock." The theme of adultery or illicit love
curiously flickers in Lowell's poetry, flaring into his translation of
Racine's *Phaedra*.

But I could not concentrate on that oddly recurring theme in
Lowell's poetry now that I was visiting that garden whose swanboats so aroused my curiosity when I first read *Lord Weary's Castle*.
At the time of my first reading I peered across distances to follow
Lowell's injunction: "Grandfather Winslow, look, the swanboats
coast / That island in the Public Gardens. . . ." Eventually I had
come to Boston to look for myself at the actual boats. They weren't
quite what I imagined, although nothing could have been. Needless
to say I did not find what Lowell strained to see:

> . . . the ghost
> Of risen Jesus walks the waves to run
> Arthur upon a trumpeting black swan
> Beyond Charles River to the Acheron
> Where the wide waters and their voyager are one.

(That Boston-Christian-pagan vision has remained both fascinating
and alien to me; the *w*s and *r*s of that last line have always seduced
me—the mythic unity insisted upon by Lowell's magisterial

repetitions.) I did not find the swanboats of either my or Lowell's
imagination.

That Public Garden, partly real and partly imaginary, is also the
place from which the fifth grader Robert Lowell had been expelled
for being a bully and a pest to other children, as he describes in his
memoir of childhood, "91 Revere Street." It is the place to which
the adult Lowell returns in his imagination: King David makes his
illicit request to Bathsheba; she, years later, laments her displace-
ment by another woman. The Public Garden in this way becomes
Lowell's mythical garden of the fall, where he too once behaved in
violation of the proper code. The place of childhood peccadillos
becomes the place of adulterous overtures. In the same Public
Garden Lowell imagines the Christian-swanboat voyaging into
redemption beyond the sin of this life. For Lowell, Boston is the
beginning after the fall.

From the Public Garden I walked to the northern end of Boston
Common, where I sought out Augustus St. Gaudens' 1897 relief in
honor of Colonel Robert Gould Shaw and his Civil War troops,
described by Lowell in "For the Union Dead," some one hundred
years after the event it celebrated. Across the street the sun dutifully
beamed on the golden dome of the Boston Statehouse.

The figure of Shaw on his horse leading his troops looms so large
in my mind that I keep on seeing that relief as a statue and so mistakenly referred to it in the first edition of this book, just as Lowell
was compelled by the situation of his grandfather to transform the
scene of Arthur Winslow by the door of Trinity Church.

Though, as Lowell says, "There are no statues for the last war
here," diagonally across Beacon Street and ceremoniously
"blocking" the way to a wing of the Statehouse, is a huge statue of
the Civil War General Joseph Hooker, subject of a poem in *Lord
Weary's Castle*. The contrasting images of Hooker and Shaw in
downtown Boston might be imagined as the public objectification
of the terror and allure of the military hero in Lowell's poetry.

Astride his horse atop a marble base about twelve feet high, the
apotheosized Hooker looks away from the Shaw relief. Gazing off
into an idealized future, Hooker might be scanning some military
heaven. None of the tension of Shaw's face clouds Hooker's. Looking at St. Gaudens' relief, even if you know nothing about Shaw,
you feel the young colonel is steeling himself for some decisive experience, his fate connected to the dark soldiers who march beside
him. We don't feel in the case of Shaw that the battle he is riding to

is somewhere offstage, for it is also inside the young colonel. Looking up at the statue of Hooker, you tend to forget, if you know, that he commanded the Union Army in its defeat at Chancellorsville. Hooker has been converted to pure statue, bronzed in history. His horse is a docile, trained statuesque steed, unlike the snorting, reined defiance that shaw is riding. The nostrils of Shaw's horse resemble the hollowed eyes of a skull. Boyishly, Hooker rides into some abstract military glory above us. He looks as if nothing can stun him; but Shaw is brave vulnerability riding to war. Appropriately, St. Gaudens' monument is alongside the very street where Shaw and his troops marched on their way to Fort Wagner.

The features of Hooker's wintry figure are also assigned to Generals Grant and Eisenhower in the *Life Studies* poem "Inauguration Day: January 1953." Grant, like Hooker, is identified with the "God of our armies," and Ike is summoned to the mausoleum of the country's heart. While the rigidity of these generals invokes in Lowell's poems the fear of the military impulse, the image of Colonel Shaw speaks for another way of life, a civilian-soldier's private dedication to the civic-military cause of his black troops.

On the stone base of the relief is carved a passage from James Russell Lowell's poem to Shaw, "Memoriae Positum":

> Right in the van of the red rampart's slippery swell
> With heart that beat a charge he fell forward as
> fits a man
> But the high soul burns on to light men's feet
> Where death for noble ends makes dying sweet. . . .

Other lines from this poem, though not inscribed on the base, are reworked by Robert Lowell in his poem to Shaw. The earlier Lowell's "Our wall of circumstance/Cleared at a bound, he flashes o'er the fight. . ." is condensed to "He is out of bounds now." A hidden element in Lowell's composition of this poem for a public occasion is that it instigated a challenge—one of many—he had to make to the family past. The words of an earlier family poet had to be sheared of their rhetoric. In any case, the poets from that family past never appealed to Lowell as much as the family's military heroes.

Flying over the figure of Shaw and his troops on the relief is a sad female spirit who waves them forward to the war, her hair flowing

over her back and her garments streaming behind her. Carrying a
bush with some berries, she is the only stock figure on the monument. The Latin motto of the Society of Cincinnati, whose
members were descendants of officers of the Revolutionary War,
and of which Shaw was a member, is printed in front of the spirit's
arm and above the heads of the troops in front. For his poem,
Lowell changed the motto from the singular to the plural, "Relinquunt Omnia Servare Rem Publicam,"—"They gave up everything
to serve the Republic"—thereby including Shaw's troops in the
praise. (In the last stanza of the poem, that word "Servare" is converted to a bitter pun as Lowell thinks of the life of contemporary
Boston.)

The troops on the relief are four abreast, pressed together in their
bronze ranks. They crowd their part of the monument as the drums
of the boys in front merge with the right border and the right feet of
the last soldiers emerge from the left edge. The troops are of
different ages: boys, young men, and older men. Each has his right
foot braced in the rear, his left foot forward, Shaw's horse in step
with the men. Shaw rides alongside his troops but also apart from
them. He almost seems removed and at a distance, as if he could be
detached from the rest of the relief. Shaw resembles Melville's "The
College Colonel" as "he guides his strong steed—how coldly too."
And about Shaw we can also feel, in Melville's words, "Self he has
long disclaimed." Even though Shaw and his men are headed in the
same direction, there is something superior in the stiff back of the
white colonel leading the blacks who do not have an officer of their
own color. Yet Shaw, as the poem also cryptically informs us, shared
a common grave with his troops. Charles Russell Lowell, a fellow
officer in the Civil War, wrote of his friend Shaw, "I am thankful
they buried him 'with his niggers.' They were brave men and they
were his men." The passage quoted by Colonel Lowell and used in
the poem refers to a remark supposedly made by a Confederate
general about Shaw: "He is buried with his niggers." Despite the
shared fate, however, Shaw dominates the monument, just as he
plays a great role in Lowell's poem.

The luck and opportunity available to Robert Gould Shaw in
1863, the opportunity to convey his conscientious objection through
a military role endorsed by his community and supported by his
family, was unavailable to Robert Lowell during World War II.
Unlike the shame, disapproval, and rejection that flowed between
the World War II-protestor Robert Lowell and his ex-naval officer

father, Robert Gould Shaw and his father commonly approved of the son's military deed, proud of the social and personal risk it took. Lowell was envious, I suspect, of the opportunity that Shaw's cultural moment afforded him. During the 1940s Lowell must have felt that a Boston courage now came in the form of refusing arms. The roots of "For the Union Dead" were deep in Lowell and the world he inhabited, a world of the past he in part admired and in part must have seen himself as struggling against or redefining.

Even that intended Confederate insult of the burial of the white officer with his black troops (all the other officers of the 54th having been "decently buried") could in time be seen as nourishing the imagination of Lowell who in *Life Studies* would relate the condition of "A Mad Negro Soldier Confined at Munich" to the fate of members of his family and of himself as conveyed in that book. Turning his back on his inherited status as conceived by his immediate family, Lowell nevertheless found some of his most compelling themes through exploring his connections to his New England-family past. The military theme in Lowell's poetry is more than a family matter as he seeks to convert his earlier portrayal of Hooker, "The blundering butcher," to the inwardly dedicated Shaw, who, having chosen to share the fate of his black troops, has "moved into position to die."

"To die is life," the dead hero Pallas cryptically advises Aeneas in Lowell's "Falling Asleep over the Aeneid." Shaw's sword in St. Gaudens' monument is out of its scabbard as he holds it across the flank of his bronze brisk-faced horse, now white-streaked by birds and green-stained by weather. (When I returned a few years later, I noticed that the sword was broken, a rusty piece of metal housing a broken piece of wood extending a few inches from the hilt.) The guns of the marching troops look like rods of lethal bamboo as they point to the stars that border the relief. Their black faces stare straight ahead; they will encounter what awaits them. The faces of both the officer and his men are firm. They are their own fate as they march to their grave, then to their monument, then into William James's speech at the dedication of the relief, and then into Robert Lowell's poem some one hundred years after the actual event. The impacts of history, monument, speech, and poem combine. The puzzling advice of Pallas to Aeneas for a moment seems clear at this northern end of Boston Common. And so does Lowell's remark about "Man's lovely, / peculiar power to choose life and die." Pallas's advice and that "peculiar power" refer, as in the ex-

ample of Robert Gould Shaw, to a man's ability to live beyond his
death by having the kind of death that springs from a chosen and
significant way of life that later men will ponder and admire.
Lowell imagines Shaw having

> . . . an angry wrenlike vigilance,
> a greyhound's gentle tautness;
> he seems to wince at pleasure,
> and suffocate for privacy.
>
> He is out of bounds now. He rejoices in man's lovely,
> peculiar power to choose life and die—
> when he leads his black soldiers to death,
> he cannot bend his back.

The conscientious objector fascinated by the military officer, Lowell
in this case has transformed that officer to a stubborn bestower of
life—a paradoxical, military Orpheus who does not look back and
delivers himself and his men to posthumous fame. Their deaths
make a claim on our lives.

Henry James objected to the setting of St. Gaudens' relief, complaining that the viewer wasn't led toward the work by way of some
appropriate milieu, but suddenly was confronted by the monument,
right by the street. But James had not considered the fact that Shaw
and his troops had marched past this spot, that historical incident
thus reinforcing the presence of the art. Also, as it turns out,
Hooker's statue across the way affords the viewer a military
counterpoint to Shaw's kind of dedication.

I study the monument again. The folded oval bedrolls atop the
packs of the men resemble short pillars lying on their side, like parts
of a toppled monument. They are rolled up behind the necks and
heads of the troops wearing their fatigue-like caps. Those crumpled,
soft bedrolls are in contrast to the resolute faces of the troops, officer, and the firm line of the horse. But I wonder why Lowell
described the troops as "bell-cheeked Negro infantry." More like
bell-lipped or bell-nosed it seems to me, certainly unlike Shaw's
thin, pursed lips, or his pointed nose that is like an arrow behind the
bridle and the horse's curly mane. Lowell's description of Shaw fits
the image of the young officer on the relief. Shaw is better and
more pointedly described than the troops, who are mainly the
backdrop for Shaw's nervous devotion to his task. Lowell's description of Shaw reinforces that terror-like dedication to turmoil con-

veyed throughout Lowell's poetry. No other officer in his poetry—General Hooker, Captain Amasa Delano, Aeneas—quite matches the figure of Shaw astride his horse by his troops. He leads them to death and immortality.

"For the Union Dead" is the only poem Lowell ever wrote for an occasion, a Boston Garden Festival in June of 1960. The occasion, it turns out, had been long nurtured within him—by childhood visits to Boston Common, casual memories of the monument, lines from a James Russell Lowell poem, memories of ancestral military officers. The poem on the public occasion has personal sources. In writing the poem Lowell returned to a childhood scene and to his early appreciation of the free verse of William Carlos Williams. The returns were renewal.

A few hundred yards back down Beacon Street along the border of Boston Common and facing the park is another relief. Less successful than the one by St. Gaudens, this relief depicts the founding of Boston. Some stock Puritans and Indians populate the relief. On the other side, the side facing the street, is a plaque containing an excerpt from Governor John Winthrop's sermon to the Puritans aboard the *Arabella* in the spring of 1630, "A Model of Christian Charity." The excerpt contains the famous words "For wee must consider that wee shall be as a citty upon a hill, the eies of all people are upon us, soe that if wee shall deale falsely [with our god] in this worke wee have undertaken . . . wee shall be made a story and a byword through the world." The tensions, the warning, the clear-cut choice between glory or damnation, as well as the Old Testament prophetic tone, make for a good introduction to the concerns and passions of *Lord Weary's Castle*, its harsh sense of judgment and betrayal. In that book Lowell is a disappointed descendant of those Puritans who heard the promises and warnings of Winthrop's sermon. Lowell looks upon what he calls "this planned / Babel of Boston," and concludes in a Puritan prophetic voice:

> . . . And all the streets
> To our Atlantic wall are singing: "Sing,
> Sing for the resurrection of the King."
> Flies, flies are on the plane tree, on the streets.

For Lowell, in *Lord Weary's Castle*, the family-national tree is subject to blight, no longer growing by righteous streams. Occasionally,

however, he found a figure from his New England-family past who
was inspiring, as was the case with Shaw.

In the *New York Times* of March 19, 1965, John Fenton reported
on a memorial rally held near Boston Common for the Reverend
James J. Reeb, a minister in Boston, who had died from injuries
received in Selma, Alabama, while on a civil rights mission. Fenton
pointed out in the article that on the Common, where an earlier
memorial rally was held, "are a number of memorials to other victims of civil rights and liberty dating from Colonial days." He
referred, first, to the memorial to Shaw; then to a monument in
memory of Crispus Attucks, a mulatto killed in the Boston
Massacre; then to a statue of Senator Charles Sumner, who was
beaten on the floor of the Senate in 1856 after delivering a two-day
speech in favor of the abolition of slavery; then to a statue of
abolitionist William Lloyd Garrison. It would have been appropriate for someone to have read Lowell's poem "For the Union
Dead" at the rally, for it also, in part, derives from the spirit of
those monuments in or around Boston Common. "To die is life."
Occasionally I think I understand what Pallas meant and why
Lowell gave him those words to utter to Aeneas, a fellow soldier,
whose martial exploits and death had to be in the service of a civic
ideal if that militarism were to sustain people who came after him.

Moving from the Shaw relief and down Beacon Street, I turned
into Charles Street going toward the river. I was looking for 91
Revere Street, where Lowell spent much of his boyhood. He had
named his prose memoir in *Life Studies* after that address. Revere
Street looked seedier than Marlborough Street, a bit of not-quite-
quaint, not-quite-rundown Greenwich Village here in Boston.
Never did I feel more like critic-become-voyeur over the old bones
of the poet's life than when I stared at number 91 from across the
street.

The facade was just as Lowell has described it: "The outside of
our Revere Street house was a flat red brick surface unvaried by the
slightest suggestion of purple panes, delicate bay, or triangular
window-cornice—a sheer wall formed by the seamless conjunction
of four inseparable facades, all of the same commercial and
purgatorial design." It still looks the same, only more so.

Lowell used to stand in the middle of the street and look through
his own windows, especially at the scarlet waistcoat portrait of his
ancestor Major Mordecai Myers. I now stood across the street, peering, peering, at the facade across the way. I saw only stone, the

front of a house. I felt myself only loitering, a critic-surrogate ghost of the poet-as-child.

A few blocks beyond and down by the river I noticed a huge blue-gray building with large white letters MGH blocked on top of it and above the neighborhood. I hadn't realized that Massachusetts General Hospital was so close to Revere Street. I remembered that Massachusetts General was associated with the private mental hospital in nearby Cambridge where Lowell went for a period, as he describes in "Waking in the Blue."

From Revere Street I retraced some of my steps, cut across Boston Common and walked along Tremont Street until I reached King's Chapel, the site of Lowell's poem "At the Indian Killer's Grave." Here is the grave of John and Mary Winslow, colonial ancestors of Lowell on his mother's side.

In the poem the beheaded Indian leader, King Philip, delivers a jeremiad to the New England settlers. After Philip's body was quartered and decapitated, his head was exhibited on a pole in Plymouth for twenty years. His wife and children were sold into slavery in the West Indies. In the poem this detached head, on a platter, warns the Indian killers of a divine judgment as if, through Philip, John Winthrop's unhappy God berates His people for having fouled their promise in the new world. Unfortunately, the tone of everybody in *Lord Weary's Castle*, even of King Philip, sounds Calvinistic.

In the graveyard a workman "paints the railing red / Forever. . . ." Forever? On my visit, the railing was black. Does Lowell mean the gates of hell or the bones and blood of the red man? The fierce iron fence in the King's Chapel graveyard poem is more like the fence Lowell describes in the family cemetery in Dunbarton: "A fence of iron spear-hafts / black-bordered its mostly Colonial grave-slates." Nor did I see Lowell's stageprop mouse as it "Cracks walnuts by the headstones of the dead / Whose chiselled angels peer / At you, as if their art were long as life." Shouldn't that mouse be a squirrel? Except for those angels, Lowell's studied decor was missing. In the poem, he ponders by the railing at this graveyard, unconvincingly trying to arrive at a Christian transcendence of the fate of the Indian killers and their descendants, one of whom is Lowell himself. He was writing the poem near the time of still another war.

In the cemetery I sensed the poem as I did not before:

Blacker than these black stones the subway bends
About the dirty elm roots and the well
For the unchristened infants in the waste
Of the great garden rotten to its root. . . .

The third line is still half a puzzle to me, but in the cemetery there
is an old well whose covering of wire mesh and iron form a kind of
cupola. The well now serves as an airshaft for an underground
trolley line; the roar and screech of the wheels can be heard through
the mesh.

"The off-scourings of the town" are both inside and outside the
cemetery as the movement of cars and people around it never seems
to end during the day. The space for the cemetery is exhausted.
Outside this iron-fenced cage, when I returned for a second look in
1973, "yellow dinosaur steamshovels were grunting" as they tore up
the street in front of the nearby Parker House.

Inside King's Chapel there is a bust relief of John Lowell, 1769 -
1840. On a white marble slab which is above one of the pews, the
memorial is written in Latin. On a diamond-shaped stone placed on
top of the slab and edging out from it is the coat of arms and motto
of the Lowell family: a hand clutching three arrows and the phrase
"*Occasionem cognosce*"—"Know the occasion," or, perhaps,
"Understand your opportunity."

In 1755, Reverend John Lowell (not the one mentioned above)
preached a farewell sermon to a colonial contingent going off to
fight in the French-Indian Wars. The sermon was printed under the
title, "The Advantages of God's Presence with his People in an Ex-
pedition against their Enemies." Although, according to Ferris
Greenslet, the Lowell family biographer, this sermon warned
against unnecessary bloodshed, it was Reverend Lowell who added
the Latin motto to the family coat of arms. Another ancestor of
Lowell, Josiah Winslow, was a noted Indian fighter and Governor of
Plymouth during the war against King Philip.

The address of King Philip to the Indian killers in the poem is
also the address of Lowell to his ancestors. For a moment he abandons his family for the voice of the conquered and mutilated Indian
chief. Lowell's visit to the graveyard at King's Chapel was his
critical visit to his "family heritage." My trip to Boston brought
home to me the compressed family-historical heritage that Lowell
had to bear. At the end of "At the Indian Killer's Grave" Lowell
asks as he leans against the railing:

> Who was the man who sowed the dragon's teeth,
> That fabulous or fancied patriarch
> Who sowed so ill for his descent, beneath
> King's Chapel in this underworld and dark?
> John, Matthew, Luke and Mark,
> Gospel me to the Garden, let me come
> Where Mary twists the warlock with her flowers—
> Her soul a bridal chamber fresh with flowers
> And her whole body an ecstatic womb,
> As through the trellis peers the sudden Bridegroom.

But the effort to transform *angst* into ecstasy (as one critic, George Nitchie, has put it) is of no avail, nor is the buried call to the name of a family ancestor, nor the invoking of Mary in Lowell's Catholic conversion mood. For peering at her pastoral body is not only Christ but the Indian who waits in ambush, wanting his revenge, the Indian we thought we killed, or hoped to disarm. No sermons, no Marian effort at peacemaking, and certainly no sense of family heritage enabled Lowell to turn aside that waiting Indian, disguised in the poem as God the final ravisher.

The Indian killers are John and Mary Winslow, buried in King's Chapel cemetery, and carriers of the same name as the cousin to whom Lowell dedicated his World War II elegy, "The Quaker Graveyard in Nantucket." How many times I was to reread *Lord Weary's Castle* before I clutched at the dragnet of its family references! Despite their formal differences, the family concerns of *Life Studies* follow from *Lord Weary's Castle*, just as both books come out of Boston, its past and present.

Lowell's Boston had been a confining yet powerful locale. Most of us are not raised in a house from which we can walk to one of the oldest churches in the country to visit the graves of ancestral Indian killers, passing on the way St. Gaudens' relief of Colonel Robert Gould Shaw, whose sister (after Shaw's death) married Charles Russell Lowell, that relative Robert Lowell said he most admired, and who in turn was killed during the Civil War. And most of us also don't have breakdowns forcing us to retreat to a mental hospital connected to a hospital just a few blocks behind our childhood home, and even if we did it is not likely that our adult post-hospital return would be to our own family home (on Marlborough Street) still within walking distance of the old graveyard, the Boston Common, and the childhood home. The Lowell family pressures were ferociously squeezed into a famous but narrow geography. No wonder Lowell felt that at some point he had to leave Boston. The move was an effort to get some distance between himself and the heavy weight of Boston, family, and national history. Lowell left Boston a year or so after writing *Life Studies*. He moved to New York in the early 1960s. And in 1972 he also fled New York, this time to live in England. A rereading of the very first poem from *Lord Weary's Castle*, "The Exile's Return," now compels us to see that poem as a camouflaged statement of Lowell's long-felt need to investigate and sustain his life after it had been shaken by an unseasoned liberation from its past. Finally, the funeral service for Lowell in October, 1977, was held in the Church of the Advent, also near the scenes of his childhood.

I thought I had now exhausted the lessons of King's Chapel and Lowell's Boston. I walked back along the Freedom Trail. At the Tremont Street edge of Boston Common I saw a group of young men and women parading in a circle. Some were ringing little bells. All wore sneakers. Most of the men's heads were shaven bald, but two had a little knot of hair, like a miniature sheaf of wheat, just below the crown. One young man was warning the curious onlookers to find spiritual peace, for material goods could not last. He recited the names of Joseph Kennedy, Jr., John F. Kennedy, and Robert Kennedy as examples of men who had died and lost the world. If even to a rich, youthful Kennedy the fall from life could come, and come even at the moment of power and success, then surely it could come to any one of us at any time. Spiritual peace, acquiescence to the rhythm of things, denial of material claims were the only answers he assured us as he stood in his Buddhist robe of tiger-lily orange. I acknowledged to myself the boy's shrewdness and even courage in invoking the names of the Kennedy brothers as examples during his subdued fire sermon in the heart of Boston. But I also instructed myself that the ghost of Jonathan Edwards would be bothered at this promise of seemingly easy spiritual peace offered by these young American monks in their robes the color of orange sherbet and with their gentle tinkling of bells. The Edwards who preached constant and painful self-examination in the face of the terrors of human experience and the Divine Will and the Robert Lowell of *Lord Weary's Castle* who demanded retribution since he couldn't find redemption in his Boston contrasted with the neat spiritual conclusions being offered near the Freedom Trail.

Standing there at the northeast edge of Boston Common and listening to those circling, tinkling American monks in their faded pumpkin colored robes as they chanted of final unities, I told myself that their message was never to be mine or Lowell's. Just as Lowell in *Life Studies* had tried to let his contradictions come through, I hoped that in writing my study I would not impose critical certainties and unities on the life of the poetry but would remember myself as a reader who ever since adolescence was confused and captured by Robert Lowell's poetry, a poetry that always spoke to me more deeply than I understood.

Now I can see that Lowell's desire to transform Boston in *Lord Weary's Castle* for purposes of accusation and betrayal, his exacerbated language, as well as his grand statements of sorrow, informed a bitter, avenging, adolescent idealism that I felt during my high school years when I first came across *Lord Weary's Castle* in a Brooklyn school library. My nervous, angry relationship to America and my suspicion that words alone were my line to life found support in that early poetry of Robert Lowell.

However, by the time of *Life Studies,* the earlier Lowell (the Lowell whose personal perplexities had been brilliantly buckled into a harsh-organic armor of form) had become a descendant of Whitman. In Lowell's shifting from *Lord Weary's Castle* to *Life Studies,* and thereby continuing the ego-work of Whitman, something had been brought forward for me. For in reading *Life Studies* I found that one of my adolescent enthusiasms—the ego-explorations of my Brooklyn-Manhattan Walt—had become attached to my adult skepticisms, even enabling me in time to find rich complexities and uncertainties in Whitman's self-projections that I had not dreamed of in my adolescent admiration of his enthusiasms and assurances. *Life Studies* had brought forward my long-time attraction to the Whitmanesque celebration of the ego nourishing itself and had combined that attraction with my other, later, conservative bent, which distrusted the luxuriating ego and found itself surprisingly regardful of Henry James and his portrayal of the encounter between self and social setting. Lowell had come, in Whitman's phrase, to "filter and fiber" my own dual tendencies. My investment in his poetry, I longed to feel, was not simply an academic one, but was a reflection of my own development. It was a development that appreciated but kept a distance from the scene of the young American monks in their pale orange circle-parade of affirmation two corners down from the march of Shaw and his black troops.

I turned from the scene. It was time to search out a place for a bite to eat and then stray back to my gray American Rambler.

Notes and References

Chapter Two

1. Frederick Seidel, "The Art of Poetry," *Paris Review*, 7 (Winter-Spring, 1961), 64, 84.
2. *Ibid.*, p. 62.
3. *Ibid.*, p. 81.

Chapter Three

1. (Ann Arbor: Univ. of Michigan Press, 1967), p. 129.
2. "Liberal Anti-Communism Revisited," *Commentary*, September, 1967, p. 54.
3. Quoted by Friedrich Heer in *The Intellectual History of Europe*, I (Garden City, 1968), p. 324.
4. "The Meaning of this Hour," in *The Judaic Tradition*, ed. Nahum Glatzer (Boston, 1969), p. 615.
5. Seidel, "The Art of Poetry," *Paris Review*, 7 (Winter-Spring, 1961), 75.

Chapter Four

1. "From the Kingdom of Necessity," *Poetry and the Age* (New York, 1955), p. 192.
2. Jerome Mazzaro, *The Poetic Themes of Robert Lowell* (Ann Arbor, 1966), p. 87.
3. In a note to the poem in their *Norton Anthology of Modern Poetry*, Richard Ellmann and Robert O'Clair suggest that the funeral at the end of the poem might refer to a commemoration at Harvard in 1865 for the Civil War dead. (It was on this occasion, as a matter of fact, that James Russell Lowell, read his "Ode" for the war dead, one more family element surrounding the poem.)
4. The Herman Melville of the Civil War Poems, T. S. Eliot, Ezra Pound and Robert Penn Warren compare with Lowell in the way history enters their work. However, a study of the historical element in the works of these poets would show, I believe, that Lowell more than the others connects his sense of history to his sense of family. Like Yeats, Lowell is attached to ancestral houses.
5. Whit Burnett, ed., *This Is My Best* (New York, 1970), p. 437.
6. *Conversations on the Craft of Poetry* (New York, 1961), p. 47.

7. Donald Keene, "Mishima," *New York Times Book Review*, January 3, 1971, p. 25.

8. "Applause for a Prize Poet," *Life*, February 19, 1965, p. 58.

9. "Robert Gould Shaw," *Memories and Studies* (New York, 1917), pp. 57 - 8.

Chapter Five

1. In "The Prose Tradition in Verse," a review of Ford's poems, Pound celebrated Ford's "instinct for prose" and the sense of prose that should be brought to the writing of poetry. It is in this essay that Pound made his famous remark: "I cannot belittle my belief that Mr. Hueffer's [Ford's] realization that poetry should be written at least as well as prose will have as wide a result." One of these results was to be *Life Studies*. For Pound's essay see *Literary Essays of Ezra Pound*, edited by T. S. Eliot (New York, 1954), pp. 371 - 377.

2. John McCormick, "Falling Asleep over Grillparzer: An Interview with Robert Lowell," *Poetry*, January, 1953, p. 274.

3. *Alms for Oblivion* (Minneapolis, 1964), p. 59.

4. *The Triumph of the Therapeutic* (New York, 1966), p. 240.

5. *The Modern Poets* (New York, 1965), p. 231.

6. Stanley Kunitz, "Talk with Robert Lowell," *New York Times Book Review*, October 4, 1964, p. 39.

7. "Nazi Draft Dodger Gets 3-Year Term," *New York Times*, October 14, 1943, p. 13.

8. See the symposium "In Clay's Corner," *Partisan Review* 34 (Summer, 1967), 460.

9. *The Poetic Themes of Robert Lowell* (Ann Arbor, 1966), p. 115.

10. In the original hard-cover edition of *Life Studies*, "Skunk Hour" is the final poem. In the Vintage paperback edition, the last poem is "Colonel Shaw and the Massachusetts 54th" (later changed to the final and title poem of *For the Union Dead*). This poem can also be seen as a culmination of *Life Studies* as Lowell's respect for the soldier Shaw contrasts with the way he questions his patriotic but unmilitary act in "Memories of West Street and Lepke" and contrasts with the image of his father as well as with his usual portrait of the military leader. Taking their places at the end of *Life Studies* "Skunk Hour" would represent the personal victory over disorder and the poem about Shaw would convey some image of a public hero despite the disorderly urban construction that is being described. But since the poem about Shaw reappeared in the book *For the Union Dead*, I will discuss it in detail in terms of that work.

11. "On 'Skunk Hour,' " *The Contemporary Poet as Artist and Critic*, ed. Anthony Ostroff (Boston, 1964), pp. 108 - 09.

12. See *The Contemporary Poet as Artist and Critic*, pp. 84 - 110, for their discussions.

13. *Robert Lowell: The First Twenty Years* (New York, 1962), pp. 82 - 83.

14. *The Continuity of American Poetry* (Princeton, 1961), pp. 134 - 35.

15. Rieff, pp. 22, 137.

16. (Boston, 1946), pp. 76, 94.

17. I am indebted to Joseph Schumpeter's *Capitalism, Socialism and Democracy* (New York, 1950), p. 137, for leading me to these considerations.

18. *The New York Review of Books*, 14 (February 26, 1970), 39.

19. "An Interview with Sartre," *New York Review of Books*, March 26, 1970, p. 26.

20. The motto of the Winslows, Lowell's mother's family—"Cut down we flourish"—befits the achievement of *Life Studies*, and the connection between motto and book of poems is enlarged by what was heretofore a puzzling biblical passage: "Truly, truly, I say unto you, unless a grain of wheat falls into the earth and dies, it remains alone; but if it dies, it bears much fruit." (John 12:24) Robert Lowell had to disown the assigned, stagnant family roles and inheritance before he could empower himself and that family through his poetry.

Chapter Six

1. "Imitations," *American Poetry Review*, Sept.-Oct., 1973, p. 35.

2. (Bloomington, Ind., 1962).

3. "Robert Lowell's *Near the Ocean:* The Greatness and Horror of Empire," *Hollins Critic*, No. 4 (February, 1967), pp. 4 - 5.

4. "Two Translations," *Language and Silence* (New York, 1967), p. 215. According to this view, the translator's achievement, through loyalty, is the transfiguring of the original, not the distorting or the improving of it. Furthermore, Lowell has complicated the situation by showing signs of wanting to eat his cake and have it too. Thus, some imitations, even those wreaking havoc with the originals, have appeared in at least one anthology of European poetry. In addition, a five-line stanza from the last poem in *Imitations*, Rilke's "Pigeons," is spread out to six lines, retitled "Epigram," and placed among the poems in *For the Union Dead*, with no indication at all of its origins or previous intentions. Surely Lowell is not trying to pass off the isolated, slightly revised stanza as a new poem. Is this effort to be viewed as Lowell imitating Lowell imitating Rilke? There is some justice, to repeat, on the side of those who criticize Lowell for his subjective and idiosyncratic renderings. Nevertheless, Steiner himself has included Lowell imitations in his anthology *The Penguin Book of Modern Verse Translation*.

5. "Philip Massinger," *Selected Essays* (New York, 1960), p. 182.

6. Olga Andreyev Carlisle, "Poems by Osip Mandelstam," *Atlantic*, June 1963, p. 63.

7. Among American writers, only Stephen Crane in *The Red Badge of Courage* describes military leaders as does Lowell. Lowell's poetry comes

close to Crane s prose: "In the eastern sky there was a yellow patch like a
rug laid for the feet of the coming sun; and against it, black and
patternlike, loomed the gigantic figure of the colonel on a gigantic horse."
"He turned toward the colonel and saw him lift his gigantic arm and calmly
stroke his mustache." (Both passages are found in the second chapter of the
novel.) To both Crane and Lowell that implacable officer is the personifica-
tion of history. One way for both writers to describe that personified force is
through an image of the commander in some human void where only his
will exists.

8. Federick Seidel, "The Art of Poetry," *Paris Review*, 7 (Winter-
Spring, 1961), 71.

9. Stanley Kunitz, "Talk with Robert Lowell," *New York Times Book
Review*, October 4, 1964, p. 38.

10. "Explication de Texte Applied to Walt Whitman's Poem 'Out of the
Cradle Endlessly Rocking,'" *Essays on English and American Literature*
(Princeton, 1962), pp. 33 - 34.

11. For a discussion of modern poetry that has sought to go beyond the
false "set" of the world, see an important study by Frank Kermode, "A
Babylonish Dialect," in *T. S. Eliot: The Man and His Work*, ed. Allen Tate
(New York, 1965), pp. 231 - 43. Kermode's intriguing examination of
"decreation" in modern poetry is not exactly the same as the infinitude
theme in Lowell's poems, but Kermode's discussion helped me in considering this theme in Lowell's imitations.

12. *Suicide* (Glencoe, III., 1951), p. 257.

13. I am indebted to and recommend a review of Pasternak's *Letters to
Georgian Friends*, by Helen Muchnic in *New York Review of Books*,
(November 7, 1968, p. 11) for some remarks about Pasternak's translations
which have a striking relationship to Lowell's imitations.

14. Lowell's remarks are quoted by Hugh Staples in *Robert Lowell: The
First Twenty Years* (New York, 1962), p. 84.

Chapter Seven

1. *Conversations on the Craft of Poetry* (New York, 1961), p. 47.

2. Frederick Seidel, "The Art of Poetry," *Paris Review*, 7 (Winter-
Spring, 1961), 79.

3. See Lowell's essay "William Carlos Williams," *Hudson Review*, 14
(Winter, 1961 - 62), 530 - 36.

4. *Conversations on the Craft of Poetry*, p. 45.

5. "Robert Gould Shaw," *Memories and Studies* (New York, 1917),
pp. 57 - 8.

6. See Peter Burchard's *One Gallant Rush* (New York, 1965),
pp. 93 - 94.

7. See Poirier's review of *For the Union Dead*, *Book Week*, October 11,
1964, p. 16.

8. *Conversations on the Craft of Poetry*, p. 47.

Chapter Eight

1. Frederick Seidel, "The Art of Poetry," *Paris Review*, 7 (Winter-Spring, 1961), 77.
2. *Literature and Revolution* (New York, 1957), p. 110.
3. Stanley Kunitz, "Talk with Robert Lowell," *New York Times Book Review*, October 4, 1964, p. 39.
4. See Chapter Two, *The Historical Novel* (Boston, 1963).
5. "In Praise of Robert Lowell," *New York Review of Books*, 3 (December 3, 1964), 8, 10.
6. *Ibid.*, p. 8.
7. *Ibid.*, p. 10.

Chapter Nine

1. (Englewood Cliffs, N.J., 1967), p. 304.
2. During one of the rehearsals of *Prometheus Bound* for its initial performance at Yale in May, 1967, those on the set of the Lowell play could hear noise from a nearby student production dealing apparently with the Russian Revolution. Cries of "Long Live the Czar!" and "Down with the Duma!" were caught by those rehearsing Lowell's play. (Reported by Jonathan Price in "The Making of Prometheus," *Yale Alumni Magazine* (June, 1967 p. 34.)

Chapter Ten

1. *Conversations on the Craft of Poetry*, (New York, 1961), p. 45.
2. *Herzog* (New York, 1964), p. 3.
3. "A Talk with Alfred Alvarez," *Encounter*, February, 1965, p. 40.
4. (Ithaca, 1973), pp. 118 - 23.
5. "'I Am that I Am,' The Ethics and Aesthetics of Self-Revelation," *American Poetry Review*, January-February, 1974, p. 38.
6. "After Enjoying Six or Seven Essays on Me," *Salmagundi*, No. 37 (Spring, 1977), p. 113.
7. *Conversations on the Craft of Poetry*, p. 35.

Selected Bibliography

PRIMARY SOURCES

1. *Books*
Day by Day. New York: Farrar, Straus & Giroux, 1977.
The Dolphin. New York: Farrar, Straus & Giroux, 1973.
For Lizzie and Harriet. New York; Farrar, Straus & Giroux, 1973.
For the Union Dead. New York: Farrar, Straus & Giroux, 1964. Reprinted with *Life Studies* (paperback). New York: Noonday Press, 1968.
History. New York: Farrar, Straus & Giroux, 1973.
Imitations. New York: Farrar, Straus & Giroux, 1961.
Land of Unlikeness. Cummington, Mass.: Cummington Press, 1944.
Life Studies. New York: Farrar, Straus & Cudahy, 1959. Reprinted, New York: Vintage Books (paperback), 1960. With *For the Union Dead* (paperback), New York: Noonday Press, 1968.
Lord Weary's Castle. New York: Harcourt, Brace & Co., 1946. Reprinted with *The Mills of the Kavanaughs* (paperback). New York: Meridian Books, 1961.
The Mills of the Kavanaughs. New York: Harcourt, Brace & Co., 1951. Reprinted with *Lord Weary's Castle* (paperback). New York: Meridian Books, 1961.
Near the Ocean. New York: Farrar, Straus & Giroux, 1967.
Notebook. New York: Farrar, Straus & Giroux, 1970. (A revised and expanded edition of *Notebook 1967 - 68.)*
Notebook 1967 - 68. New York: Farrar, Straus & Giroux, 1969.
The Old Glory. New York: Farrar, Straus & Giroux, 1965. Reprinted, New York: Noonday Press (paperback), 1966. Revised Edition, 1968.
The Oresteia of Aeschylus. New York, Farrar, Straus & Giroux, 1979.
Phaedra. New York, Farrar, Straus & Cudahy, 1961.
Prometheus Bound. New York: Farrar, Straus & Giroux (hardback and paperback editions published simultaneously), 1969.
Selected Poems. New York: Farrar, Straus & Giroux, 1976.
The Voyage. New York: Farrar, Straus & Giroux, 1969.

2. *Prose Articles (Selected)*
Since most of these articles are not discussed in the text, those selected are listed here in order of their appearance and annotated in order to suggest a chronology for Lowell's interests and activities.

"A Review of *Four Quartets.*" *Sewanee Review,* 51 (Summer, 1943), 432 -
35. Lowell praises Eliot's long poem "as one of the very few great
poems in which craftsmanship and religious depth are equal."
"A Note." *Kenyon Review,* 6 (Autumn, 1944), 583 - 86. Lowell celebrates
Hopkins's exuberance and sanctity and the dedication of his poetry to
both human action and the quest for perfection.
"The Verse of Thomas Merton." *Commonweal,* 42 (June 22, 1945), 240 -
42. Lowell assesses an important Catholic poet.
"Current Poetry." *Sewanee Review,* 54 (Winter, 1946), 145 - 53. Particular-
ly useful for Lowell's comments on war poetry.
"Imagination and Reality." *The Nation,* 164 (April 5, 1947), 400 - 02.
Lowell expresses praise and reservations in reviewing Wallace
Stevens's *Transport to Summer.*
"Thomas, Bishop and Williams." *Sewanee Review,* 55 (Summer, 1947),
493 - 503. Lowell has praise for Dylan Thomas's ear (despite some
reservations about his rhetoric), and further appreciates Elizabeth
Bishop's poems as observations and William Carlos Williams's dedication to experience.
"Paterson." *The Nation,* 166 (June 19, 1948), 692 - 93. Praise for Williams's
poem and the effort of the poet to place himself inside America.
Lowell is, however, disappointed in the way people melt into voices in
recent long American poems.
"Homage to John Crowe Ransom." *Sewanee Review,* 56 (July-September,
1948), 374 - 77. Lowell honors Ransom's language: its urbanity, its
"pushing of utterance to the limits of one's abilities," and its quality of
good conversation.
"Prose Genius in Verse." *Kenyon Review,* 15 (Autumn, 1953), 619 - 25. An
important review of Robert Penn Warren's *Brother to Dragons.* Lowell
is particularly alert to Warren's (and any modern poet's) effort to get
plot and character into a long poem and his effort to bring the genius
of prose to verse.
"The Muses Won't Help Twice." *Kenyon Review,* 17 (Spring, 1955), 317 -
24. In this review of a new translation of Ovid's *The Metamorphoses,*
Lowell indicates his interest in the use of couplets and the writing of
the long poem.
"Visiting the Tates." *Sewanee Review,* 67 (Autumn, 1959), 557 - 59.
Lowell's candidly amusing reminiscence of his first visit to Allen Tate.
"I. A. Richards as Poet." *Encounter,* 14 (February, 1960), 77 - 78. Lowell's
receptivity to Richards's poetry bears upon some of his own inclinations in *Life Studies.*
"William Carlos Williams." *Hudson Review,* 14 (Winter, 1961 - 62), 530 -
36. (Reprinted in *William Carlos Williams: A Collection of Critical
Essays.* Ed. J. Hillis Miller. Englewood Cliffs: Prentice-Hall, 1966.) In
a moving appreciation of Williams, Lowell honestly and finely tries to
indicate what Williams has meant to him.

"The Cold War and the West." Symposium in *Partisan Review*, 29
(Winter, 1962), 47. Lowell opposes any use of the atomic bomb and
views sovereign nations as obsolete.
"On the Gettysburg Address." In *Lincoln and the Gettysburg Address*. Ed.
Allan Nevins. Urbana: University of Illinois, 1964, pp. 88 - 9. A word
of praise for Lincoln, the statesman who could use words, and for his
address which was "a symbolic and sacramental act."
"On Stanley Kunitz's 'Father and Son' " and "On 'Skunk Hour.' " *The
Contemporary Poet as Artist and Critic*. Ed. Anthony Ostroff. Boston:
Little, Brown, 1964, pp. 71 - 75, 107 - 110. In a brief comment on
Kunitz's poem Lowell expresses some skepticism about critical analysis
and indicates some of the things that he looks for in a poem: organiza-
tion yet unpredictability; in the second piece, Lowell reacts to the
critical discussion of his poem and talks about its genesis.
"A Tribute." *Agenda*, 4 (April-May, 1965), 221. A brief salute to Pound.
Forward to *Ariel* by Sylvia Plath. New York: Harper & Row, 1966.
Lowell briefly pays his respects to Sylvia Plath's poetry, only realizing
now her "appalling and triumphant fulfillment."
"On Two Poets." *New York Review of Books*, May 12, 1966, 3. Lowell's ap-
preciation of Ford Madox Ford, especially those qualities in the old
writer which attracted Lowell as a young poet. (In addition, there is a
discussion of Sylvia Plath, which is reprinted in *Ariel*.)
"Randall Jarrell, 1914 - 1965. An Appreciation." In *The Lost World* by
Randall Jarrell. New York: Collier Books, 1966. (Reprinted in *Randall
Jarrell 1914 - 1965*. Eds. Lowell, Peter Taylor and Robert Penn
Warren. New York: Farrar, Straus & Giroux, 1967.) Lowell tenderly
conveys his appreciation of his friend, fellow student, and fellow poet.
"What s Happening to America" [symposium]. *Partisan Review*, 34
(Winter, 1967), 37 - 38. Lowell's half-dour, half-longing sense of the
American situation, some of his comments reflecting the concerns of
his poetry.
"On Freedom in Poetry." *Naked Poetry*, Eds. Stephen Berg and Robert
Mezey. Indianapolis: Bobbs-Merrill, 1969, p. 124. A brief but instruc-
tive comment on the writing of free verse.
"Liberalism and Activism." *Commentary*, 47 (April, 1969), 19. Lowell's
sympathetic but complex attitude toward campus and political protest.
"For the Union Dead." In *This Is My Best*. Ed. Whit Burnet, New York:
Doubleday, 1970, p. 437. A brief note by Lowell about the genesis of
the poem.
"For John Berryman." *New York Review of Books*, April 6, 1972, pp. 3 - 4.
A wayward, affectionate reminiscence.
"Supplement: On Rhythm from America." *Agenda*, 11 (Spring-Summer
1973), 51 - 2. Prejudices and inclinations concerning meter, free verse,
and line length.
"Tribute to John Crowe Ransom." *The New Review*, 1 (Aug., 1974), 3 - 6.
Lowell's fond memories of Ransom and soft interest in his poetry.

"The Meaning of Vietnam." *New York Review of Books*, June 12, 1975, p. 27. Brief contribution to a symposium.

"On Hannah Arendt." *New York Review of Books*, May 13, 1976, p. 6. One of the best of Lowell's obituary memoirs, mixing remembrances and appraisals, tinged by affection, respect, and sadness.

"Digressions from Larkin's 20th Century Verse." *American Poetry Review*, 6 (Jan. - Feb., 1977), 33 - 4. Under the guise of a review of *The Oxford Book of Twentieth Century Verse*, Lowell achieves some flickering brilliant phrases about American and English poetry, also giving homage to some poets who have particularly moved him.

"After Enjoying Six or Seven Essays on Me." *Salmagundi*, No. 37 (Spring, 1977), pp. 113 - 15. Notes on influences, attitudes, ambitions, with a brief tracing of his own career: changing styles, but the same quest.

3. *Interviews (arranged chronologically).*

McCORMICK, JOHN. "Falling Asleep over Grillparzer: An Interview with Robert Lowell." *Poetry*, 81 (January, 1953), 269 - 79. Interview during Lowell's sojourn in Europe between the publication of *The Mills of the Kavanaughs* and *Life Studies*.

SEIDEL, FREDERICK. "The Art of Poetry." *Paris Review*, 7 (Winter-Spring, 1969), 56 - 95. (Reprinted in *Writers at Work*, Second Series. New York: Viking Press, 1963, pp. 335 - 68.) Very important interview, during which Lowell speaks of autobiographical and literary matters pertinent to his poetic concerns and achievements. This interview affords valuable insights into Lowell's thought and craft.

Conversations on the Craft of Poetry. New York: Holt, Rinehart & Winston, 1961. This pamphlet includes a conversation (also available on tape) that Lowell has with Cleanth Brooks and Robert Penn Warren on the craft of poetry. The discussion illuminates Lowell's ideas on writing poetry.

KUNITZ, STANLEY. "Talk with Robert Lowell." *New York Times Book Review*, October 4, 1964, pp. 34 - 38. Interview with Lowell at the time of the publication of *For the Union Dead* and just before *The Old Glory* was first presented. Lowell comments on the writers who have influenced him, on the kind of poetry he is interested in writing, and on his dramatic trilogy.

ALVAREZ, ALFRED. "A Talk with Robert Lowell." *Encounter*, February 24, 1965, 39 - 43. Lowell speaks of those themes and concerns—such as power, idealism and violence—which occupy the mind of a contemporary writer.

"Applause for a Prize Poet." *Life*, February 19, 1965, pp. 49 ff. Pictures of Lowell and a number of pithy comments by him about such matters as ancestors and poetry.

Gilman, Richard. "Life Offers No Neat Conclusions." *New York Times*, May 5, 1968, Section 2, pp. 1, 5. Brief interview during which Lowell comments on his writing of plays and his engagement in politics.

CARNE-ROSS, D. S. "Conversation with Robert Lowell." *Delos*, 1 (1968), 165 - 75. The discussion of Lowell's techniques of translation and his thoughts about translation assist the reader in considering Lowell's imitations.

NAIPAUL, V. S. "Et in America Ego—The American Poet Robert Lowell Talks to the Novelist V. S. Naipaul. . . . ." *The Listener*, 82 (September 4, 1969), 302 - 4. On "art, power and the dramatisation of the self."

YOUNG, DUDLEY. "Talk with Robert Lowell." *New York Times Book Review* April 4, 1971, pp. 31 - 32. Lowell refuses to accede to the public role of poetry.

HAMILTON, IAN. "A Conversation with Robert Lowell." *Modern Occasions*, 2 [Winter, 1972], 24 - 48. Reprinted in *The Review*, No. 26 (Summer, 1971) pp. 10 - 29; Lowell talks of living in England and comments on his past religious and literary associations as well as the contemporary poetry scene.

ALVAREZ, ALFRED. "A POET Talks About Making History Into Theater." *New York Times*, April 4, 1976, Section 2, pp. 1, 5. On the occasion of a revival of *The Old Glory* Lowell discusses the making of the three plays.

4. *Tapes and records of Lowell reading his poetry*
An Album of Modern Poetry. Lowell reads "Where the Rainbow Ends." Library of Congress.
Conversations on the Craft of Poetry (available from Holt, Rinehart & Winston). In addition to discussing poetry with Cleanth Brooks and Robert Penn Warren, Lowell reads parts of "The Quaker Graveyard in Nantucket," "Terminal Days at Beverly Farms," and all of "For the Union Dead."
Robert Lowell Reading His Own Poems. Lowell reads and comments on "The Quaker Graveyard in Nantucket," "For the Union Dead," and other poems. Two-record set. (Available from Library of Congress, Recording Laboratory, Box E, Washington, D.C. 20540.)
Treasury of 100 Modern American Poets. Vo. 13, Side 2, Lowell reads from his poems, including "Falling Asleep over the Aeneid." (Available from Spoken Arts Inc., New Rochelle, New York, 10801.)
Yale Poetry Series (Carilon Records, YP 301). Lowell reads "The Quaker Graveyard in Nantucket" and all the poems from part four of *Life Studies*.
YMHA Poetry Center Series. Lowell reads poems from *For the Union Dead* and *Notebook*. (Available from Jeffrey Norton Publishers, Inc., Audio Division, 145 E. 49th St., New York, N.Y. 10017.)

5. *Television Film*
National Educational Television has produced a film interview with Lowell. (Available from Audio Visual Center, Indiana University, Bloomington, Indiana 47401.)

SECONDARY SOURCES

1. *Bibliography*

MAZZARO, JEROME. *The Achievement of Robert Lowell: 1939 - 1959.* Detroit: University of Detroit Press, 1960. A bibliography of works by and about Lowell, through *Life Studies.*

————. "Checklist: 1939 - 1968." In *Robert Lowell: A Portrait of the Artist in His Time,* eds. Michael London and Robert Boyers. New York: David Lewis, 1970. Lists interviews, biographical material, and criticism.

2. *Books*

AXELROD, STEVEN GOULD. *Robert Lowell: Life and Art.* Princeton: Princeton University Press, 1978. Especially good in analyzing the differing influences of Allen Tate and William Carlos Williams on Lowell's work and career.

COSGRAVE, PATRICK. *The Public Poetry of Robert Lowell.* New York: Taplinger Publishing Co., 1972. The faults of Lowell's poetry are due to "the undisciplined entry of the personality of the poet into the poetry . . . brought about by the collapse of the controlling tradition of moral reference established by the earlier tradition of English poetry."

CRICK, JOHN. *Robert Lowell.* New York: Barnes & Noble, 1974. A judicious survey of Lowell's career, presenting the range of critical reactions to Lowell's poetry over the years.

LONDON, MICHAEL and ROBERT BOYERS, eds. *Robert Lowell, A Portrait of the Artist in His Time.* New York: David Lewis, 1970. A generous selection of critical material on Lowell's work plus an excellent checklist of material about Lowell, 1939 - 1968.

MARTIN, JAY. *Robert Lowell.* Minneapolis: University of Minnesota, 1970. Pamphlet on Lowell in the University of Minnesota series on American writers.

MARTZ, WILLIAM J., ed. *The Achievement of Robert Lowell.* Glenview, Ill.: Scott Foresman (paperback), 1966. Includes a selection of poems with criticism.

MAZZARO, JEROME. *The Poetic Themes of Robert Lowell.* Ann Arbor: University of Michigan, 1965. Thoughtful summary and critique of Lowell's development from a Catholic esthetic to a more secularized and a more personal art. Particularly useful on the sources of a number of Lowell's poems.

————. *Profile of Robert Lowell.* Columbus: Charles E. Merrill Pub. Co., 1971. Mainly useful for its reprinting of a number of interviews with Lowell, several of them not otherwise easily available.

MEINERS, R. K. *Everything to be Endured.* Columbia: University of Missouri Press, 1970. A study of Lowell's poetry in terms of the directions of modern poetry.

PARKINSON, THOMAS, ed. *Robert Lowell: A Collection of Critical Essays.* Englewood Cliffs: Prentice-Hall, 1968. The essays display the various critical reactions to Lowell's poetry.

PERLOFF, MARJORIE G. *The Poetic Art of Robert Lowell.* Ithaca: Cornell University Press, 1973. Mostly stylistic studies of Lowell's poetry.

PRICE, JONATHAN. ed. *Critics on Robert Lowell.* Coral Gables: University of Miami Press, 1972. A selection of criticism of Lowell's work from *Land of Unlikeness* to *Notebook.*

Salmagundi. No. 37 (Spring, 1977). Special issue devoted to Lowell on his sixtieth birthday. Philip Booth's reminiscences of Lowell in Castine, Maine, and Robert Hass's nimble inspection of "The Quaker Graveyard" poem stand out in this collection.

STAPLES, HUGH. *Robert Lowell: The First Twenty Years.* New York: Farrar, Straus & Cudahy, 1962. First book-length study of Lowell; discussion of "The Quaker Graveyard in Nantucket" and the elegiac tradition is the most valuable piece of criticism. Especially useful are the detailed notes to the poems and the bibliography of Lowell's poems.

WILLIAMSON, ALAN. *Pity the Monsters.* New Haven: Yale University Press, 1974. A study of the psychosexual, political concerns of Lowell's poetry, especially after *Life Studies,* viewing Lowell somewhere between Freud and the later, radical Freudians, such as Brown and Marcuse.

YENSER, STEPHEN. *Circle to Circle.* Berkeley: University of California Press, 1976. Especially alert to the ways in which motifs, themes, and images in the separate poems of a Lowell book reinforce and intensify themselves, thus encouraging the reader to detect a unity of concern in the particular book.

3. Articles and chapters of books discussing Lowell

ANON. "From Genesis to Robert Lowell." [London] *Times Literary Supplement,* August 10, 1973, 917 - 19. Beginning the laborious comparisons of *History* and *Notebook,* but does Lowell's "cannibalizing process" result in poems?

AXELROD, STEVEN. "Colonel Shaw in American Poetry: 'For the Union Dead' and its Precursors." *American Quarterly,* 24 (October, 1972), 523 - 537. A comparison of poems about Shaw by J. R. Lowell, W. V. Moody, Berryman, and Robert Lowell.

BAKER, MARY JANE. "Classes with a Poet." *Mademoiselle,* November, 1954, pp. 106 ff. A glimpse, through the eyes of an undergraduate at the University of Iowa, of the way Lowell taught courses in poets in translation, which were part of his preparations for the writing of *Imitations.*

BAYLEY, JOHN. "Robert Lowell: The Poetry of Cancellation." *London Magazine,* 6 (June 1966), 77 - 85. Lowell's theme of cancellation and the poem's alienation from itself are the major concerns of this study.

BELITT, BEN. "*Imitations:* Translation as a Personal Mode." *Salmagundi*, No. 1 (1966 - 67) pp. 45 - 56. View of *Imitations* as translation; particular attention to Lowell's translation of Montale.

BEWLEY, MARIUS. "Some Aspects of American Poetry." *The Complex Fate.* London: Chatto and Windus, 1952. Despite the integrity of *Lord Weary's Castle* and its contact with American history, the poet often exploits his technical skill at the expense of intelligibility.

CAMBON, GLAUCO. "Dea Roma and Robert Lowell." *Accent* 20 (Winter, 1960), 51 - 61. What Rome and history mean to Lowell.

————. "Robert Lowell: History as Eschatology." *The Inclusive Flame.* Bloomington: University of Indiana, 1963. A brief discussion of Lowell's quarrel with history.

CARRUTH, HAYDEN. "A Meaning of Robert Lowell." *Hudson Review*, 20 (Autumn, 1967), 429 - 47. Sympathetically but critically considers the poetic failures of *Near the Ocean* as a means of detecting the true sources of Lowell's art and concerns, which Lowell has not dealt with clearly and resolutely enough since *Life Studies*.

CHADWICK, C. M. "Meaning and Tone." *Essays in Criticism*, 13 (October, 1963), 433 - 35. Examples of Lowell's solecisms in his imitations of French poets.

EHRENPREIS, IRVIN. "The Age of Lowell." *American Poetry*. London: Edward Arnold, 1965. (Stratford-Upon-Avon Studies 7). Survey of Lowell's poetry up to *Imitations;* this discussion illuminates several poems and contains helpful biographical information.

EILERS, HAZEL KRAFT. "Lowell Coat-of-Arms." *Hobbies*, 72 (March, 1967), 120 - 21. Description and interpretation of the Lowell coat-of-arms as well as a genealogy of the Lowell family from its first arrival in America in 1639 to James Russell Lowell.

FITZGERALD, ROBERT. "Robert Lowell, 1917 - 1977." *New Republic*, October 1, 1977, pp 10 - 12. A brief, tender memory of Lowell; telling personal details combined with a sure sense of Lowell's poetic stature.

FRIED, MICHAEL. "The Achievement of Robert Lowell." *London Magazine*, 2 (October, 1967), 54 - 64. Challenging argument that Lowell can be best understood in the tradition of New England Puritanism

GIOVANNINI, G., *et al.* "Lowell's 'After Surprising Conversions.'" *The Explicator*, 9 (June, 1951), item No. 53. Presentation and discussion of a letter by Jonathan Edwards, the source of "After the Surprising Conversions."

GOLDMAN, ERIC F. "The White House and the Intellectuals." *Harpers*, 238 (January, 1969), 31 45. Discusses Lowell's refusal to join the June, 1965, White House Festival of the Arts. Contains Lowell's letter to President Johnson.

GREENSLET, FERRIS. *The Lowells and Their Seven Worlds.* Boston: Houghton, Mifflin, 1946. A history of the Lowells in America.

GROSS, HARVEY. *Sound and Form in Modern Poetry*. Ann Arbor: University

of Michigan Press, 1964. Discussion of meter in Lowell's poetry up to
Life Studies.

HALL, DONALD. "Robert Lowell and the Literature Industry." *Georgia
Review*, 32 (Spring, 1978), 7 - 12. A rejection of Lowell's poetry after
For the Union Dead and of reviewers who have praised that poetry.

HARDISON, O. B. "Robert Lowell: The Poet and the World's Body."
Shenandoah, 14 (Winter, 1963), 24 - 32. Traces Lowell's efforts, not
always successful, to achieve in his poetry "the image of a particular
man at a particular moment in history."

HARDWICK, ELIZABETH. "Boston." *A View of My Own*. New York: Noonday
Press, 1963. From this description of Boston by Lowell's wife, the
reader gets an idea of what Lowell was escaping when he moved to
New York.

Harvard Advocate. November, 1961. Of special interest in this issue
devoted to Lowell are the comments by Anne Sexton, Donald Hall and
John Crowe Ransom.

HEANEY, SEAMUS. "On Robert Lowell." *New York Review of Books*
February 9, 1978 pp. 37 - 8. A modest, brief memoir of Lowell—an intimate sense of loss, moments with the poet, and his comments elegiac-
ly recalled.

HOCHMAN, BARUCH. "Robert Lowell's *The Old Glory*." *Tulane Drama
Review*, 11 (Summer, 1967), 127 - 38. The trilogy is viewed as Lowell's
statement about the discords of civilization, authority, and protest being part of one tragic situation.

HOFFMAN, DANIEL. "Robert Lowell's *Near the Ocean:* The Greatness and
Horror of Empire." *Hollins Critic*, No. 4 (February, 1967). Lowell's
career is traced from *Imitations* to *Near the Ocean* in this sympathetic
and intelligent account of Lowell's ability to change and adjust his
styles to his developing concerns and attitudes.

HOLDER, ALAN. "The Flintlòcks of the Fathers: Robert Lowell's Treatment
of the American Past." *The New England Quarterly*, 44 (March,
1971), 40 - 65. Lowell's interest in his family's historical past is declining in his work, being replaced by his own personal past and present
situations.

HOLLOWAY, JOHN. "Robert Lowell and the Public Dimension." *Encounter*,
30 (April, 1968), 73 - 79. The problem of the poet's relationship to
social or historical themes is raised through a consideration of Lowell's
poetry.

ILSON, ROBERT. "*Benito Cereno* from Melville to Lowell." *Salamagundi*,
No. 1 (1966 - 67), pp 78 - 86. Comparison reveals a change from
Melville's innocent and self-deceiving Captain Delano to Lowell's
cynical and violent Delano.

JARRELL, RANDALL. "From the Kingdom of Necessity." *Poetry and the Age*.
New York: Vintage Books, 1955. Major essay on Lowell's poetry, especially on *Lord Weary's Castle*, in which Jarrell points out the forces

at work in Lowell's early poetry and the implication of those forces for
his development.

JONES, A. R. "Necessity and Freedom." *Critical Quarterly,* 7 (Spring, 1965),
11 - 30. Lowell, Sylvia Plath, and Anne Sexton compared as confessional poets.

JUMPER, WILL C. "Whom Seek Ye? A Note on Robert Lowell's Poetry."
Hudson Review, 9 (Spring, 1956), 117 - 25. Some reservations are ex-
pressed about the lack of clarity in some of the major themes from
Lord Weary's Castle.

KALSTONE, DAVID. "Robert Lowell: The Uses of History." *Five
Temperaments.* New York: Oxford, 1977. Pp. 41 - 76. The place of
History in the development of Lowell's poetry and praise of the book's
ability to frame an elegiac autobiography.

KAVANAUGH, PAUL. "The Nation Past and Present: a Study of Robert
Lowell's 'For the Union Dead.' " *Journal of American Studies,* 5
(1971), 93 - 101. A comparison of "For the Union Dead" and James
Russell Lowell's "Memoriae Positum," also about Shaw.

KUNITZ, STANLEY. "The Sense of a Life." *New York Times Book Review*
October 16, 1977, pp. 3, 34, 36. An unsentimental memoir about
Lowell with a strong sense of the commitment of his life to writing.
Glimpses into Lowell's personal problems, the drive behind his art.

LEIBOWITZ, HERBERT. "Robert Lowell: Ancestral Voices." *Salmagundi,* No.
1 (1966 - 67), 25 - 43. Vigorous survey of Lowell's poetry up to *For the
Union Dead;* particularly intelligent for its discussion of Lowell's
relationship to Puritanism and the past.

LUTYENS, DAVID BULWER. "Robert Lowell: Poet of Reconciliation." *The
Creative Encounter.* London: Secker & Warburg, 1960. Pp. 128 - 199.
Despite bibliographical errors, contains some useful close readings of
poems from *Lord Weary's Castle.*

MAILER, NORMAN. *The Armies of the Night.* New York: Signet Books, 1968.
Contains passages in which Mailer uniquely describes Lowell during a
peace march in Washington.

MAZZARO, JEROME. "Imitations." *The American Poetry Review,* 2
(September/October, 1973), 35 - 41. A difficult, overwritten, but
rewarding essay (the best yet) on the unified intentions of *Imitations*
and the book's relationship to Lowell's development.

――――――. "Robert Lowell's Early Poetry of Apocalypse." *Modern American
Poetry: Essays in Criticism.* Ed., Jerome Mazzaro. New York: David
McKay & Co., 1970. Pp. 321 - 350. A study of the apocalyptic temper
of Lowell's early poetry.

McCLATCHY, J. D. "Robert Lowell: Learning to Live in History."
American Poetry Review 6 (January-February, 1977), 34 - 8. An assessment of the strategies of *Selected Poems* also offers the critic the opportunity to assess Lowell's achievement to date.

McFADDEN, GEORGE. " 'Life Studies'—Robert Lowell's Comic

Breakthrough." *PMLA*, 90 (January, 1975), 96 - 106. An intriguing explication of the *Life Studies* poems in terms of the "Freudian myths of maturation and the family romance" and of Lowell's "comic strategy."

MILLER, TERRY. "The Prosodies of Robert Lowell." *Speech Monographs*, 35 (November, 1968), 425 - 34. Analysis of the shift in prosody from "The Quaker Graveyard in Nantucket" to "Skunk Hour."

MILLS, JR., RALPH J. "Robert Lowell." *Contemporary American Poetry*. New York: Random House, 1965. Elementary survey of Lowell's poetry up to *Life Studies*.

NEWLOVE, DONALD. "Dinner at the Lowells." *Esquire*, September, 1969, pp. 128 - 29, *passim*. A fictive conversation with the Lowells and dinner guests: a clever, semi-malicious, and worldly-wise spoof, not without its keen points.

NITCHIE, GEORGE. "The Importance of Robert Lowell." *Southern Review*, 7 (January, 1972), 118 - 132. Lowell's poetry is inextricably connected to historical and contemporary issues.

OBERG, ARTHUR. "Lowell Had Been Misspelled Lovell." *Modern American Lyric*. New Brunswick: Rutgers University Press, 1977. Pp. 5 - 47. Concentrating on the volumes of 1973, the article is especially good in pointing out the relationship between Lowell's sense of his life and his use of the sonnet form.

OSTROFF, ANTHONY. "On Robert Lowell's 'Skunk Hour.' " *The Comtemporary Poet as Artist and Critic*. Boston: Little, Brown and Company, 1964. Fascinating, illuminating discussions of Lowell's poem by Richard Wilbur, John Frederick Nims, and John Berryman, with a concluding reaction to their criticism by Lowell, who also discusses the genesis of the poem.

PARKINSON, THOMAS. "*For the Union Dead*." *Salmagundi*, No. 1 (1966 - 67), pp. 87 - 96. Judicious rejection of the impatient, incomplete poetry found in this book along with a recognition of how even Lowell's artistic failures deeply reflect the era.

PEARSON, GABRIEL. "Robert Lowell." *The Review*, No. 20 (March, 1969), pp. 3 - 36. An insightful critical survey of the verbal texture of Lowell's poetry and of the relationship between the use of language and attitudes in the poems.

PERLOFF, MARJORIE. "Death by Water: The Winslow Elegies of Robert Lowell." *Journal of English Literary History*, 34 (March, 1967), 116 - 40. A carefully reasoned critique of the family elegiac theme in Lowell's poetry.

RICKS, CHRISTOPHER. "Profile: The Poet Robert Lowell—seen by Christopher Ricks." *The Listener*, 89 (June 21, 1973), 830 - 2. Lowell's poems of marriage and ex-marriage compared to Meredith's *Modern Love*, the risks and achievements of such exposure.

ROSENTHAL, M. L. "Poetic Theory of Some Contemporary Poets or Notes from the Front." *Salmagundi*, No. 1 (1966 - 67), pp. 68 - 77. Discussion of the confessional esthetic of *Life Studies* in the context of some critical theorizing about the making of poems by some contemporary poets.

————. "Robert Lowell and 'Confessional' Poetry." *The New Poets.* New York: Oxford, 1967. First-rate discussion of *Life Studies;* includes the esthetic implications of the way Lowell ordered his experience.

————. "Robert Lowell and the Poetry of Confession." *The Modern Poets.* New York: Oxford, 1965. Confessional impetus in Lowell's poetry placed within the context of the poetry of this century.

SIMON, JOHN. "Abuse of Privilege: Lowell as Translator." *Hudson Review,* 20 (Winter, 1967, 8), 543 - 62. Rejection of *Imitations* and *Prometheus Bound* on the grounds that Lowell's adaptations distort the original works.

SNODGRASS, W. D. "In Praise of Robert Lowell." *New York Review of Books,* December 3, 1964, pp. 8, 10. Perceptive review of *The Old Glory* in which the power and the faults of the trilogy are warmly examined.

SOLOMON, SAMUEL. "Racine and Lowell." *London Magazine,* 6 (November, 1966), 29 - 42. Detailed attack on Lowell's inaccurate and overdone translation of *Phaedra;* it is more Lowell than Racine.

SPACKS, PATRICIA MEYER. "From Satire to Description." *Yale Review,* 58 (Winter, 1969), 232 - 48. An informative comparison of Lowell's and Samuel Johnson's versions of Juvenal's "Vanity of Human Wishes," which points up the differences between the classical and modern uses of satire.

STAPLES, HUGH. "Beyond Charles River to the Acheron: An Introduction to the Poetry of Robert Lowell." *Poets in Progress.* Ed., Edward Hungerford. Evanston: Northwestern University Press, 1967. Elementary survey up to *Life Studies;* contains some biographical information.

STEINER, GEORGE. "Two Translations." *Language and Silence.* New York: Atheneum, 1967. Lowell is charged with substituting himself and Seneca for Racine in his translation of *Phaedra;* he distorts and "improves" the original work.

STEPHANCHEV, STEPHEN. "Robert Lowell." *American Poetry Since 1945.* New York: Harper & Row, 1965. Survey of Lowell's poetry.

THOMPSON, JOHN. "Robert Lowell, 1917 - 1977." *New York Review of Books.* October 27, 1977, pp. 14 - 15. A jumble of reminiscences; the careless, restless, ambitious role of the poet. Raw glimpses for the future biographer.

VENDLER, HELEN. "The Difficult Grandeur of Robert Lowell." *Atlantic.* 235 (January, 1975), 68 - 73. A defense of *History, For Lizzie and Harriet,* and *The Dolphin* in terms of Lowell's ability to develop from an earlier harshness and urge for transcendence to a self-acceptance and a portrayal of the ordinary condition of men.

WEALES, GERALD. "Robert Lowell as Dramatist." *Shenandoah* 20 (Autumn,

1968), 3 - 28. A sympathetic but also critical review of Lowell as dramatist.

WEATHERHEAD, A. KINGSLEY. "Imagination and Fancy: Robert Lowell and Marianne Moore." *Texas Studies in Literature and Language,* 6 (Summer, 1964), 188 - 99. Application of the famous Coleridgean terms to two modern poets.

WIEBE, DALLAS E. "Mr. Lowell and Mr. Edwards." *Wisconsin Studies in Contemporary Literature* 3 (Spring-Summer, 1962), 21 - 31. A reading of the two Edwards poems in *Lord Weary's Castle;* relationship of these poems to the entire book.

WILLIAMSON, ALAN. " 'I Am That I Am': The Ethics and Aesthetics of Self-Revelation." *American Poetry Review,* 3 (January-February 1974), 37 - 39. An effort to isolate the function of the ego in "confessional poetry" so as to avoid moral judgments in evaluating such poetry.

WILLIS, G. D. "Afloat on Lowell's *Dolphin.*" *Critical Quarterly* 17 (Winter, 1975), 363 - 76. A tour through *The Dolphin* in terms of the women to whom Lowell is attached.

Index

219

220

Lowell, James Russell, 18, 28, 189, 193, 201n3
Lowell, John, 196
Lowell, Lawrence, 29
Lowell, Robert: biography, 28-32; relationship to family, 28-32, 38, 42, 55-59, 66-67, 69-75, 77, 78, 88-92, 114, 116-17, 123, 130, 189, 190-91, 193-94, 196-97

WORKS:
"The Abyss," 104
"Alfred Corning Clark," 114, 116
"At a Bible House," 42
"At the Indian Killer's Grave," 42, 56, 195-97
"Ballad for the Dead Ladies," 99
"The Banker's Daughter," 64
Benito Cereno, 26, 135-55, 165, 181-82
"Between the Porch and the Altar," 37, 46, 179
"Beyond the Alps," 50, 64, 68, 114, 123, 172
"Buenos Aires," 123
"Buttercups," 56
"Caligula," 119-20
"Central Park," 65, 108
"The Chess Player," 105
"Children of Light," 42, 129
"Child's Song," 116
"Christmas Eve Under Hooker's Statue," 44, 46, 64, 99, 101-103, 107
"Colloquy in Black Rock," 43-44, 68
"Commander Lowell," 56
"Concord," 42, 129
"David and Bathsheba in the Public Garden," 65
Day by Day, 174-77
"The Dead in Europe," 99, 165
"Death from Cancer," 107
"The Death of the Sheriff," 35, 179
"The Dolphin," 173-74
The Dolphin, 166-74
"Dora Markus," 21, 104
"The Drinker," 65
"Dropping South: Brazil," 120, 123
"The Drunken Boat," 104

"During Fever," 70
Endecott and the Red Cross, 135-39, 164
"Epigram," 203n4
"Evil," 99
"The Exile's Return," 30, 39, 41, 111, 129, 130, 174, 177, 198
"Eye and Tooth," 115
"Fall 1961," 116, 122
"Falling Asleep over the Aeneid," 48, 54-60, 61, 90, 120, 180, 182, 191
"The First Sunday in Lent," 122
"The Flaw," 114, 123
"Florence," 122
"Ford Madox Ford," 67
"For George Santayana," 67
For Lizzie and Harriet, 167-74
"For Sale," 122
"For the Union Dead," 46, 55, 57, 58, 90, 99, 107, 115, 122-23, 125-34, 181, 182, 185-86, 188-94
For the Union Dead, 60, 101, 113-34, 187
"France," 22-23, 99
"Grandparents," 70, 71
"The Great Testament," 101-103
"Hamlet in Russia: A Soliloquy," 109
"Hawthorne," 117-19
"Helen," 99
"Hell," 173
"Her Dead Brother," 49, 62
History, 56, 57, 122, 166-74, 184
"Home After Three Months Away," 78, 186-87
Imitations, 93-112, 119, 169
"Inauguration Day: January 1953," 64, 131, 172, 189
"In the Cage," 42
"The Infinite," 103-104
"In Memory of Arthur Winslow," 23-24, 29, 50, 70, 185
"Jonathan Edwards in Western Massachusetts," 119
"July in Washington," 123
"Lady Raleigh's Lament," 114, 116
Land of Unlikeness, 30, 38, 41, 50, 99
Life Studies, 25-27, 29, 30, 31, 45, 46-47, 48, 49, 50, 53, 55, 62, 63-92,